BEIHEFTE ZUR IBEROROMANIA

Herausgegeben von
Heinrich Bihler, Dietrich Briesemeister, Rolf Eberenz,
Horst Geckeler, Hans-Jörg Neuschäfer, Klaus Pörtl,
Michael Rössner

Band 10

Meg H. Brown

The Reception of Spanish American Fiction in West Germany 1981–1991

A Study of Best Sellers

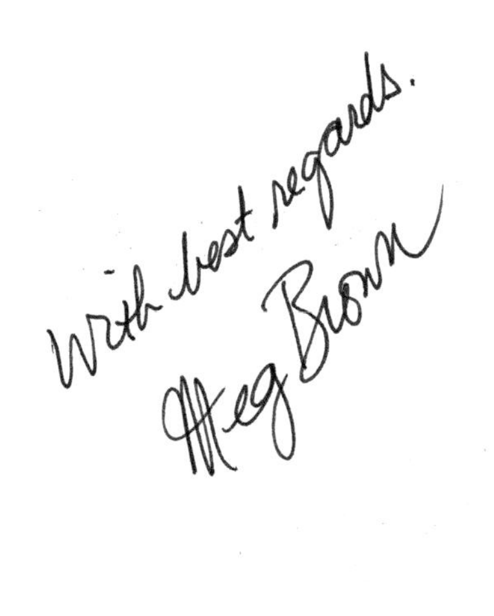

MAX NIEMEYER VERLAG TÜBINGEN
1994

Die Deutsche Bibliothek – CIP-Einheitsaufnahme

[Iberoromania / Beihefte]
Beihefte zur Iberoromania. – Tübingen : Niemeyer
Früher Schriftenreihe.
Fortlaufende Beil. zu: Iberoromania
NE: HST
Bd. 10. Brown, Meg H. : The reception of Spanish American fiction in West Germany 1981 – 1991. – 1994

Brown, Meg. H.:
The reception of Spanish American fiction in West Germany 1981 – 1991 : a study of best sellers / Meg H. Brown. – Tübingen : Niemeyer, 1994
(Beihefte zur Iberoromania ; Bd. 10)

ISBN 3-484-52910-5 ISSN 0177-199X

Printed in Germany.
Druck: Weihert-Druck GmbH, Darmstadt
Einband: Hugo Nädele, Nehren

Table of Contents

Part II

Acknowledgements

The research for this project was made possible by a Fulbright-Hayes grant from the Fulbright Commission and through a Presidential Research Fellowship from the Committee on Institutional Studies and Research at Murray State University, both of which allowed me to utilize the resources at the Universität Mannheim in Mannheim, Germany, and to travel in Germany and Switzerland as part of my research. I am indebted to Dr. Walter B. Berg and particularly Dr. Vittoria Borsò, who greatly assisted me during my association with the Lehrstuhl Romanistik III at the Universität Mannheim.

I would furthermore like to express my gratitude to Suhrkamp Verlag and Kiepenheuer & Witsch Verlag for allowing me access to their archives. Special thanks are extended to Frau Ursula Müller, Dr. Jürgen Dormagen, Dr. Christoph Groffy, and Dr. Michi Strausfeld with Suhrkamp Verlag and to Frau Dünkel and Dr. Bärbel Flad with Kiepenheuer & Witsch Verlag for their continuous aid. In Germany and Switzerland, a number of people granted me interviews, for which I am most grateful. In particular I wish to acknowledge Prof. Dr. Gustav Siebenmann in St. Gallen, Switzerland, who was most generous with his time and his thoughts.

Sally Mahoney of Paducah, Kentucky, deserves recognition for her diligent reading of my manuscript. At the University of Texas at Austin, I would like to thank Dr. Peter Hess and Dr. André Lefevere for their suggestions and input regarding genre theory. Additionally, I am appreciative of Drs. Walter Wetzels, Naomi Lindstrom, André Lefevere, and Hubert Heinen, for their careful reading. A special word of thanks goes to Hans-Bernhard Moeller for his help and expertise and to my husband, Barry T. Brown, whose patience and encouragement know no bounds.

Introduction

Lateinamerikanische Romanciers haben sich in den letzten Jahren einen festen Platz auf dem deutschen Buchmarkt erobert [...] (Börsenblatt 11 July 1989)

Bestsellers are produced [...] on scales which we have never witnessed before. Such efficiency and magnitude will be hard to ignore for much longer. (John Sutherland, Bestseller 247)

"Lateinamerika ist 'in'!" Thus begins a German review of *Mexikanischer Tango* written in October of 1988.[1] Indeed, for almost half of that year, four novels by three Spanish American authors were best sellers in West Germany. This seems strange when we consider that during the decades of the 1950s, 1960s, and 1970s, West German sales and readership of Spanish American works lagged decidedly behind those of most other countries. What brought about such a radical change in readership taste? What were the West Germans looking for in the Spanish American works during the '80s, and what were they finding? What special literary needs did West Germans of the 1980s have, and how were the Spanish American books answering these needs?

Although little or no distinction is made in West Germany between literature from Spain, Spanish America, and Latin America, I plan to investigate only Spanish American works of fiction as opposed to those from Spain or from Brazil. The simple reason for this is that during the 1980s, novels from Ibero-America made the German hardcover fiction best seller list, and novels from Spain and Luso-America did not. As noted above, "Latin American" (Spanish American) authors and literature achieved a popularity in West Germany during the 1980s that had not been witnessed in earlier decades. I intend to examine the extent to which novels from Spanish America were read in West Germany during the 1980s, which Spanish American works were most read there, why Germans read these books, and what it suggests about the contemporary West German literary needs and desires.

Both "Spanish America" and "Latin America" are employed here. Since little distinction is made between the two expressions in Germany, I use "Latin America" to indicate Central and South America, the Caribbean, and Mexico and their similar culture, society, politics, history, and literature as opposed to those of West Germany. "Spanish America" is then applied to mean those countries of the Western Hemisphere where Spanish is the principal language--or one of the principal languages--spoken, Indian dialects constituting the other languages.

"Works of fiction" is the correct term to describe the books that I analyze. All of them are novels except Isabel Allende's *Geschichten der Eva Luna*, which is a book of stories. In many ways, it closely resembles her prior novel, *Eva Luna.* Since ten of the eleven works are novels, I will occasionally refer to all of the works as "novels."

For simplicity's sake, I use "West Germany" to indicate the Federal Republic of Germany before unification and that which was called "western Germany" thereafter. The occasional use of "German" and "Germany" may refer to the whole of the German culture but is intended to include specifically only the area of Western Germany. The purpose of investigating the reception of the works only in West Germany is two-fold. First, the German (East and West together) historical background is different from that of Austria and Switzerland. These countries have a different cultural heritage which in turn influences their world outlook and thus affects their reception of literature. Specifically the role of Germany in World War II and the psychological consequences in the aftermath of the war are shown here as creating an environment in which West Germans perceive certain aspects of literary works that readers in other countries--even in other German-speaking countries--would be less likely to focus on. Second, post-World War II West Germany became a highly-industrialized, technological, and capitalistic Western European country with a strong socialist opposition to the ruling class. This again marked its reception of Spanish American fiction as very different from the reception of these works in the German Democratic Republic. The conditions under which novels in West Germany were read were totally different from those in East Germany. The government-controlled book market in the East had very little in common with the West's book market system. Furthermore, the fall of the Wall on 9 November 1989 did not have a significant impact on the reception of Spanish American works in former West Germany in the time I have specified through 1991. Unification signals a potentially different perspective on literature as economic stability comes to the whole of the new Federal Republic.

While many novels achieve international best seller status, what any one particular country's readers perceive in those works varies according to that country's heritage, history, and world outlook. A study of this type of reception in the German-speaking countries of Austria, Switzerland, East Germany, and West Germany would constitute four different investigations. Therefore, I am examining here the case of West Germany alone.

The time frame of 1981 to 1991 was selected simply because these were the inclusive years of the Spanish American works on the German best seller list as a noticeable trend. In the decades before the '80s, there were no Latin American best sellers in West Germany. In fact, as I will illustrate, before 1981 there was a dearth of reception of Spanish American/Latin American narrative fiction in West Germany. The 1980s marked a decided reversal in this reception: Twelve Spanish American works were placed on the West German hardback belletristic best seller list of *Der Spiegel* beginning in 1981. This turnaround indicates that there was a change in the West German attitude toward Spanish American literature and/or a change in the narrative prose itself. As a result, the popularity of this literature suggests a trend that popularized Spanish American fiction in West Germany. The "Latin American wave" in itself continued through a period of decline in 1990, and after March 1991 there were no more Spanish American works of fiction on the best seller list for a year and a half.

Earlier studies have been done on the subject of the reception of Latin American literature in German-speaking countries. Their focus, purpose, and methodology varied, but their conclusions were similar: They lamented the lack of reception of Latin American literature in West Germany.

In 1972 Gustav Siebenmann published *Die neuere Literatur Lateinamerikas und ihre Rezeption im deutschen Sprachraum*, an empirical study in which he compiled extensive statistics covering the reception of Latin American literature in the German-speaking countries: published titles, price, number of editions, and so forth. This definitive study on the subject concludes that the lack of reception of Latin American literature in German-speaking countries could be attributed to 1) the cultural *Fremdheit* of Latin America in the German-speaking countries; 2) the publishers who are in turn dependent on agents, translators, and Hispanists; 3) the reader: "Dem deutschen Durchschnittsleser [...] fehlt letzten Endes doch das Verständnis für die romanische Mentalität" (80); and 4) critics who did not know enough about Latin American literature. Siebenmann thus convincingly documents German indifference to Latin American literature.

In 1976 Dieter Reichardt presented a paper entitled "Bestandsaufnahme der Rezeption lateinamerikanischer Literatur in den Ländern deutscher Sprache" at the Lateinamerika-Colloquium. In the essay, Reichardt confirmed the underrepresentation of Latin American literature in the German book market, concentrating on the critic, his or her lack of knowledge about this literature, and his or her perceived role as an authority of "good taste" (64-65). Reichardt, however, discussed the reader only peripherally.

In contrast, Yolanda Broyles's dissertation *The German Response to Latin American Literature and the Reception of Jorge Luis Borges and Pablo Neruda*, published in 1981, concentrates specifically on reader response. She studied the reception of said literature in Germany, primarily since World War II. Broyles focused on the West German readers in their interaction with Latin American works of literature through the West German socio-eco-political and cultural situation. The first part of her study examined and reprimanded the Germans for their "non-reception" of Latin American literature. Chapters 3 and 4 analyzed reader response toward Borges (Argentina) and Neruda (Chile). The group of readers studied was made up of newspaper literary critics: Broyles analyzed the qualitative content of reviews published on German translations of Borges and Neruda. She came to the conclusion that Borges had been well received in West Germany as a result of his ideological views while Neruda, on the same basis, had not. This may be an oversimplification: In my research I found constant positive references to Neruda, and I maintain that much more is involved in an author's cross-cultural reception than his or her ideological views.

Michi Strausfeld's 1983 essay "Lateinamerikanische Literatur in Deutschland. Schwierigkeiten und Kriterien für ihre Vermittlung und Veröffentlichung" summarized the reception of Latin American literature in the Federal Republic and compared it to that in other West European countries. In the latter half of the 1970s, Latin American literature was considered to be either exotic and readable or else avant-garde, innovative in form, of powerful expression, and elitist. Strausfeld wrote that the European expectations concerning Latin American literature demanded certain themes and certain directions in style: magic realism, accusations, and denunciations. To some degree these are the expectations of the European reader and, more specifically, of the elite West German reader of Latin American literature. However, it is my intention to show that the general reading public in Germany is not as drawn to those features as is generally assumed. Strausfeld concludes with the hope that Germans would begin reading Latin American literature:

> Die jüngste der zeitgenössischen Literatur der Welt hat sich in knapp dreißig Jahren an die Spitze geschrieben--auch wenn sie in Deutschland noch nicht die Rezeption gefunden hat, die sie aufgrund ihrer Vielseitigkeit und Qualität verdient. Aber dies ist nur eine Frage der Zeit--sie kommt. (938)

Rafael Gutiérrez Girardot's article "La recepción de la literatura latinoamericana en la República Federal Alemana," published in 1989, is not as optimistic. He observes no change in this reception and indeed condemns German reception. Gutiérrez Girardot also affirms that between

> a distant Latin America without a future [as perceived in West Germany] and a nearby Spain with a future that is its own [as a result at least in part of its joining the Common Market], the German public reader and consequently the publishers prefer literature from the second. (32)

He thus sees a preference in West Germany for literature from Spain over that from Latin America.[2]

In her 1989 article "La recepción de la literatura hispanoamericana del 'boom' en Alemania," Claudia Wiese offers a thorough overview of the reception of the authors of the Spanish American "boom" (Julio Cortázar, José Donoso, Alejo Carpentier, Juan Rulfo, Guillermo Cabrera Infante, Carlos Fuentes, Mario Vargas Llosa, and Gabriel García Márquez, among others) in West Germany. She begins with the reasons for the lack of West German preparation for reading Spanish American literature of the "boom" and goes on to list several events that helped open the way for this literature in Germany after 1976. Wiese's discussion of the various stages in the publication of this literature in Germany covers the publishers, translators, and literary critics. She concludes by saying, "We find ourselves at the beginning of a true reception in the sense of receiving, learning, and understanding" (translation is mine) (53). Here I will demonstrate that the West German general reading public indeed has taken the initiative toward this type of reception.

Wiese continues her investigation into the "boom" in her book *Die hispanoamerikanischen Boom-Romane in Deutschland. Literaturvermittlung, Buchmarkt und Rezeption.* In this publication, Wiese combines discussion specifically of the Spanish American *boom*, covering roughly the decades of the '60s and the '70s, with an overview of the German book market. She reviews the *nueva novela* and the *boom* both in Latin America and in the international context. Finally, she focuses with pain-staking detail on the Spanish American *boom* on the German literary scene, examining Spanish American literary events in Germany, German publishers of Spanish American works, various forms of publicity for the Spanish American authors in Germany, translators and translations, and the critics. Wiese uses an interdisciplinary approach and concentrates on "kontextuelle Fakten und Daten [...], die als Symptome und Indizien für die Rezeptionsmotivation gelten können" (22). Wiese's study and mine were written at approximately the same time and complement one another in time frame and content.

Here I will also employ an interdisciplinary approach with an emphasis on the reception aesthetics theory of Hans Robert Jauß in conjunction with genre theory in order to focus on the West German readers in their interaction with Spanish American novels. Jauß's theory is applied here and measured against empirical research, which forms the body of this investigation. Furthermore, the neopositive approach utilized here lends itself to the study of reception aesthetics, the genre, and best sellers since it provides the cultural setting in which the works are read. In the meeting of the reader and the text, each has certain attributes which exist independently of their interaction. In reception analysis, text variables, reader variables, and their interaction must be taken into account. Each reader has his or her own set of variables that differ from those of other readers. However, the aggregate set of variables of the readers from a common cultural background, from any one country, may be studied as a composite set to be distinguished from the composite set of variables of readers from other countries. Jauß explains:

> The interpretative reception of a text always presupposes the context of experience of aesthetic perception: the question of the subjectivity of the interpretation and of the taste of different readers or levels of readers can be asked meaningfully only when one has first clarified which transsubjective horizon of understanding conditions the influence of the text. (Jauß, "Challenge" 23)

Thus, West German readers collectively have a different set of variables from Mexican, Colombian, Chilean, and Peruvian readers, and those from other Spanish American countries. Furthermore, the horizon of understanding of a general audience will vary from that of an elite set of readers. This set of collective average West German reader variables will be shown to influence the West German reading of these Spanish American texts.

In *Literary History as a Challenge to Literary Theory* (*Literaturgeschichte als Provokation*), Jauß utilizes Thomas Kuhn's concept of the paradigm in natural sciences and the periodic shifts in paradigms to explain literary history. A paradigm is used to indicate the thought construct in any given historical period. Jauß applies a term coined by Mannheim, *Erwartungshorizont* ("horizon of expectations"), to both the reader and the work. Jauß's three-part model examines the interaction between the production of a work, the product as the work itself, and the audience's reception of that work. The audience's set of expectations and its reception of the work is then said to influence future production of later works.

Influence is sometimes quite difficult to prove. It should be noted that Jauß's theory discusses the scenario in which the production and reception phases are intracultural, whereas my analysis is cross-cultural. It is also difficult to show how precisely reception influences production, whether cross-cultural or intracultural. Furthermore, Jauß uses historical examples, while I will be focusing on works written recently, making the identification of any discernable influence even more difficult.

In the literary process, the *Erwartungshorizont* can be described by the following: 1) the recognized norms of the literary genre to which a work belongs as established by the literary canon, 2) the implicit relationship known to other works of the time, and 3) the opposition between fiction and reality as expressed in poetic versus practical language. The distance between the *Erwartungshorizont* and a new work is called the *ästhetische Distanz* (aesthetic distance). According to Jauß, great literature will create a *Horizontwandel* ("horizon transformation"), i.e., will lead to new reader expectations. The aesthetic distance between a great work of literature and its *Erwartungshorizont* will be greater than the aesthetic distance between a work of popular fiction and its *Erwartungshorizont.*

Due to the difficulty in constructing a general *Erwartungshorizont* for any given moment in the literary process, Jauß later switched his emphasis to the concept of concretization inspired by the structuralists.[3] The concretization of a work is the public and accepted view of an author or a work, presumably reflecting the interaction of the work with an existing *Erwartungshorizont* (Zeller 16). The critical reactions to the text, together with evidence of the extent of its audience, provide a reasonably accurate foundation for the *Erwartungshorizont.*

By switching his emphasis to concretization, Jauß justifies the use of published literary criticism as the primary factor influencing the concretization of a work. My study employs reviews published in newspapers and magazines and presented on the radio to determine the concretizations of these works in West Germany. This aspect of the influence of critical reviews combined with indications of the large German audience reading the Spanish American works allows us to arrive at conclusions concerning the *Erwartungshorizont* and concretization of these novels.

Jauß's reception theory, concretization, and *Erwartungshorizont* construct are in part influenced by one of the prevailing theories of the concept of the genre, the theory that is used here. Consistent with the general lines of Jauß's model, a genre may be considered as a form that has similar characteristics and has become historically concrete; the creation of genres may likewise be viewed as the dynamic interaction between the producer (the author), the work, and the recipient (the reader) as a constant process of the establishment of norms and deviation from these norms.

In literary study today, there is no agreement on the exact meaning of "genre." During the 1960s, literary critics contended that works of a recognized genre should meet very specific criteria, while during the late 1960s and the 1970s the socio-historical approach maintained that a genre defines itself by norm and deviation. Harald Fricke, in his book *Norm und Abweichung*, bases his definition of a genre on the dialectic between deviation and norm formation and contends that a genre is defined by a set of deviations from general language norms, whether they be phonetic, morphological, lexical, syntactic, semantic, textual, or thematic deviations.

Once textual features positively influence reception--i.e., once there is a generic model and reception has been established--then there exists a genre; and this concept of genre is based on generic expectation. We find here the triadic model of the producer, the work, and the receiver where the author is influenced by the expectations of the public and critics to write within a recognized norm, or genre, but with deviation, or variation.

Works within a particular genre establish a set of similar characteristics which the public and the critics come to expect and continue to consume based on this set of shared features and on reader expectations (*Erwartungshorizont*). Each new work in that genre then reinforces for the readers that set of cohesive similarities that they have come to expect, but the new work also offers variation, thus forming the basis of the genre as norm and deviation. This is a process of pluralistic forces in which the publisher, the media, and the critic can also initiate and promote the idea of shared characteristics of a group of works. In addition, an overlapping of genres is possible; works can belong to more than one genre, such as a historical novel that is also a detective novel. Usually one genre will predominate over another.

In his essay "Genres and Medieval Literature," Jauß likewise departs from the traditional concept of the genre. He believes that literary genres are to be understood not as *genera* (classes) but as groups or historical families (79-80). Thus, a literary genre is independently able to constitute texts, and this constitution must be "synchronically comprehensible in a structure of nonsubstitutable elements, as well as diachronically in a potential for forming a continuity" (81-82).

Hence, beyond the canonized major and minor genres, other series of works that form a continuity and that appear historically may be considered as constituting a genre. Jauß says that the continuity formative of a genre can lie not only in the acknowledged texts of one genre but also in the succession of the works of one author or in the cross-sectional phenomena of a period style (80-81). In addition, a work can also be grasped according to various generic aspects, and Jauß maintains that this mixing of genres can be made into a methodologically productive category. He goes on to explain that not all elements of a generic structure must be found in all later works of a genre (93).

Jauß further discusses the origin of any one genre. He addresses the case where there is no initially posited and described generic norm, as was the case of the Spanish American novel as perceived in West Germany in earlier decades: A generic structure must be gained from the perception of individual texts in a continually renewed preconceiving of an expectable whole or regulative system for the series of texts (93-94). He sees literary forms and genres as neither subjective creations of the author nor just retrospective ordering-concepts, but rather as primarily social phenomena, which means that they depend on functions in the lived world (100). The lived world experiences may be interpreted as referring both to the production phase and to the receptive stage of a genre, including cross-cultural reception:

> A work which is ripped out of the context of the given literary system and transposed into another one receives another coloring, clothes itself with other characteristics, enters into another genre, loses its genre; in other words, its function is shifted.[4]

As an extension of this thought, such a work, or more specifically a series of works, transposed into a different cultural literary system from the one in which it was produced, could also take on the characteristics of a perceived genre. In concentrating on the study of reception aesthetics, I suggest that the cross-cultural reception of Spanish American best sellers in West Germany from 1981 to 1991 created an environment in which the works were perceived to share certain characteristics which distinguished them from other types of novels read in Germany.

The concept of the genre employed here is based on historical and geographical factors and is used to classify the group of Spanish American works of fiction that became best sellers in West Germany. Since genres can be considered primarily social phenomena depending on functions in the lived world, the neopositive approach provides the necessary background for examining the context in which a body of fiction is read. I will concentrate on the case study, i.e., on the empirical aspect of the reception and concretization of these novels more than on the genre theory aspect. Neopositivism and genre theory are used here to lay the foundation for understanding how the Spanish American works were collectively received in Germany. It is not my intention to establish new parameters of reception or genre theory.

With regard to Spanish American best sellers in West Germany, we may assume that the general scope of readership is significant based on best seller status. With one exception (Mario Vargas Llosa's *Lob der Stiefmutter*, in Spanish *Elogio de la madrastra*), all the books have decidedly Latin American features, themes, descriptions, and settings; and some of these same qualities were even occasionally attributed by German critics to *Lob der Stiefmutter*. Yet the fact that those works became cross-cultural best sellers is testimony to the additional fact that they were successful in a very different culture from the one in which they were written. Best seller status does not measure readership; however, best sellers are at least a fair indication of the most read books in a country. To rely on sales figures, particularly in the case of novels written in or translated into German, would not provide adequate documentation. Such figures would include sales from other German-speaking countries, whereas the best seller lists are based on sales in bookstores in the limited, determined geographical area of the Federal Republic.

The danger in focusing on best sellers is, of course, the association of best sellers with *Trivialliteratur*. Many intellectuals and literary critics tend to arbitrarily equate best-selling novels with this deprecated type of fiction, especially in Germany. West Germans have a long history of exalting "good" literature (*hohe Literatur*) while scorning *Trivialliteratur*, more so than do the people of many other countries.

Such categorization of literature in German began in earlier centuries as the growing middle class and even some of those from the lower class learned to read. Their taste in literature deviated from that of the relatively closed audience of the upper or middle-upper classes. Eventually, writers of "good" (*hohe*) literature and their readership endeavored to segregate themselves from that type of writing produced for the larger audiences; thus originated the distinction between *hohe Literatur* and *Trivialliteratur*, a distinction still in effect today.[5]

Nevertheless, there is a third category of fiction: *Unterhaltungsliteratur*, popular literature, which generally lies between *hohe Literatur* and *Trivialliteratur*. More recently, there have been indications from some scholars and critics that there is a "changing definition of literature and culture which does not distinguish between elite culture and popular culture."[6]

While it is true that many books that become best sellers in West Germany are considered *Trivialliteratur*, that does not mean that a novel is *Trivialliteratur* by virtue of the fact that it appears on the best seller list. Respected authors such as Günter Grass, Heinrich Böll, Martin Walser, Siegfried Lenz, Umberto Eco, and Gabriel García Márquez, to name a few, have appeared on the list.[7] In fact, a classic may become a best seller; the terms are not mutually exclusive.[8]

The Spanish American works examined here are, for the most part, not classics, but neither are they *Trivialliteratur*. *Hundert Jahre Einsamkeit* by García Márquez is, in fact, already considered a classic of world literature. The quality of Isabel Allende's *Von Liebe und Schatten*, *Eva Luna*, and *Geschichten der Eva*

Luna is described in various West German reviews as approaching that of *Trivialliteratur*. However, literary critics who write for respected newspapers in Germany would not have reviewed these books if they were truly "trivial."[9] Therefore, the novels studied here are considered to be those works attaining best seller status covering the spectrum from classics through the range of *Unterhaltungsliteratur*.

Twelve Spanish American works became best sellers in West Germany from 1981 to 1991; I will discuss eleven of them. The authors of these works are the Colombian Gabriel García Márquez, the Chilean Isabel Allende, the Mexican Angeles Mastretta, and the Peruvian Mario Vargas Llosa. The novels, listed in order of their German publication, are:

Hundert Jahre Einsamkeit, Gabriel García Márquez, 1970, translated by Curt Meyer-Clason; originally published as *Cien años de soledad*, 1967.

Chronik eines angekündigten Todes, Gabriel García Márquez, 1981, translated by Curt Meyer-Clason; originally published as *Crónica de una muerte anunciada*, 1981.

Das Geisterhaus, Isabel Allende, 1984, translated by Anneliese Botond; originally published as *La casa de los espíritus*, 1982.

Von Liebe und Schatten, Isabel Allende, 1986, translated by Dagmar Ploetz; originally published as *De amor y de sombra*, 1984.

Die Liebe in den Zeiten der Cholera, Gabriel García Márquez, 1987, translated by Dagmar Ploetz; originally published as *El amor en los tiempos del cólera*, 1985.

Mexikanischer Tango, Angeles Mastretta, 1988, translated by Monika López; originally published as *Arráncame la vida*, 1986.

Eva Luna, Isabel Allende, 1988, translated by Lieselotte Kolanoske; originally published as *Eva Luna*, 1987.

Lob der Stiefmutter, Mario Vargas Llosa, 1989, translated by Elke Wehr; originally published as *Elogio de la madrastra*, 1988.

Der General in seinem Labyrinth, Gabriel García Márquez, 1989, translated by Dagmar Ploetz; originally published as *El general en su laberinto*, 1989.

Geschichten der Eva Luna, Isabel Allende, 1990, translated by Lieselotte Kolanoske; originally published as *Cuentos de Eva Luna*, 1990.

Der Geschichtenerzähler, Mario Vargas Llosa, 1990, translated by Elke Wehr; originally published as *El hablador*, 1987.

That Spanish American work which became a best seller but which I am excluding is García Márquez's *Das Abenteuer des Miguel Littín. Illegal in Chile* (1987, translated by Ulli Langenbrinck). It is neither a novel nor a work of fiction, even though it was on the "Belletristik" best seller list. The book is a compilation of hours of audio cassette narration by Chilean film-maker Miguel Littín for García Márquez. García Márquez then transcribed and edited the narration from the cassettes and published the book, which appeared about the same time as Miguel Littín's documentary-type movie filmed during his clandestine trip to his homeland. Since I only intend to examine works of fiction, I have omitted this work.

I will divide this survey into two parts. Part I establishes the context for my analysis and illustrates the Spanish American best seller as a product of the West German market system. The neopositive theoretical structure in Part I establishes the context for reception aesthetics in Part II. Neopositivism allows us to examine first the cultural-historical background of the collective set of West German reader variables and how the values then guided the German reception and interpretation of the Spanish American works. Part I provides the definition of the term "best seller" as applied here, discusses the Spanish American works of fiction that became best sellers in West Germany in their content and West German marketing, provides an explanation of the shift in the reception of Spanish American literature in West Germany, and explores the various stimuli that motivate Germans to buy books together with the specific role that the German critic plays in the motivational and concretizational processes. Part II, utilizing Jauß's idea of concretization in reception aesthetics, examines the shared characteristics that came to be associated with the Spanish American novel in West Germany as viewed through the body of reviews of these works.

The overall goal of my investigation is to demonstrate the increased reception of Spanish American works in West Germany during the 1980s; to consider the marketing of these novels targeted for the German public; to ascertain the similar characteristics shared by these novels as these features were perceived, promoted, and perpetuated by West German critics; and to test the norm and deviation concept of the genre and Jauß's reception aesthetics theory in a cross-cultural circumstance. I will also determine what differences may exist in how the Spanish American works are reviewed in liberal, moderate, and conservative publications. The critics' reviews served to influence readers' opinions; at the same time, the critics are representative readers of the given cultural context (von Bülow 10). The features attributed by Germans to the works were then concretized, and this led to the set of expectations that caused the Spanish American novels to be perceived as if they constituted a sub-genre in West Germany.

Notes

[1] Ennely Schmidt, "Warten auf den Tod," *Stadtblatt Osnabrück* Oct. 1988: N. pag.

[2] For a contrasting opinion, see Ray-Güde Mertin's article "Desbrozando el camino a la literatura latinoamericana en Alemania. La labor de una agente literaria," in the same edition of *Humboldt* 97 (1989): 38-45.

[3] See Hans Robert Jauß, "Racines and Goethes Iphigenie. Mit einem Nachwort über die Partialität der rezeptionsästhetischen Methode," *neue hefte für philosophie* 4 (1973), 3.

[4] Juri Tynjanov, "Die Ode als oratorisches Genre," *Texte der russischen Formalisten, II*, ed. W.-D. Stempel, (Munich, 1972), 273-337; quoted in Jauß, "Genres and Medieval Literature" 106-107.

[5] For further background material on this subject, see Ralf Schnell, *Literatur der Bundesrepublik. Autoren, Geschichte, Literaturbetrieb* (Stuttgart: J.B. Metzlersche Verlagsbuchhandlung, 1986) 36-37; Lynda J. King, *Best-Seller by Design. Vicki Baum and the House of Ullstein* (Detroit: Wayne State University Press, 1988) 20-21: Rolf Engelsing, *Der Bürger als Leser. Lesergeschichte in Deutschland 1500-1800* (Stuttgart: J. B. Metzler, 1974) 183; Herbert G. Göpfert, *Vom Autor zum Leser. Beiträge zur Geschichte des Buchwesens* (Munich: Carl Hanser, 1977) 36.

[6] Mark W. Rectanus, *Literary Series in the Federal Republic of Germany from 1960 to 1980* (Wiesbaden: Otto Harrassowitz, 1984) 170. See also Bernhard Zimmermann, "Das Bestseller-Phänomen im Literaturbetrieb der Gegenwart," *Literatur nach 1945, II: Themen und Genres*, ed. Jost Hermand (Wiesbaden: Akademische Verlagsgesellschaft Athenaion, 1979) 121-22 and Joachim Kaiser, "Die neue Lust am kulinarischen Roman," *Stern* 16 Feb. 1989: 70-71.

[7] Werner Faulstich presents many best seller examples of the more aesthetic, "literary" literature from 1700 to the mid-1960s in *Bestandsaufnahme Bestseller-Forschung* (Wiesbaden: Otto Harrassowitz, 1983) 30-31.

[8] Malcolm Cowley 25. In this article written in 1947, Cowley is criticizing Frank Luther Mott's conception of best sellers since Mott "would like to abolish the distinction between classics and best-sellers." While Cowley's statement concedes that classics and best sellers are not mutually exclusive, he maintains that the two should not be confused. I agree with Cowley about the distinction between classics and best sellers, but I believe it is important to note that they are indeed not mutually exclusive.

[9] See Chapter 4, section 4.2 for a more detailed explanation. On the basis that critics do not review works that they consider to be *Trivialliteratur*, one might determine that Allende's *Geschichten der Eva Luna* is indeed regarded as *Trivialliteratur* since fewer critics reviewed the work.

Part I

Chapter 1

Best Sellers

Kultur und Kommerz werden eins. (Dieter E. Zimmer, Die Zeit, 1971)

"Man macht seine anderen Bücher, die kleineren, mit der Bestsellerei kaputt," gestand der Verleger Willy Droemer einmal--und bestsellerte eifrig weiter. (Schnell, Literatur der Bundesrepublik 28)

"Best seller" is a universally understood term; the expression, however, can and does mean different things to different people. The literal meaning is, of course, a book purchased and read by a sufficient number of people to be ranked in the top 10 or 15 by any one of several ranking institutions. What other meanings, whether literal or connotative, can be implied by the term "best seller"?

Intellectuals and scholars come to no consensus on how the term should be defined. For some scholars, best sellers are so called because they have been sold in sufficient quantities, whether over a short period of time or over an extended period of time. Nor is the term limited to books: "Best seller" may refer to books, a style of books, or an author of books (Sutherland 6). Best seller scholar John Sutherland confirms that "the word 'bestseller' and its derivatives (bestsellerism, bestsellerdom) are not governed by any agreed definitions" (5), and West German best seller scholar Werner Faulstich has written several books on the subject, including one focusing on the many definitions of "best seller": *Bestandsaufnahme Bestseller-Forschung.*

Many have discussed what may be understood under the term "best seller." While the various definitions each contributes to the concept, most are in some way deficient. After I have surveyed a selection of these definitions and commented on their merits and flaws, I will choose the definition or combination of definitions best suited to my study. Most earlier definitions take into consideration only one or two aspects of bestsellerism, e.g., sales figures and time frames, whereas a greater range of facets, such as best-selling author, best-selling genre, and best seller lists, needs to be considered. I will also discuss the West German *Spiegel/Buchreport* best seller list, how the books on this list are chosen, and the interaction of the West German society with this ranking to show the role of the best seller list in the West German literary market system.

1.1 Definitions of "Best Seller"

Even the simplest definitions of the term "best seller" vary greatly and offer no definitive explanation of the expression. Sonja Marjasch provides one of the least complicated definitions. For her a "best seller" indicates "sehr guter Umsatz innerhalb einer bestimmten Meßzeit: Woche, Monat oder Jahr" (15). Marjasch's explication points to two components beneficial for a definition of best sellers: relative sales and a time frame. While her inclusion of the time frame is a helpful delimitation, we are left uncertain about the exact meaning of "sehr guter Umsatz." She offers no indication of what is considered very good sales, no numerical figure, nor any authority that might establish guidelines for describing when a book advances from normal sales to very good sales.

Others concentrate on the sales figures to the exclusion of all other qualifiers. They prefer to judge best sellers by specific figures of numbers of copies produced and/or sold. Dieter E. Zimmer wrote in 1971:

> Ein Bestseller ist ein Buch, das die Normalauflage von fünfhundert bis fünftausend Exemplaren gleich um das Zehn- bis Hundertfache übertrifft. Der Abstand zwischen dem normalen Buch und dem Bestseller ist in den letzten Jahren immer größer geworden. ("Die Herzen" 98)

Ralf Schnell provides more exact figures:

> "Bestseller" nennt man Bücher, von denen sich auf Anhieb mindestens 30 000 Exemplare verkaufen lassen, "Best-Bestseller" solche, die Auflagen von über 100 000 erleben, "Steady-" oder "Dauer- Seller" schließlich jene Publikumserfolge, die ihre hohen Auflagen über Jahre hinweg halten. (26-27)

In contrast to Marjasch's definition, in those of Zimmer and Schnell we encounter figures to differentiate between normal books, best sellers, and "steady sellers." The problem, however, lies in the lack of a consensus on the specific figures and the need for a time frame. The set minimum of the number of copies of a book could be valuable if we could find agreement on the figures, particularly if they could be combined with a time frame to substantiate a comparison between the sales of different books. An adequate definition would need to provide more comprehensive guidelines as established by an acknowledged authority. These two definitions, then, remain too vague.

In searching for an appropriate definition, we can turn to a nominal definition found in Faulstich's *Bestandsaufnahme* and taken from Gero von Wilpert's *Sachwörterbuch der Literatur*, Stuttgart, 1969:

> Bestseller (engl. = das am besten, d.h. meisten Verkaufte), ein Buch, das sofort oder kurz nach seinem Erscheinen einen durch Aktualität, Mode, Geschmack, Bedarf, Propaganda u.ä. bedingten bes. schnellen und hohen, wenn auch im Ggs. zum sog. Steadyseller meist kurzlebigen Absatz findet. Als unterste Grenze gelten etwa 100 000 verkaufte Exemplare der Originalausgabe (ohne Taschenbücher und Buchgemeinschaften) in den ersten Monaten nach Erscheinen [...] (Faulstich 29)

The benefit of this definition is that it includes some of the causes of a book becoming a best seller ("Aktualität, Mode, Geschmack, Bedarf, Propaganda u.ä.") as well as a numerical minimum for what may be considered a best seller (even though it differs greatly from the figures listed previously). It furthermore differentiates between the "best seller" and the "steady seller." Two problems immediately arise, however, in studying those Spanish American novels that the reading public and the publishers considered to be best sellers in West Germany through 1991. First, *Hundert Jahre Einsamkeit*, originally published in West Germany in 1970, did not become a best seller there until 1982, somewhat later than "sofort oder kurz nach seinem Erscheinen," as stated in the above *Sachwörterbuch* definition. Second, *Chronik eines angekündigten Todes*, *Mexikanischer Tango*, *Lob der Stiefmutter*, *General in seinem Labyrinth*, and *Geschichtenerzähler* did not attain the 100,000 quota before they were considered best sellers.

The approach of Frank Luther Mott in *Golden Multitudes* concentrates not on the minimum figure but rather more on the fact that best sellers are in actuality those books which have higher sales figures than other books in their class. Burkhart R. Lauterbach tells us that in Mott's study,

> [man] findet keine grundsätzliche Erörterung des Begriffs "Bestseller" statt. Vielmehr geht der Autor sofort von einer "Loslösung" des Begriffs aus; er beruft sich auf *Webster's New International Dictionary*: "A book, and, hence, any article of merchandise, whose sales are among the highest of its class," und führt dementsprechend aus, daß es eine Gruppe von sehr erfolgreichen Büchern gibt, die Bestseller genannt werden. Eine untere Grenze, mit deren Hilfe man sehr erfolgreiche Bücher von anderen Bücher unterscheiden kann, nennt er nicht. (Lauterbach 9)

By using Webster's definition and then operating on the principle that there does exist a type of book that is distinguished from other books in its class, Mott could offer an important component to the concept of the best seller. However, in discussing *Golden Multitudes*, John Sutherland offers a different perspective:

> [Mott's] test for bestselling status is that a book shall sell a quantity equal to 1 per cent of the population of the US for the decade in which it was published. The advantage of Mott's calculus is that he can include in his discussion long-term steady-sellers which move too slowly to figure on weekly, monthly and annual lists, or which are too unglamorous to be included, since the essence of bestsellerism, [...] is that there should be hectic change and turnover. The disadvantage of Mott's approach is that for him the bestseller is not a distinct genus but an ordinary book which succeeds to an extraordinary degree. Whereas for the book trade, of course, the bestseller stands in the same relation to other books as does a star to a supporting player. It is importantly *different* from the run of merchandise. (6)

Sutherland's analysis of Mott's method demonstrates the use of Mott's specific definition to include steady-sellers. Sutherland's observations also indicate that best sellers should be studied as a distinct genus. As Sutherland states, the "hectic change and turnover" is a part of bestsellerism, and best sellers should be examined with their more prominent selling status in relation to other books in their class. However, the authority which records and reports on the change, turnover, and superior sales must be established.

To solve some of the problems of the aforementioned definitions, we could attempt to apply Alice P. Hackett's approach in her various books on the American best seller. Hackett "summarizes the works which have figured in the New York lists and makes up an annual 'ten bestsellers of the year' [...] For Hackett, bestsellers are books which have had the honour of appearing in American bestseller lists" (Sutherland 6). When viewed in relation to the context of the Spanish American best seller in Germany, Hackett's definition would allow us to look at those Spanish American works which have appeared on the *Spiegel/Buchreport* Best Seller List, generally considered the German equivalent of *Publishers' Weekly* or the *New York Times* Best Seller Lists, without the limitation of an arbitrary minimum number of copies sold. There are explicit benefits to Hackett's delimitation.

Faulstich addresses the advantages of Hackett's type of definition, classifying one kind of nominal definition as "der Listen-Bestseller. Gemeint sind jene

Romane und Sachbücher, jene Bücher, die in wöchentlichen, monatlichen und jährlichen Listen [...] genannt werden" (*Bestandsaufnahme* 7). In his *Bestseller als Marktphänomen*, Faulstich further discusses best sellers as list best sellers:

> Zugrundegelegt ist die Auffassung des Bestsellers als Listen-Bestseller. Bei dieser Nominaldefinition ist es unerheblich, ob die Listenangaben korrekt jeweils den Titelverkauf wiedergeben, also ob der Listentitel wirklich der Bestseller im echten Wortsinn ist. Ausschlaggebend ist vielmehr allein die Nennung des Titels in einer Liste. [...] Innerhalb des Systems Literatur hat sich hier ein Subsystem mit ganz bestimmten Regeln eingespielt. [...] Sein zentrales Organisationsprinzip ist die Liste, die für die verschiedenen Instanzen des Literaturbetriebs (für Verleger und Buchhändler ebenso für Kritiker und Leser) ganz bestimmte direktive Funktionen übernimmt. Mit der Liste ist zumindest einer der dominanten Referenzfaktoren des Regelkreises ROMAN-Bestseller bestimmt. [...] Mit "Referenzsystem" ist quer durch alle Literaturarten und Medien zunächst diese Orientierung an der Liste gemeint: der Liste-Bestseller. (20)

Faulstich goes on to say that the advantage of the list best seller is

> die Objektivität der erzielbaren Ergebnisse. Bezogen auf einen bestimmten Zeitraum und auf einen bestimmten Verbreitungsbereich, die jeweils noch bestimmt werden sollen, läßt sich zweifelsfrei ermitteln, welche literarischen Werke in den verschiedenen Medien--als Listen-Bestseller--am erfolgreichsten waren. (20-21)

The simplicity and objectivity of the "Listen-Bestseller" offers certain benefits: The time frame distinguishes the best sellers from the steady sellers and would exclude the latter. Furthermore, we can see how the sales of Spanish American works compare in direct competition, comparison, and turnover with native German-language best sellers and with novels translated from other languages into German which then became best sellers in Germany. I will include the "list best seller," then, in the definition of "best seller" in my analysis. This definition, however, is limited to the list best seller and offers no further information on the best-selling author or the best seller as a genre, i.e., a best-selling line or type of books (Sutherland 8).

In contemplating the Spanish American fiction as best sellers, both best-selling author and the best seller as a genre should be considered. Gabriel García Márquez and Isabel Allende are best-selling authors (that is, authors who have produced several best sellers) in West Germany. German audiences have come to expect a certain kind of literature from Allende and García Márquez, who had four and five books, respectively, on the West German best seller list from 1981 to '91.

Sutherland identifies the best seller as a genre in the collective sense of certain types of novels that become best sellers. The best seller as a genre can be understood on an individual basis to mean a particular type of novel bearing special similar characteristics which hold a special appeal and expectation for a broad-based reading audience, which thus enables these novels to become best sellers.

Here, the Spanish American novel is considered to demonstrate a certain combination of features which, although found separately in other works and genres, have aggregately combined to answer specific expectations of West German readers. As such, these attributes have contributed to the best seller status of twelve Spanish American novels and to the distinction of being perceived in West Germany as a best-selling sub-genre. We must thus look further to find a definition that includes the best seller as author and as genre as well as list best seller.

Sutherland and Faulstich do not limit their approaches to the term and concept of best sellers to just the books themselves. Sutherland writes:

> I would contend that bestsellers are usefully approached by an examination of the apparatus which produces them (bestseller lists, the publishing industry, publicity), an apparatus which is called here, for convenience, "bestsellerism." (8)

He maintains that the word "sell" in the term "best seller" connotes the common American usage of "persuaded to buy." Sutherland continues, "This dynamic sense of selling by crashing through sales resistance [...] is inherent in the bestseller system" (18). In light of West German marketing of the Spanish American novels, the inclusion of the broader idea of the best seller system has its definite merits.

Faulstich adopts and expands John Sutherland's use of the term "best seller" to provide a more detailed definition. He sees the best seller as a book market phenomenon in the sense that the best seller is not considered a single product. He continues:

> Bisher lassen sich vor allem drei verschiedene Inhalte von "Buchmarkt-Phänomen" namhaft machen: der Bestseller als Bestseller-Autor, als neues Genre neben anderen Literaturgenres und als System. [...]

> [...] Bestseller-Autoren vermögen ihre Produkte in regelmäßiger Folge in die Listen schreiben zu können, scheinen den literarischen Erfolg geradezu zu besitzen. [...] Der Leser weiß präzise, was er zu erwarten hat [...]; der literarische Erfolg zeugt den Erfolg. [...]
>
> Umfassender ist demgegenüber das Verständnis des Wortes Bestseller als ein Genre, "eine neue Buchart, [...]" gleichrangig bzw. übergeordnet zu bekannten wie Lyrik, Humoristische Bücher, Praktische Ratgeber oder Klassiker hinzukommt. [...]
>
> Dabei steht Sutherland bereits an der Schwelle eines Wortverständnisses, nach dem der Bestseller nicht nur Genre, sondern System ist. [...]
>
> Beim Bestseller als Buchmarkt-Phänomen, vor allem im Sinn des Markts als System, wird wieder jene geschichtliche Einschränkung gemacht, die auch das Verständnis des Bestsellers als Listenbestseller kennzeichnet. (*Bestandsaufnahme* 24-28)

Faulstich thus offers the most complete definition and comprehensive meaning of the best seller and one which best identifies the material that is examined here: the best seller as list best seller, as author, as genre, and as a system within the West German literary market process. Viewing the best seller as a system enables us to contemplate the author's production, the publishers' marketing, the critics' published opinions, and the readers' expectations and reception of the texts and thus the concretization of the works.

I consider the "best seller," then, to be the hardback fiction list best seller and as such to be recognized as a system as defined by Werner Faulstich. The individual Spanish American works that made the West German best seller list from 1981 to 1991, the best selling authors, the best seller lists themselves, the publishers, the publicity and marketing as well as contemporary events influencing book sales are all viewed here as the system that produced Spanish American works as best sellers in West Germany during the ten year period. Collectively, these Spanish American novels are judged here as emanating special similar qualities that distinguish them from other best-selling novels read in West Germany, i.e., qualities that classify them as a separate type, and that meet certain expectations that West Germans have of this kind of novel. This principle then caused them to be perceived in West Germany, from the viewpoint of the recipients, as if they constituted a best-selling sub-genre. I will present the specific characteristics of these novels in more detail in Part II. The best seller list used here is the *Spiegel/Buchreport* Best Seller List.

1.2 *Spiegel/Buchreport* Best Seller List

While there is a variety of sources of best seller lists available in West Germany, I chose the *Spiegel/Buchreport* Best Seller List for three primary reasons. First, when one speaks of "the best seller list" in West Germany, the list most frequently meant is the *Spiegel/Buchreport* list. Second, publishers of the Spanish American novels covered in this study refer to the *Spiegel/Buchreport* list when they discuss "the best seller list." Third, the *Spiegel/Buchreport* list is a part of the best seller market system in West Germany: It not only records and reports the information on best sellers, but it also helps generate best sellers in that it is used as a reference guide to recommend to the general public to buy certain books.

Under the title "Orientierung für Millionen. Woche für Woche mit dem Computer ermittelt," the trade magazine *Buchreport* reported in October 1988 the history of the best seller list in *Spiegel* and how data for the *Spiegel/Buchreport* best seller lists is collected. The article begins

> Als *Der Spiegel* am 18. Oktober 1961 begann, regelmäßig Bestsellerlisten für Bücher zu veröffentlichen, war damit ein Signal für den Buchhandel gesetzt: Das Nachrichtenmagazin verabschiedete sich von der über Generationen hinweg hochgehaltenen, einseitigen Betrachtung des Buches als Transportmittel "wertvoller" Inhalte und fügte ihr den Warenaspekt hinzu; von nun an wurde nicht nur sichtbar, was Kritiker mochten, sondern es wurden Montag für Montag die meist*gekauften* Bücher im *Spiegel* aufgeführt. (5 Oct. 1988: 34)

The article continues with the account of the new data collection system (34-35). A review of the changed profile of bookstores in West Germany in the years prior to 1988 showed that some smaller bookstores had disappeared, others had become large bookstores, and still others had sprung up from nowhere. In order to get a random sample of bookstores, a representative panel was chosen based on tax information from *Buch und Buchhandel in Zahlen.* Those with sales of less than 500,000 DM per year were discarded since it was felt that they would not be able to provide precise enough information.

Of the total of 1621 bookstores which could then be considered, 220 were chosen to be the representative participants based on the various sales figures and regions of the country. The panel remains relatively constant, although it is checked and adjusted each year as needed.

The participants then fill out and return the survey sent them each Friday by the following Thursday. The survey is divided into "Belletristic" and "Non-Fiction" and contains approximately 75 best selling titles from the previous week. The bookstores then rank the books from one to fifteen based on sales for the week in question. Should the bookdealer encounter a title with substantial sales but one which did not appear on the previous week's list of 75 titles, the book dealer writes in the title by hand.

Once the list is sent in, a computer sorts and compiles the data. The weekly lists are prepared and published, and the information is stored for the yearly best seller list that appears in the first issue each new year.

At the time of the Frankfurt Book Fair in 1987, the list that appears in *Spiegel* was lengthened from ten works per category to fifteen. The purpose of the extension was to expose the names of more of the best-selling novels to the public. *Buchreport* is not for sale to the general public; bookstores may subscribe to it. In each issue there is a large inset with the "Spiegel Bestseller" List of hardcover books and the "Gong Taschenbuch Bestsellerliste" of paperbacks. Most bookstores either display the lists in the store or at least indicate the rankings of the best seller hardcover books according to the "Spiegel Bestseller" list. The list reporting the best sellers then in turn becomes itself a recommendation to buy certain books and as such plays a role in the book market as a system.

1.3 Interaction Between Best Sellers and Society

What is the interplay between the best seller as a system and its consumers in society? What is the relationship between the best seller and society itself? How does the best seller function as a suggestion to buy certain works?

Faulstich describes the best seller list as a recommendation to purchase books. He quotes a researcher of the German book trade process, Horst Machill, who discusses book dealers and the best seller lists as a motivating factor to buy:

> Hierzu eine Stimme von vielen [Buchhändlern]: "Wir merken diese Wirkung immer deutlicher, sogar bei unseren Stammkunden, die sich bisher immer von uns beraten ließen, und sind dabei sicher, daß diese abweisende Haltung gegenüber dem Verkaufsgespräch nur an der dringlichen Empfehlung durch die 'List,' aber keinesfalls an einer Enttäuschung über unsere bisherigen Empfehlungen liegt." (Qtd. in Faulstich *Bestandsaufnahme* 129)

Machill goes on to say that the influence of the list in the field of belletristic literature is especially strong. "Einkäufe mit dem Wunsch 'geben Sie mir die ersten fünf Titel der Bestseller-Liste aus der Zeitschrift [...]' sind durchaus keine Sonderfälle" (129).

The reasons behind customers wanting to buy books on the best seller list vary. First, customers who are somewhat intimidated by bookstores can enter a bookstore with more confidence and request a book that thousands of others have already purchased:

> Solche Käufer sehen in der Liste einen besonders guten Weg, ihre Unsicherheit gegenüber dem beratenden Buchhändler zu verdecken und finden dabei in der Möglichkeit, einen bestimmten Wunsch entschlossen zu äußern, das Gefühl einer 'Pseudo-Sicherheit.' (Machill, qtd. in Faulstich, *Bestandsaufnahme* 130)

Historically, bookstores in Germany have been considered "ein sehr hoch angesehenes Einzelhandelsgeschäft" (Hooge, personal interview). While this general opinion is different now--due to the democratization of the bookstores--for some buyers the lack of self-assurance has been eased by the best seller lists.

Faulstich lists three sources of motivation for book buying through the best seller lists: 1) the "snob effect" as an elite dissociation from the masses, "der sich letztlich aus dem zeitlichen Vorsprung der Konsumtion herleitet," 2) the "Veblen effect," again a dissociation of an "elite" group in that the higher price of a hardcover book actually increases its demand, the desire to have what others do not or cannot possess. Faulstich says that the "snob effect" and the "Veblen effect" have two characteristics in common: topicality ("Aktualität") and the high price of the hardcover editions. The last source of motivation is 3) the "bandwagon effect," "nämlich für diejenigen, die 'in', die 'up-to-date' sein oder mitreden wollen" (*Bestandsaufnahme* 166).

Others who have written on best sellers agree on this last function. Hohendahl explains:

> Die Aufgabe des Verlags besteht darin, das Buch als Gesprächstoff anzubieten. Denn der Bestseller erhält als Kontaktmaterial in einer arbeitsteiligen, hochspezialisierten Gesellschaft eine wichtige Funktion. Die besondere Gratifikation für seinen Leser besteht darin, mit anderen Lesern desselben Buches, mit denen ihn im übrigen wenig verbindet, ein gemeinsames Gesprächsthema zu haben. (173-74)

Similarly, Dieter Zimmer maintains, "Kennen immerhin sollte man [Bestseller] schon, wenn man mitreden will" (Qtd. in Faulstich, *Bestandsaufnahme* 18).

Indeed, society and the best seller stand in direct relation to each other. The best sellers of a society are often a reflection of a contemporary way of thinking, of the hopes, dreams, and fantasies of the society as a whole.[1] "Super-Bestsellers," Faulstich states, are characterized as contemporary forms of a "Mythos, als kollektive Träume [...] Träume entweder 'öffentlicher' oder 'privater' Art" (*Bestandsaufnahme* 168). Heinz Ludwig Arnold remarks in the "Vorbemerkung" to his *Deutsche Bestseller, deutsche Ideologie*,

> "Das Ereignis 'Bestseller' ist also immer das Zusammentreffen ganz bestimmter innerer Bedingungen und äußerer historischer: sozialer, psychischer, politischer usw. Verhältnisse." (5)

And in the words of Kracauer we learn:

> Der große Bucherfolg ist das Zeichen eines geglückten soziologischen Experimentes, der Beweis dafür, daß wieder einmal eine Mischung von Elementen gelungen ist, die dem Geschmack der anonymen Leserschaft entspricht. (Qtd. in Hohendahl 173)

We can apply the aforementioned statements on the relationship of best sellers and society to the case of the Spanish American best seller in West Germany. As will be shown in Chapter 3, there was a decided increase in the reception of Spanish American fiction in Germany during the 1980s. These novels echoed a shift in German contemporary way of thinking about Latin American literature. The works likely mirrored and at the same time gave rise to the "hopes, dreams, and fantasies" of the German public with regard to Latin America. Chapter 3 and Part II illustrate the interest in Spanish American literature and culture during the '80s as collective dreams, hopes, fantasies, and expectations emanating from these texts.

If the best seller is a successful sociological experiment, the fact that a number of Spanish American novels have become best sellers in West Germany indicates that the German general reading public found in the Spanish American novels that mixture of elements that can create cross-cultural best sellers.

Notes

[1] See Bernhardt Zimmermann, *Neues Handbuch der Literaturwissenschaft: Literatur nach 1945, II: Themen und Genre*, ed. Jost Hermand (Wiesbaden: Athenaion, 1979) 121-22 and Imogen Seger, "Bestseller-Soziologie--eine Forderung unserer Zeit," in *Für Willi Droemer zum 18 Juli 1971* (Munich: N.p., 1971) 191.

Chapter 2

Spanish American Best Sellers Marketed in West Germany

[D]er traditionelle Verleger als Hüter des kulturellen Grals [verweist] ängstlich auf das Verlagsgeschäft als "ein großes Lotteriespiel." (Werner Faulstich, *Thesen zum Bestseller-Roman* 43)

What are the elements that have caused so many Spanish American novels to attract the attention of West Germans? This chapter examines the publisher's role in producing a marketable cross-cultural novel for the West German public. I plan to discuss the individual works in their content, style, translation, packaging, and marketing. The translation and packaging are a product of that part of the best seller market system that is responsible for targeting the novels specifically for the German marketplace. Marketing has the further effect of reinforcing and perpetuating the West German association of certain characteristics with these Spanish American novels as a collective type, or subgenre. Later chapters draw on the information presented here to discuss the perceived similar intrinsic elements in the success of these novels in Germany.

2.1 "Creating" Best Sellers

If there is such a close relationship between society and the best seller, it would seem that best sellers could be created, that a formula for best sellers in a particular society and at any particular point in time could be composed and that best sellers could be produced on the basis of this formula. However, there is a difference between best-selling authors and a publisher-produced formula for creating best sellers. Some authors can create best sellers; publishers market the product.

In examining best-selling authors, that is, authors who have consistently written best-selling novels in West Germany, one finds that most of these authors continue to write novels that fulfill certain expectations on the part of their readers. However, each author uses his or her own formula, and what works for one author likely would not work for another. In West Germany, best-selling authors--in this case, those who had two or more of their novels on the yearly best seller list of *Spiegel/Buchreport* in the 1980s--were Christine Brückner, Ephraim Kishon, Ilse von Bredow, Johannes Mario Simmel, Heinz G. Konsalik, Frederick Forsyth, Otto Waalkes,[1] Brösel (Rötger Werner Feldmann), James Clavel, Stephen King, John Jakes, Kristiane Allert-Wybranietz,

Günter Grass, Siegfried Lenz, Umberto Eco, Michael Ende, Patrick Süskind, Gabriel García Márquez, and Isabel Allende. In most cases, the author clearly has a certain formula, a particular style that is appealing to the general public. The success of best-selling authors generates further success, i.e., best-selling authors can create more best sellers.

In contrast, the consensus among many scholars and publishers is that the publisher cannot create a best seller, that there is no formula emanating from the publisher that would guarantee best seller success (Dormagen, personal interview 18 May 1989; Faulstich, *Bestandsaufnahme* 139; King 74). It is, however, the publishers' job to convince as many people as possible to purchase the books they produce, and the publishers exercise the control that they have to attract customers.

What can the publisher do to influence the public to buy certain books in the first place? Once the publisher has accepted a text, there are many facets of the marketing process that must be considered. Should preprints be given to newspapers and magazines? When should book clubs be offered rights to the text? Should the author make a reading tour?

More concretely, the publisher must consider the form in which the book will be presented to the public.

> Wichtiger für den Erfolg eines Buches als sein Inhalt und als die Intensität der Werbung ist der Verlag, der hinter ihm steht, und ist seine Verpackung: Titel, Klappentext, Schutzumschlag. (Zimmer, "Die Herzen" 112)

The title, the book jacket blurb, and the book jacket design itself are part of the marketing, and the targeted consumer must be considered in the marketing process. "Whereas the text itself is said to offer a functional value (*Gebrauchswert*), advertising offers an exchange value (*Tauschwert*) or nonfunctional value" (King 76). Whether or not the publisher has been successful in choosing author, text, and marketing strategies is ultimately decided by the consumer.

In dealing with the Spanish American novels that have already become best sellers in West Germany, we have the advantage of knowing that the publishers have utilized some combination of the above to successfully market the authors and the texts. The next step is to determine what was successful and why.

2.2 The Spanish American Best Sellers

This section includes a brief description and history of the German career of each of the Spanish American best-selling works of fiction. I will examine how each work came to be published in Germany and how each author came to his or her publisher. The German title, book jacket blurbs, book jacket design, and general marketing are also taken into account. Furthermore, the quality of the translations will be discussed, as well as some of the difficulties the translators experienced in translating from the American Spanish into German.

2.2.1 Gabriel García Márquez

The popularity of García Márquez built up slowly in West Germany, but in recent years his name has become synonymous with literary quality in best sellers. He has visited the country a few times but has not been there for a number of years. His absence, however, has not adversely affected the sales of his books (Flad, personal interview 13 Feb. 1989).

Hundert Jahre Einsamkeit, published in Spanish in 1967, was published in German in 1970. It is the story of a family, a town, a country, a continent, and mankind. José Arcadio Buendía and his wife Ursula, who is also his cousin, found the town of Macondo, and the novel follows their story throughout several generations, to the last Buendía family member. Under the leadership of the family, Macondo experiences futile revolution, Yankee imperialism, exploitation, the arrival of technology, and uncontrollable natural elements. Condemned to a life without love or reflection, the Buendía family dies out when the last of the Buendías is born with a pig's tail and is carried off and devoured by ants.

As the last adult Buendía, Aureliano, manages to decipher an old manuscript in the last pages of the novel, readers learn that they have been reading the history of Macondo and of the Buendías as recorded by Melquíades, a Gypsy who has appeared several times in the novel--indeed, coming back from the dead more than once. Melquíades has held the past, present, and future as if they were but an instant of thought. The first paragraph of the novel best illustrates the interplay of time sequences as well as the innocence of a distant, paradisiac, Eden-like time:

> Viele Jahre später sollte der Oberst Aureliano Buendía sich vor dem Erschießungskommando an jenen fernen Nachmittag erinnern, an dem sein Vater ihn mitnahm, um das Eis kennenzulernen. Macondo war damals ein Dorf von zwanzig Häusern aus Lehm und Bambus am Ufer eines Flusses mit kristallklarem Wasser, das dahineilte durch ein Bett aus geschliffenen Steinen, weiß und riesig wie prähistorische Eier. Die Welt war noch so jung, daß viele Dinge des Namens entbehrten, und um sie zu benennen,

> mußte man mit dem Finger auf sie deuten. Alljährlich im Monat März schlug eine Familie zerlumpter Zigeuner ihr Zelt in der Nähe des Dorfes auf und gab mit einem gewaltigen Getöse aus Pfeifen und Trommeln die neuesten Erfindungen bekannt. (9)

The style of the book has been as acclaimed as the content. Written by an author who understands, feels, and is capable of conveying the essence of Spanish American life, *Hundert Jahre Einsamkeit* is not just a chronicle of a family. With its many episodes, the book is a string of many stories. Some of the stories are based on fact (e.g., the incident of the banana cutters), and some fall into the realm of magic realism. With magic realism, the magical, the fantastic, and the phenomenal (e.g., yellow butterflies flitting around a seducer, a girl's ascension into heaven while hanging the sheets out to dry one day) are accepted as perfectly natural events.[2] They are almost understatements, another of García Márquez's techniques.

A further aspect of García Márquez's style is his humor, which takes form not only in understatements but also in overstatements. We find, for example, Aureliano Buendía's seventeen sons by seventeen different women, the thirty-three revolutions he survived, and the rain that continued for four years, eleven months, and two days. García Márquez's humor can be grotesque as well, reminiscent of that of Franz Kafka, who influenced García Márquez. *Hundert Jahre Einsamkeit* is not an easy book to read for most average readers; the baroque complexity and the confusing repetition, although in fact one of the themes of the novel (that we are nothing more than a reflection of those who have come before us and of those yet to come), does not seem to lend itself to mass readership.

Two other facets of García Márquez's literary world that should be mentioned are the influence of the matriarch (more specifically, that of his grandmother) and the "macho" lifestyle on the author, both of which are reflected in his works. Like Mario Vargas Llosa and Isabel Allende, García Márquez had lived with his grandparents when he was a child; and his grandmother's storytelling inspired him to tell stories. In many of his works, including *Hundert Jahre Einsamkeit*, female characters tend to be strong and matriarchal. At the same time, García Márquez frequently portrays the macho world. Sometimes he depicts it as a natural part of Latin American life (as with Colonel Aureliano's seventeen illegitimate sons in *Hundert Jahre Einsamkeit*), and other times he focuses on the macho way of life in order to condemn it (*Chronik eines angekündigten Todes*). Good story-telling, the prominence of the strong female characters, and the literary treatment of machismo are also found in works by Isabel Allende, Angeles Mastretta, and Mario Vargas Llosa.

A translator for Kiepenheuer & Witsch was instrumental in introducing *Cien años de soledad* to the German public. The translator was in Santiago, Chile, in 1968/1969 when the book was recommended to her, and she brought it back to Germany. Two recommendations were obtained for publishing the book, and Kiepenheuer & Witsch paid 5,000 DM for the rights to the novel in German. Since the tendency is to keep an author from abroad with the one publisher, a contract was signed for Kiepenheuer & Witsch to be García Márquez's publisher in German.

Cien años de soledad thus appeared in German as *Hundert Jahre Einsamkeit* and was translated by one of the premier translators of Spanish and Portuguese into German, Curt Meyer-Clason. The translation was praised in the numerous reviews of the novel, by Walter Haubrich, Hans-Jürgen Heise, and Gustav Siebenmann, among others.

There have been three different versions of the book jacket. The book jacket of the first edition showed a skeleton surrounded by flowers. A later edition had a motif of men in Latin American clothing and hats constructing or repairing a building. Most recently, the dust jacket featured a painting of a tropical jungle with green plants, red flowers, and birds. The border and remainder of the jacket is black. This last book jacket design looks very similar to the book jacket for *Die Liebe in den Zeiten der Cholera* and *Der General in seinem Labyrinth.* All three have similar paintings of tropical flora with a thick black border. This tropical setting may have been more inviting to the Germans than the skeleton motif.

In contrast to *Cien años de soledad,* García Márquez's *Crónica de una muerte anunciada* (1981, in German *Chronik eines angekündigten Todes,* 1981) is much shorter and easier to read. Although not a linear narrative, the novel does not draw on the suspense of who will be killed, nor how or when. The book opens with the sentence,

> An dem Tag, an dem sie Santiago Nasar töten wollten, stand er um fünf Uhr dreißig morgens auf, um den Dampfer zu erwarten, mit dem der Bischof kam. (9)

The first phrase of the Spanish original reads, "El día en que lo iban a matar, [...]," suggesting with more certainty that the murder would take place. García Márquez wanted to avoid "vulgäre Spannung";[3] to do this, he decided not to withhold basic plot data until the end. By starting the novel with the first sentence announcing that the murder will take place, García Márquez sustains the suspense throughout the book. What draws the reader to the book is the question: How can a town have known that a murder would take place and not have prevented it?

A newcomer to town, Bayardo San Román, decides to marry Angela Vicario. Since his father is rich, he spares no expense for the wedding and for their house. On their wedding night, Bayardo claims that Angela is not a virgin, and he returns her to her family. After threats from her brothers, Angela names Santiago Nasar as the one who has disgraced her. Her twin brothers, Pedro and Pablo, then announce to everyone they meet that they have to kill Santiago Nasar to avenge the lost family honor. The conventions of the honor code make it inevitable that someone would be killed, even though there is an attempt to keep the affair a bloodless ritual. The townspeople support the avenging of honor but want it to take place on a more theatrical level. By the time the murder is committed, almost everyone knows the murderers' intentions, and still the murder takes place. Not all answers are provided: Santiago Nasar's "guilt" is never established, and the reader never learns why Angela names him, who it was if not he, or if, in fact, she had even been violated at all.

The novel is written in a journalistic style: the language is concrete, realistic, and objective. The sentences are simple, and every possible detail is included. The narrator constantly reminds the reader of the time in relation to the murder. Although the reader knows from the beginning that a murder will happen, the story is intriguing and humorous. The story is based on an incident that happened in a town in Colombia, and García Márquez mentions real relatives of his own. At the same time, a reference is made to Colonel Aureliano Buendía, a fictional character in *Hundert Jahre Einsamkeit.*

Kiepenheuer & Witsch was already the publisher in Germany for García Márquez, but that did not prevent an unauthorized printing in the alternative magazine *Pflasterstrand* under the name "G. de Aracataca" (Aracataca is García Márquez's hometown in Colombia) with the title "Novela." The printing is, however, not likely to have significantly hurt the sales of the authorized publication since the book received publicity from the incident.

Curt Meyer-Clason also translated *Chronik eines angekündigten Todes*, but this time the reviews of the translation were not laudatory. He was accused of having translated the work too hurriedly and of making a number of translating mistakes.[4] While the editor at Kiepenheuer & Witsch tried to catch as many mistakes as possible, a number went on to be published. Later, a dispute occurred between Meyer-Clason and the head of Kiepenheuer & Witsch. Although Meyer-Clason had previously translated all of García Márquez's works into German, *Chronik eines angekündigten Todes* was the last.

The book jacket is again black, this time with a photograph instead of a painting. The picture shows a house at twilight with festive colored lights in a tree next to the house. Behind the house is the outline of a palm tree. The blurb on the back cover states:

> Ein Dorf an der kolumbianischen Karibikküste feiert ein rauschendes Hochzeitsfest, doch noch in der Hochzeitsnacht wird die Braut ins Elternhaus zurückgeschickt; sie war nicht mehr unberührt. Der mutmaßliche "Täter" muß sterben. In seiner atemberaubenden Chronik, einem in sich geschlossenen Meisterwerk, beschreibt Gabriel García Márquez die Stunden zwischen Ankündigung und bitterem Vollzug dieses Todes.

The book jacket cover and blurb convey the Caribbean setting (the palm tree, Latin American wedding celebration, Caribbean coast) and suggest mystery and suspense (twilight and darkness, "der mutmaßliche Täter," "atemberaubenden Chronik").

García Márquez's *El amor en los tiempos del cólera*, 1985 (in German *Die Liebe in den Zeiten der Cholera*, 1987), actually begins with the death of two men; but the theme, the subject, and the tone are lighter than those in *Chronik eines angekündigten Todes*. It has a much more traditional and, for the most part, linear structure and is therefore accessible to the average reader.

The content is relatively simple and on the surface would not seem to support 509 pages. For over fifty years, Florentino Ariza, the illegitimate son of a ship owner and a haberdasher, has waited to declare his undying love to Fermina Daza, whom he had courted and almost won when they were young. Unfortunately, he makes his declaration at the funeral of Fermina's husband, one of the most respected men of the community and a professor of medicine, who had been a leader in the fight against the cholera epidemics that had ravaged the country. García Márquez then shifts back in time to the days when Fermina and Florentino met, fell in love, courted, and separated.

The author traces their respective lives as they develop over the years until they are reunited when they are in their seventies. In spite of their age and Fermina's rebuff, Florentino pursues her relentlessly. His persistence is rewarded as the pair takes a cruise on a river ship that belongs to Florentino's ship line company. The novel ends with the decision that Florentino, Fermina, and the captain of the ship will continue traveling on the ship indefinitely with the cholera flag raised to "protect" it from intruders:

> Der Kapitän [...] erschrak über den späten Verdacht, daß nicht so sehr der Tod, vielmehr das Leben keine Grenzen kennt.
>
> "Und was glauben Sie, wie lange wir dieses Scheiß-Hin-und-Zurück durchhalten können?"
>
> Florentino Ariza war seit dreiundfünfzig Jahren, sieben Monaten und elf Tagen und Nächten auf die Frage vorbereitet:
>
> "Das ganze Leben", sagte er. (508-509)

With the theme of the love story comes the more conventional style. "It is a novel that deals confidently in cliché and improbable exaggeration" (Minta 126). The novel combines reality, bringing in real events in the lives of García Márquez's parents and the history of Colombia, while again creating a fictional work full of fantasy. Humor and irony are mixed with the tragic. (At the beginning and again near the end of the novel, characters commit suicide.) Still, the novel has a happy ending. It is interesting to note how Stephen Minta relates the two main male characters to what he believes to be García Márquez's intention in writing the novel in relation to literature:

> Juvenal Urbino, the symbol of correctness in literature as in everything, is condemned by his position to read only what is best in the field of contemporary writing, whereas Florentino reads simply for the love of reading, without caring about distinctions between good and bad. He has been brought up on the volumes of the *Biblioteca Popular*, a series which can be found everywhere and which contains everything, from Homer to the most derisory of local poets. It is this kind of freedom that García Márquez is seeking in the novel [...] (143)

In light of *Liebe in den Zeiten der Cholera* becoming an international best seller that remained on the West German best seller list the second longest of any of the Spanish American novels, it would appear that García Márquez has found and justified "this kind of freedom."

Since Kiepenheuer & Witsch was no longer using the services of Meyer-Clason as translator, a new translator had to be engaged. The translation was offered to Dagmar Ploetz, who had already translated Isabel Allende's *Von Liebe und Schatten* for Suhrkamp Verlag, and she accepted the undertaking. A few reviewers criticized her rhythm and her choice of words, particularly when she uses compound words in an attempt to move away from García Márquez's very frequent use of the genitive. The Spanish "amores de emergencia," for example, is translated into German as "Erste-Hilfe-Liebe." However, there was not an outcry against the overall quality of the translation as there had been with *Chronik eines angekündigten Todes*, and Dagmar Ploetz became the translator of García Márquez into German.

García Márquez himself chose the painting to be used on the cover of the novel in Spanish and in many of the translations, including the German translation. (The English version deviates from the norm and uses instead Edward J. Steichen's *Poster Lady*, 1906.) The painting shows, again, a tropical jungle scene in various shades of green with red flowers and a red bird. In the lower left is Cupid with his arrow drawn. There are mountains in the background, and a body of water in the center. García Márquez had a steam boat with a hoisted yellow flag added on the body of water. In contrast to the Spanish version's light blue background frame, the German places the picture and the author's, publisher's and novel's names on a black background. The picture itself is complementary to the plot, and it also draws attention to the book, emphasizing the love theme and the tropical setting. Even with the same picture, the black border communicates a different impression from that of the light blue on the Spanish version.

Both Ulla Brümmer, in charge of dust jacket design at Kiepenheuer & Witsch, and Jürgen Dormagen, in charge of the Latin American Program at Suhrkamp Verlag in Frankfurt, note that they usually have to make changes in the jackets from the Spanish original to adapt them to the tastes of the German public. The appeal of the design differs from culture to culture: What is aesthetically in vogue in Latin America is often less enticing or conveys a different message in Germany. Kiepenheuer & Witsch recognize their German public's need to associate a book with a classical literary appearance (Brümmer, personal interview). To market Spanish American fiction in Germany, both publishing houses wrap the books in jackets that are viewed by the German public as less frivolous and more elegant than the Spanish original, whether in the color of the background border or in the elimination of the discordant colors in the picture.

Kiepenheuer & Witsch conducted an extensive advertising campaign for *Liebe in den Zeiten der Cholera.* Postcards of the picture on the book jacket were inserted into copies of the books and transparent stickers of the Cupid figure were used on envelopes mailed from the publisher. The public eagerly anticipated the publication of the novel.

The book jacket blurb draws on García Márquez's fame from his earlier masterpiece as well as on the novel's theme of a love story:

> Gabriel García Márquez, der Autor von *Hundert Jahre Einsamkeit,* hat einen großen Liebesroman geschrieben. Eine Geschichte voller Lebenskraft und Poesie, die von der lebenslangen Liebe Florentino Arizas zu Fermina Daza erzählt.

Certain key words like "Liebesroman" and "Liebe" in the book jacket blurb hold particular interest for many readers in general (Eckard Hooge, personal interview), while "Lebenskraft," is presumably a characteristic in Latin American novels that draws German readers (personal interviews: Maria Bamberg, 3 Apr. 1989; Jürgen Dormagen, 18 May 1989; Bärbel Flad, 13 Feb. 1989).

The German version of *El general in su laberinto*, *Der General in seinem Labyrinth*, was published the same year that the original appeared, 1989. The work deviates significantly from García Márquez's earlier novels. This "historical novel" recounts the last seven months in the life of Simón Bolívar, known as the "Libertador" of what became Ecuador, Colombia, and Venezuela. It describes Bolívar's forced resignation as President of "Gran Colombia," his departure for the capital Santa Fe de Bogotá, and his last trip down the Magdalena River (the same river figuring in the ending of *Liebe in den Zeiten der Cholera*), accompanied by a few loyal people, with the goal of exile in Europe. Before he reaches the sea, Simón Bolívar dies, a sick "old" man, at the age of 47. The book relates Bolívar's preoccupations, reflections, ramblings, and memories of grander times. His dream of a United South America was never realized, and his illness and feeling of betrayal acerbate his bitter disappointment.

García Márquez purposefully selected the last days of Bolívar. While all of the *Libertador*'s life is thoroughly documented through his myriad of detailed letters, there is virtually no record of the last few months except for two or three letters. García Márquez said, "My fantasy had no boundaries; I could invent everything."[5] He was able to add fiction to history.

García Márquez's journalist background again contributes to the work: At the end García Márquez describes the detailed research he did in preparation for writing the novel. The generic context is different from the other novels, and therefore so is the style. It was not written to be suspenseful; gone too are the hyperboles and the fantastic of magic realism typical of García Márquez's works. The critics compliment Dagmar Ploetz's German rendition of the novel.

The dust jacket, similar to that of *Liebe in den Zeiten der Cholera*, was taken from the Spanish original. This time with a dark green border, it shows a porch with a hammock and a pair of boots. Looking out from the porch, one sees tropical vegetation on both sides of blue water, yellow flowers, and a colorful bird in a tree. Kiepenheuer & Witsch bolstered the image in the illustration with postcards and posters with the same representation of the porch and hammock.

On the back cover is information about the Simón Bolívar:

> Simón Bolívar, der glorreiche General des südamerikanischen Unabhängigkeitskrieges gegen die spanische Krone, ist der Held von Gabriel García Márquez's neuem mitreißenden Roman. Vom großen Ruhm bis zur bitteren Niederlage entsteht in einem spannungsreichen Geflecht historischer Ereignisse das faszinierende Leben dieses Liebhabers schöner Frauen und der Macht. Der kolumbianische Nobelpreisträger entwirft das gegreifende Porträt

eines Menschen im Labyrinth seiner Leiden und verlorenen Träume.

Likely to entice the potential German reader are phrases such as "mitreißenden Roman," "spannungsreichen Geflecht historischer Ereignisse," and of course "das faszinierende Leben dieses Liebhabers schöner Frauen und der Macht," together with the name "Gabriel García Márquez," by now a "trade name" (Ripken, personal interview, 9 June 1992). The German public was willing to buy the book based on the name of the author.

2.2.2 Isabel Allende

With Isabel Allende the focus shifts from Kiepenheuer & Witsch to Suhrkamp's Latin American Program, which will be discussed in more detail in the next chapter. Three of the four Spanish American authors (Isabel Allende, Angeles Mastretta, and Mario Vargas Llosa) whose novels became best sellers in West Germany between 1981 and 1991 are published by Suhrkamp.

Allende at first had some difficulty in getting her first novel, *La casa de los espíritus*, 1982, published. The novel was rejected by various Latin American publishers before she sent it to the agent for several other Spanish American writers, Carmen Balcells, in Barcelona. *Casa de los espíritus* was consequently published by Plaza & Janés in Spain, and it won the Premio Mazatlán, a prize for literature. At a presentation in Barcelona, Michi Strausfeld, scout for Suhrkamp Verlag, met Allende and received a copy of the novel from her. Strausfeld read the book and wrote a recommendation to Suhrkamp. Suhrkamp bought the German rights to the novel soon thereafter, and the translated version, *Das Geisterhaus*, was published in 1984.

Since *Geisterhaus* has been published, Allende has been to West Germany several times, and each time her circle of fans has been greater. Germans respond well not only to her novels but also to her personal and open public appearances; in 1989 her public readings were sold out in cities across the country.

Geisterhaus describes the rise and fall of three generations of a bourgeois family, the Truebas. After Rosa del Valle's death, her younger sister Clara marries Rosa's fiancé Esteban Trueba. A polarity arises between them as Esteban builds his estate, becomes a senator for the conservatives, and has many illegitimate children while Clara knits for the poor and remains unpolitical. For three generations she works against class privileges. Esteban and Clara have three children: two sons, one of whom becomes a doctor for the poor and friend of "the President" (Salvador Allende, although he is never named), and a daughter, Blanca. Blanca has an illegitimate child by a farm hand, whom she loves all of her life. Their daughter, Alba, who becomes friends with a young revolutionary, is arrested after the putsch overthrowing "the President;" and one of Esteban Trueba's numerous illegitimate grandchildren, who has become a colonel, tortures her. Alba survives and writes the family history together with her grandfather Esteban Trueba, whom she understands and loves in spite of their differences.

The novel is a series of anecdotes in the lives of the family members. Allende mixes fantasy with history--both Chilean history and the history of her own family--and politics. She incorporates fantasy, exaggeration, the grotesque, humor, and tragedy into her writing. The end result is a very readable, consumable product.

Geisterhaus was translated into German by another of the most respected translators in Germany, Anneliese Botond, and the translation has been praised. Botond won the *Johann-Heinrich-Voß-Preis* from the Akademie für Sprache und Dichtung for her translation of the novel. The editor of the Latin American Program at Suhrkamp noted that *Geisterhaus* is a title that suggests expectation, distinctive images, and animated feelings (Dormagen, personal interview 18 May 1989).

The novel was not originally promoted by Suhrkamp Verlag any more than its other Latin American works, and there was nothing to indicate that *Geisterhaus* would become so popular in West Germany. The original version of the book jacket contained the following words in large print and in this configuration:

Isabel
Allende Das
Geisterhaus
Roman
Suhrkamp

Below the words was a picture of a street scene with the central figure being an armed soldier standing in front of a building. Suhrkamp had felt that the novel would only sell several thousand copies. But after the second edition, that is, after about 20,000 to 30,000 copies had been sold, they decided that they might increase readership by "de-militarizing" the dust jacket. The original picture was removed, and the first two sentences of the novel were placed where the picture had been, overlain by a wrap-around strip below the title, author, and publisher and covering the words of the sentences. On the strip was a photograph of Isabel Allende in the sun. The later book design with Allende's photograph combined well with the German title "Geisterhaus," a neologism in German. The book jacket blurbs on the back of the book are two quotes from reviews praising the novel.

Allende's second novel, *De amor y de sombra* (1984), was published in German in 1986 as *Von Liebe und Schatten.* The novel combines political awakening and a love story with an incident that in reality happened in Chile after Salvador Allende's overthrow and Isabel Allende's flight from Chile.

Irene's father had abandoned her and her mother some years before the novel begins. Growing up in a bourgeois lifestyle, Irene is a journalist for a fashion magazine and is engaged to an army officer, whom she rejects in favor of Francisco Leal. Francisco, an unemployed psychologist, applies for and gets a job as a photographer for the magazine. Irene and Francisco work together and begin to fall in love. The pair becomes involved in an incident in which a peasant girl is carried off by the military. They investigate the girl's disappearance and discover an abandoned mine in which they find a number of bodies buried. The discovery brings Irene and Francisco even closer; after finding the bodies, they make love a short distance from the mine. Francisco and his politically active family (his father had fought in the Spanish Civil War) help awaken Irene's political sensibilities. Aided by others, including a mutual friend of theirs, a homosexual hairdresser, Francisco and Irene expose the mine full of bodies and the military personnel responsible for the murders. Irene is shot as she leaves the building where she works, but she recovers sufficiently to escape the country with Francisco.

For the most part, the style of *Von Liebe und Schatten* is similar to that of *Geisterhaus.* One again finds folklore, spiritualism, real events, and fantasy. Allende, whose own background is evident in her writing, took the story from newspaper and personal accounts. The language is simple but fervent, and the descriptions are vivid.

Von Liebe und Schatten was the first novel that Dagmar Ploetz translated. Several reviewers criticized the translation, but there was some question as to whether it was the translation or the Spanish original that did not reach the quality expected.[6]

The book jacket for *Von Liebe und Schatten* is taken from a painting by Pablo Picasso entitled "Portrait d'Olga dans un fauteuil" and takes up the lower half of the cover, with the name of the author and that of the novel covering the top half. Later, a wrap-around strip was placed below the title and author. On the band is Allende's picture and the announcement

> Isabel Allende: 'Autorin des Jahres 1986'
> "[...] ein Werk, dessen Originalität und Ausgewogenheit einen Markstein in der lateinamerikanischen Literatur setzen wird."
> Neue Züricher Zeitung

Allende's third novel, *Eva Luna*, was published in Spanish in 1986 and in German under the same title in 1988. *Eva Luna* delves more into fiction and the process of writing than into historical events. Allende never names in her works the country in which the novels take place, but because of the events and descriptions found in them, the country usually becomes evident. While *Geisterhaus* and *Von Liebe und Schatten* develop in Chile, *Eva Luna* takes place in Venezuela. However, most German readers probably are not familiar enough with Venezuela to have decoded the signs, so they would have assumed that the novel takes place either in an unnamed Latin American country or in Chile.

Eva Luna is the illegitimate daughter of a maidservant and an Indian. After her mother dies when the girl is still very young, Eva spends her childhood in the employ of a series of households. From her godmother she learns that as a female, an orphan, and an illiterate, she is destined to a life of poverty.

Eva's adventures bring her in contact with a wide variety of characters. She meets and befriends a street-wise boy, Humberto Naranjo, who grows up to be the leader of guerrillas who oppose the military dictatorship. After leaving the city for several years, Eva returns and by chance meets an old friend, Melicio, now Mimí, a transsexual who is now a beautiful and successful actress. The two decide to share Mimí's apartment, and Mimí encourages Eva to use her ability to tell stories to become a scriptwriter of soap operas. Because of their success, the two become financially well situated and move to a more luxurious apartment. Eva meets Rolf Carlé, who grew up in Nazi- and postwar Austria before coming to Latin America and who is now a cameraman. Carlé also knows the guerrilla leader Naranjo and has gained his trust.

Carlé and Naranjo contribute to Eva's and Mimí's political awakening. The climax of the novel is the attack on a military prison to enable political prisoners to escape. Naranjo's guerrillas orchestrate the break-in, Carlé films it, and Eva writes it into a soap opera script so that the event can be shown on national television. The romance between Eva and Carlé also finds a happy ending.

The style of the novel is like that of a soap opera; it is intended to be so since the novel is the soap opera that Eva Luna is writing. The book is therefore easy to read, it is told in episodic form, and it includes exaggeration, colorful characters, and stereotypes. Humor, an inherent element of Allende's style, is also found in picaresque novels.

Lieselotte Kolanoske translated the novel into German. She was a *Lektorin*, an editor, in East Germany before retiring and moving to West Germany. She has translated other works from Spanish into German, both in East and West Germany. The translation is considered to be a good one; the reviewers do not criticize the translation in their articles, and a favorable report of the translation was given to Allende (Allende, personal interview).

Simpler than the other two Allende book jackets, that of *Eva Luna* carries the wording in the top third and a sketch of the back of a girl with red hair in the middle. The book jacket blurb on the back of the book is taken from the novel:

> Damals hatte ich beschlossen, mein Schicksal in die eigenen Hände zu nehmen, und seither waren mir so viele Dinge geschehen, mir schien, ich hätte mehrere Leben gelebt, hätte mich jede Nacht in Rauch aufgelöst und wäre jeden Morgen neu geboren worden.

Following *Eva Luna* came the book of short stories *Cuentos de Eva Luna*, in German *Geschichten der Eva Luna*, both published in 1990. Allende never mentions the locations of the twenty-three stories, whose settings vary geographically from the mountains, the jungle, the desert, to the coast. The book begins with the words of Rolf Carlé, Eva Luna's lover in the preceding novel, with the last line of this introduction being his request: "Erzähl mir eine Geschichte, die du noch niemandem erzählt hast" (11). The half page of Carlé's introduction, including this sentence, were placed on the back cover of the dust jacket.

A very brief summary of some of the stories follows: A young girl falls in love with her mother's lover and tries to seduce him. -- A woman travels across the land and sells words to illiterates, including two words to "the Colonel," a renegade known for his brutality, to help him be elected president. -- A woman is held for almost 50 years in an abandoned factory by her lover; and upon her release when her plight is made known, she says, "He never let me go hungry." -- The wife of an embassador is taken by an old dictator to his palace in the jungle, and she achieves her own realization as nature reclaims the structure over the years. -- A rich landowner and his daughter are attacked during a raid; years later she falls in love with the man who raped her and killed her father, and she becomes incapable of seeking revenge. Instead, she commits suicide. -- The wife of a judge allows a bandit to make love to her so she can save her children. -- A Jewish couple that had left Europe during the Hitler years settles in South America, and the husband becomes a famous doctor who commits euthanasia when his wife is about to die from cancer; he asks Eva Luna for help in killing himself so he can be with his wife. -- Inés asks Riad Halabi, both characters in *Eva Luna*, for help in disposing of the body of the man she killed, the former townsperson who was responsible for her son's death years before. -- An unwed mother sells her much-loved deaf and dumb son to an organization that promises to help him, but it is later learned that the handicapped children are being delivered to an organ bank. -- A man and a woman meet and make love; and as they slowly share their secrets, they learn that both had been the victims of torture. -- Based on a true story, a little girl is stuck in a volcanic mud slide, and reporter Rolf Carlé is one of the first on the scene. He is traumatized as they share past and present experiences and fears, and the girl dies.

Geschichten der Eva Luna is so similar to Allende's previous novels, especially *Eva Luna*, that many critics did not feel that Allende was offering anything new either in style or in content. Again the language is simple and descriptive. Characters and places found in *Eva Luna*, especially the town of Agua Santa, reappear so often in her *Geschichten* that the stories are referred to as "episodes" by a number of German critics. Erotic descriptions are prevalent in most of the stories, and we find the frequent Allende theme of "love conquers all" alongside social discussion of euthanasia, organ banks, the church, ecology, machismo, and female solidarity. In *Geschichten*, Allende brings together reality and fiction only in the last story. While numerous reviewers are critical of *Geschichten der Eva Luna*, Lieselotte Kolanoske's translation remains unmentioned, indicating that the translation is a solid one.

The dust jacket has a white background border like most of the other Spanish American best sellers published by Suhrkamp. In red lettering at the top are the author's name and the title of the book with "Suhrkamp" in smaller lettering in the lower left-hand corner. The picture is an abstract design in red, yellow, gold, and tan, and pastel blues and aquas. The motif is a yellow bird on red on light blue and below a gold star. Around three sides are yellow and aqua geometrical figures with points, reminiscent of mountain peaks and the leaves of lush vegetation. The multi-faceted abstract reflects the multiplicity of a collection of South American short stories.

2.2.3 Angeles Mastretta

Like Isabel Allende, Angeles Mastretta had won the Premio Mazatlán for her first novel, *Arráncame la vida* (1986), the title of which she took from a Mexican tango. When Michi Strausfeld, Suhrkamp's scout, was in Mexico, she discovered the novel and brought it back to Germany. The Latin American editor at Suhrkamp, Jürgen Dormagen, read it and wrote a recommendation for it. Suhrkamp published the novel in 1988 under the title *Mexikanischer Tango*. Mastretta did not visit West Germany until 1990; a planned visit in 1989 had to be canceled due to illness. In spite of this, her first novel was successful in Germany before her visit.

Mexikanischer Tango relates a relatively uncomplicated story on the surface. At an early age Catalina marries Andrés Ascencio, who is twice as old as she is. He decides everything for his wife, and she allows him to do so because she is so inexperienced and because that is the custom in post-revolutionary Mexico. Andrés becomes governor of Puebla, and he brings home several of his children by other women so that Catalina can raise them along with their own two children. Catalina learns quickly and soon finds out how Andrés abuses his power. She realizes that she is just as weak and resigned to a passive lifestyle as her friends are. She begins to assert herself and to establish her own identity. Catalina falls in love with Carlos, a director and childhood friend of Andrés. But Andrés becomes jealous, and Catalina learns that even Carlos has his hand in politics. Andrés arranges to have Carlos kidnapped and killed, just as he had had others removed. The novel reveals the relationship in Latin American culture between the all-powerful men and the weak and oppressed women, most of whom acquiesce to the male-dominated world rather than try to resist, as Catalina does. The closing of the novel shows Catalina observing Andrés's downfall without compassion. After Andrés's funeral at the end of the novel, Catalina finds herself free, without having anyone to tell her what she has to do.

Mastretta's novel offers the reader a different perspective on Latin American power and violence from that of Allende's. The time period of the political focus is earlier than that in the more contemporary novels of Allende, and the more traditional role of the woman is therefore a reflection of this. Like García Márquez and Allende, Mastretta overlays history with fiction as she mentions by name some historical figures (for example, President Carranza) while she gives fictional names to others. (President Cárdenas is called Aguirre in the novel.) The author used accounts from her aunt and others to form the basis of the plot, thus using her journalistic training quality with her laconic way of writing. This, in turn, makes the novel easy to read. Mastretta presents events in the novel as a series of events in Catalina's life; the style is both humorous and somber.

Monika López translated the novel into German. She is an experienced and talented translator who has a feel for the Spanish language (Dormagen, personal interview 12 Feb. 1990). López relates that Mastretta's novel was the "flüssigste, schmissigste, 'leichteste'" of the works that she has translated and notes that this was the book, "[d]as ich am lustvollsten übersetzt habe" (letter 14 May 1990). López's translation finds both occasional criticism and praise in the reviews of the novel, but for the most part the translation remains unmentioned in the reviews.[7]

Changes were made from the original both in the title and in the book jacket. Although some critics translated *Arráncame la vida* either as "Reiß mir das Leben aus" or "Nimm mein Leben" in their reviews of the novel, these translations do not carry the same meaning or musical and social connotations as the

Spanish original, so the decision was made at Suhrkamp to entitle the novel *Mexikanischer Tango.*

The original sketch on the Spanish book jacket was retained; but the pink-blue-lavender background color with tango dancers and an orchestra was replaced by a white background with only three figures: a violinist and the two tango dancers. This cover and title probably more closely corresponded to the German taste and expectations than the translation of the original title and the cover. The German book jacket and title have thus aided in the marketing process.

2.2.4 Mario Vargas Llosa

Mario Vargas Llosa, in contrast to Angeles Mastretta, is not a new name to many German readers. Most of Vargas Llosa's works have been translated into German, and his novel *Tante Julia und der Kunstschreiber*, 1985 (*La tía Julia y el escribidor*, 1977), became a "longseller" in Germany as a paperback. Suhrkamp has been his publisher in Germany for a number of years, and Vargas Llosa has frequently visited West Germany, including a stay in Berlin from October 1991 to July 1992. He himself said that he was very warmly received by the Berliners (Vargas Llosa, conversation 24 June 1992).

Like that of *Mexikanischer Tango*, the plot of *Elogio de la madrastra*, 1988 (*Lob der Stiefmutter*, 1989), is fairly simple. Don Rigoberto has married for a second time. There is some concern that his son, the prepubescent Alfonsito, will reject his stepmother, Doña Lukrezia, but just the opposite occurs: The boy apparently falls in love with Doña Lukrezia and threatens suicide if she does not return his love. While the father attends to his business trips and his ritualized ablutions, Doña Lukrezia and Alfonsito go to bed together. One day when Don Rigoberto asks his son about his schoolwork, Alfonsito shows his father an essay he has written. The essay, entitled "Lob der Stiefmutter," describes the sexual relationship between the boy and his stepmother. Don Rigoberto throws Doña Lukrezia out of the house, and Alfonsito turns his attention to Justiniana, his nursemaid.

The style and the theme of the novel are intriguing to the reader. Besides being short and "leserfreundlich,"[8] the novel is multitextual. Vargas Llosa has inserted six paintings--by artists Jacob Jordaens, Francois Boucher, Tiziano Vecellio, Fra Angelico, Francis Bacon, and Fernando de Szyszlo--between the chapters. The paintings are then "narrated" or described by either Rigoberto or Lukrezia as erotic fantasies or as a counterpart to what is happening in the novel. The tone is ironic and humorous; and allegory, myths, and obviously eroticism and fantasy come into play.

The novel was translated by Elke Wehr, who has translated two of Vargas Llosa's other recent works into German. She is a professional translator who studied Romance languages, has translated from both French and Spanish, and is currently living in Madrid. The quality of the translation is for the most part not discussed in the reviews, which is generally a favorable sign.

Like the cover of the Spanish original, that of the German edition carries a detail of the painting "Allegorie von Venus und Cupido" by Bronzino. The detail shows Cupid kissing Venus on the lips, caressing her hair with one hand and her naked breast with another. The Spanish edition from the series "La sonrisa vertical" ("The vertical smile"), which publishes erotic novels, shows the detail of the painting with a narrow border of white against a pink background. Suhrkamp isolated the figures from the detail of the painting and put them in the lower two-thirds of the front of the book jacket on a white background. Around the lower fourth of the book, a semi-transparent band partially covers Cupid's hand on Venus's breast. On the band are the words "Der erotische Roman des großen peruanischen Schriftstellers." Representatives at Suhrkamp relate that the purpose of the band was additional publicity to acquaint the public with the subject and the author (Jürgen Dormagen and Christoph Groffy, personal interviews 12 Feb. 1990).

The alluring nature of the book jacket cover and the title are complemented on the back with the book jacket blurb:

> "Ich habe ihm den Titel gegeben: Lob der Stiefmutter. Wie findest du ihn?"
> "Sehr schön, ein guter Titel", antwortete Don Rigoberto. Und er fügte mit einem gekünstelten Lachen hinzu, fast ohne nachzudenken: "Wie der Titel eines erotischen Romans."
> "Was heißt erotisch?" erkundigte sich das Kind mit großem Ernst.
> "Bezogen auf die körperliche Liebe", klärte Don Rigoberto ihn auf.

Like *Elogio de la madrastra*, *El hablador*, 1987 (in German *Der Geschichtenerzähler*, 1990) takes place in Peru, but there end the similarities between the novels. *El hablador* was published in Spanish before *Elogio de la madrastra*; in German the reverse was true. More complex in theme, content, and style than *Lob der Stiefmutter*, *Geschichtenerzähler* can be read on different levels. The novel is related in the first person by a narrator who shares Vargas Llosa's name and who bares strong resemblance to the author.[9]

Vargas Llosa wanted to write something particular to Peru. He is very conscious of the fact that Peru is inhabited by many "tribes" and that at the same time Peru is being westernized with technology that destroys its diversity and creates two disparate worlds in one country. Besides this collision of different lifestyles, languages, and *Weltanschauungen*, he also wanted to write about a conversion, intense in nature, from one of these worlds to the other. Vargas Llosa decided that the central figure had to be a Jew, a member of one of the smallest and most unified groups in Peru.

Since his university days, the narrator has been curious about the world of the Indians who live in the jungle, and particularly the role of "Geschichtenerzähler." This revered personage was not at all political, religious, or magical, but rather traveled from settlement to settlement telling anecdotes, histories, occurrences, and carrying information about births, marriages, and deaths. Thr "Geschichtenerzähler" constituted knowledge and community; "story-telling" was not just a diversion. The narrator, as a writer, is fascinated by this idea.

The narrator has had long conversations with his Jewish friend Saúl Zuratas, who had developed a deep-seated interest in the Machiguenga Indians. Saúl is nicknamed "Mascarita" ("Little Mask") because of the liverspot that covers one side of his face, and he has a parrot called Gregor Samsa, the name of the protagonist of Franz Kafka's "The Metamorphosis." Saúl gives up a promising career as an ethnologist to spend months at a time with the Indians. He strongly defends the rights of the "uncivilized" people and speaks out against any interference in their lives from the "civilized" world, especially the missionaries and North American linguists. One day Saúl's friends lose all trace of him; apparently he has migrated to Israel.

Twenty years later, now in the early 1980s, the narrator has the opportunity to travel to the area of the Machiguengas. He talks with the missionaries who work at the "Institute for Linguistics," whose goal it is to evangelize the Indians and to teach them to read, and he interviews a couple of the Indians. From the Indians there is no more word about the "Geschichtenerzähler;" it is as if the institution no longer exists. But in further conversation, Vargas Llosa learns that one of the missionaries had seen two "Geschichtenerzähler," one of them with red hair and a large liver spot on his face.

In a parallel narration, the "Geschichtenerzähler" relates incidences about the history, the people, the gods, and the way of life of the Indians. It becomes clear that Saúl had become the "Geschichtenerzähler" for the Machiguengas. Thus is Saúl's conversion, or metamorphosis, the coming together of two radically different cultures in Peru.

The multi-layered style and theme of *Geschichtenerzähler* reflect the clash of the "primitive" and the "modern" worlds. The epics, myths, and tales of everyday life of the Indians are filled with Indian names. Irony, fantasy, and philosophical dialogue further allow the readers concerned about the impact of modern technology on the environment access to a remote world that would otherwise remain closed to them. Elke Wehr's translation of *Geschichtenerzähler* is lauded by the critics. With the many Indian and specifically Spanish terms, even when some exist in German (i.e., "Kazike"), the novel appears difficult to translate.

The book jacket, again with a white background, shows the right side of the face of an Indian with black hair and dark eyes and wearing a mask of feathers of white, red, orange, and yellow hues. The picture draws attention to the subject of the novel; even though the Indian is behind the mask, the close-up makes him a human being, an individual, and not just a unknown entity. On the back cover is the very beginning of the work, beginning thus:

> Ich war nach Florenz gekommen, um Peru und die Peruaner eine Zeitlang zu vergessen, und da begegnete mir dieses verflixte Land heute morgen auf denkbar unerwartete Weise.(9)

The reader should be as drawn to the enigmatic situation in Peru as is the narrator, who would try to forget it.

2.3 Commonality of Features

In these individual Spanish American best sellers, West German readers discerned a commonality of qualities. When read in the West German context, these perceived similar features combined with the shared Spanish American origin of these books to identify the novels as being of a particular type of novel. The transfer from one culture to another of a body of particular characteristics and the cross-cultural reception of that corpus shows that works of fiction from Spanish America met certain German audience expectations of Spanish American literature. The Spanish American novel is thus perceived by the average West German reader as if it were a sub-genre which became a trend in the 1980s and as such a best-selling sub-genre. In Part II these commonly perceived features are examined within the West German context to present the intrinsic reasons for their success there as a reflection of the response of the West German general reading public.

Having surveyed the individual novels, the question of their increased reception must now be posed. How did the public respond to the Spanish American novels and the publishers' marketing of these books? Why was there an increase in reception during the 1980s?

Notes

[1] Waalkes's success on the book market is undoubtedly related to his popular movies, comics, and television appearances.

[2] This concept was not totally new to the Germans. The Romantics of the nineteenth century had envisioned a similar conception. Novalis formulated in his *Fragmenten* (1799-1800):

> Die Welt muß romantisiert werden. So findet man den ur[sprünglichen] Sinn wieder. Romantisieren ist nichts als eine qualit[ative] Potenzierung. Das niedre Selbst wird mit einem bessern Selbst in dieser Operation identifiziert [...]

Novalis believed that everyday life should be marveled at and viewed with a sense of the distant, strange, and higher, while wondrous events should be viewed as commonplace. Latin American magic realism, on the other hand, is not an imposed philosophy but rather a depiction of seemingly magical events that are seen as commonplace occurrences in Central and South America and the Caribbean. It had its origins in the Indian and African cultures and had the purpose of enabling people to deal with strange events that occurred on a regular basis. While there are similarities between the two conceptions, they should not be considered as inherently parallel philosophies. In contrast to the philosophy of the Romantics, which would lend a more familiar base for the average German, Latin American magic realism is stranger and more difficult for the average German reader to conceptualize.

[3] García Márquez, quoted in Walter Boehlich, "Fuenteovejuna in der Karibik," *Der Spiegel* 3 Aug. 1981: 132.

[4] For a detailed listing of weaknesses in the translation, consult Walter Boehlich, "Fuenteovejuna in der Karibik," *Spiegel* 3 Aug. 1981: 132-36.

[5] Walter Haubrich, "*Der General in seinem Labyrinth*," *Frankfurter Allgemeine Zeitung* 20 April 1989: N. pag.

[6] Willi Zurbrüggen, personal interview; Eckhard Heftrich, "Naiv und pathetisch," *Frankfurter Allgemeine Zeitung* 26 July 1986: N. pag.

[7] See Wolf Scheller, "Hochtönende Liebe," *Rhein-Neckar-Zeitung* 9/10 July 1988: N. pag.; Hans-Jürgen Schmitt, "Reiß mir das Leben aus," *Süddeutsche Zeitung* 11/12 June 1988: N. pag. for criticism of the translation. For praise see Rosemarie Bollinger, "Ein Tanz um die Macht," *Deutsches Allgemeines Sonntagsblatt* 13 Mar. 1988: N. pag. and Wolfgang Kauer, "Mitgefühl und Entsetzen," *Die Rheinpfalz* 12 Aug. 1988: N. pag.

[8] Volker Hage, "Piep, piep," *Die Zeit* 11 Aug. 1989: N. pag.

[9] At a public reading in Düsseldorf on 24 June 1992, Vargas Llosa said that many critics attribute more autobiographical information to his books than there really is.

Chapter 3

A Shift in Reception of Spanish American Literature in West Germany

"The Europeans think that only that which Europe invents is good for the whole world and that everything that is different is abominable." (Simón Bolívar in Gabriel García Márquez's novel El general en su laberinto)

"Von allen außerdeutschen zeitgenössischen Literaturen scheint mir die lateinamerikanische sicherlich für das nächste Jahrzehnt die wichtigste zu sein." (Siegfried Unseld, Suhrkamp Verlag, 1976.)

"Endlich habe ich die Deutschen erobert." (Gabriel García Márquez, 1988)

Was there indeed an increase in the reception of Spanish American novels in West Germany during the 1980s? What concrete proof is there that the West Germans were reading more literature from Latin America in the '80s than they had read in the prior ten, fifteen, or twenty years prior? As we shall see, statistical data, together with the reactions to sales of Spanish American novels in West Germany in recent years, suggest that there was.

This chapter focuses on the reception of Spanish American literature in West Germany, first during the 1960s and '70s and then during the 1980s to 1991. I will also examine the image of Latin America in Germany in the early '70s and the literary horizons of expectation which the Germans had at that time regarding literature from Spanish America. Statistical evidence demonstrating the increase in sales and thus theoretical readership of the Spanish American works during the 1980s will be given. I offer several factors that contributed and led to increased readership. This section will be followed by accounts of the image of Latin America in the '80s in order to identify the actual differences between earlier decades and the 1980s. I will begin by examining the state of Latin American literature in West Germany in the '60s and '70s.

3.1 Lack of Reception

To say that Latin American literature was relatively unknown in Germany prior to 1976 would be an understatement. During the 1960s, publication of Latin Americans was minimal. Works by Jorge Luis Borges and Pablo Neruda were being published, but in very small quantities, that is, small numbers of copies published. Editions of their works were being produced primarily for a small, elite circle; the average German reader seemed unable to come to terms with Latin American literature (Strausfeld, "Lateinamerikanische" 930). The 1960s was the period of the international "boom" of Latin American literature. But according to Gustav Siebenmann the number of literary works translated from Spanish and Portuguese into German within the field of "Schöne Literatur" during that period amounted to only 2 percent (Siebenmann, *Neuere Literatur* 38). Siebenmann's calculations furthermore include the whole Iberian Peninsula and almost all of the South American continent as opposed to that portion of the Spanish-speaking South American continent that I cover here.

In a table presented by Menén Desleal and covering 1964, the number of translations of Greek and Latin classics into German were double those from Spanish into German (Desleal, "Situation" 73). In 1976 Dieter Reichardt pointed out that even if one included detective novels, school texts, and pornography to reduce somewhat the blatancies of the statistics, the disproportion of the underrepresentation ("das Mißverhältnis der Unterrepräsentation") of one of the largest cultural areas in the world on the German book market could not be overlooked ("Bestandsaufnahme" 64). In an even more decisive statement, Günter W. Lorenz wrote in an article published in 1974 of the "Nichtexistenz lateinamerikanischer Literatur in den Ländern deutscher Sprache" ("Krise" 100). Concurring with Lorenz's sentiment, Michi Strausfeld, the scout for Suhrkamp Verlag's Latin American Program, writes in an essay:

> Damals, 1975, galt die lateinamerikanische Literatur in Deutschland als ein Exotikum, als Steckenpferd einiger Experten und Passion der wenigen Liebhaber, war ansonsten jedoch unbekannt: ein weißer Fleck in der Literaturlandkarte. Die übersetzten Romane der an zwei Händen aufzuzählenden Autoren verstaubten längst wieder in den Lagern oder im Modernen Antiquariat, und selbst der gebildete Leser hätte vermutlich höchstens Borges und vielleicht noch Pablo Neruda oder García Márquez unter den südamerikanischen Literaten nennen können. [...] Alle anderen Versuche der Verleger (vor allem während der 60er Jahre), die zeitgenössische Literatur des Kontinents zu verbreiten, konnten höchstens einen Achtungserfolg verbuchen, stießen jedoch weitaus häufiger auf gelangweiltes Desinteresse. [...] Die Schriftsteller des "Booms"--Cortázar, Fuentes, García Márquez, Vargas Llosa und viele andere, auch jüngere--zählten in Frankreich längst zu den Großen der zeitgenössischen Literatur und wurden intensiv gelesen. In Deutschland hingegen waren sie zum Großteil nicht

> einmal publiziert, und von einer Rezeption konnte schon gar nicht die Rede sein.[1]

Finally, it should be noted that Yolanda Broyles's 1979 dissertation (published 1981) on the German response to Latin American literature actually examined the "chronic West German disregard for Latin American literature" (18) and the West German reader's "disinterest or the 'non-reception' of Latin American literature" (81).

As Broyles demonstrates in her study, the concept of attitude may "correspond to the concept of reader disposition or horizon of expectations (*Erwartungshorizont*) more commonly used in receptive research" (82). She cites Floyd Henry Allport's 1924 definition of attitude as "preparation of response" or "preparation in advance of the actual response" (Allport 320) and notes that Allport's definition has undergone virtually no modification since then (Broyles 83).

Allport's definition can be used here to help us examine the reasons behind the poor reception of Spanish American literature prior to the 1980s and those behind the much improved response during the '80s. The "preparation in advance of the actual response"--or lack thereof--figures prominently in the reception of this literature. The West German "preparation" preceding the response is seen here as having shifted, and therefore as having changed Germany's response to Spanish American literature. Much of the literature from Latin America was very different from European and North American literature during the 1960s and '70s, and the German preparation was not considered to be adequate. A change must therefore have occurred in preparation for the increased reception in the '80s.

Alberto Wagner de Reyna detailed in 1976 three primary obstacles keeping the West Germans from understanding Latin American literature. The first is one of language difficulties: the structural differences between German and Spanish, especially in literary expressions; the spoken language that differs from country to country in Latin America; and the use of Indian and possibly African expressions and dialectal forms that are not found in the dictionary. Wagner de Reyna lists the second barrier as the lack of objective information on Latin America in West Germany. The third impediment is more complex and deals with psychological differences between the cultures. Wagner de Reyna describes the third obstacle:

> Psychologisches Unverständnis und Mißverständnisse
> a) Die psychologische [...] Verschiedenheit der betroffenen Völker. Nicht nur Nord und Süd, nicht nur das urwüchsige Germanische und das landschaftsgebundene Indianische, nicht nur Geschichte

> und Vorgeschichte stehen sich hier gegenüber, sondern Haltungen und Ansichten in bezug auf Welt, Leben und Tod. Die mathematisch- wirtschaftliche Einstellung, die heutzutage für Europa charakteristisch ist, hat [...] wenig übrig für die schwärmerisch-heroisch-magische Seinsart, die Lateinamerika noch, [...] Profil gibt.
> b) Die [...] europäische Einstellung [...] des Haschens nach Pittoreskem [...], bringt einen Hauch paternalistischer Überlegenheit mit sich, der sich in [...] Literatur und in [...] Auswahl der zu übersetzenden Autoren manifestiert.
> c) [...] Lateinamerika wird [...] der Dritten Welt zugeschlagen [...] jedoch [...] erweist sich Lateinamerika, trotz seines indianischen Untergrundes und seiner afrikanischen Wahlverwandtschaften, in kulturellem, historischem und menschlichem Zusammenhang als ein Stück des Okzidents (46-48).[2]

Others in the field of literature also recognize the cross-cultural and linguistic difficulties in literary reception. Broyles notes that the lack of familiarity with Latin American reality reduces understanding and motivation in a variety of ways: Names of writers, characters, and place names can be "so irritatingly foreign that German readers face problems in pronouncing and retaining them," and "connotative meanings or even metaphors or symbols [...] have referents in a concrete reality foreign to the West German reading public" (104). On this subject Dieter Zimmer wrote during the Frankfurt Book Fair in 1976:

> Der deutsche Leser, auf den in diesen Tagen nun Namen über Namen lateinamerikanischer Autoren niederprasseln, die er nicht behalten und nicht aussprechen kann und bei denen er oft nicht einmal weiß, wo der Vorname aufhört und der Nachname beginnt [...], wird sich irritiert fragen: Muß er denn? Muß er das nun alles lesen? Wo soll er anfangen? (Qtd. in Strausfeld, "Multiplikatoren" 6)

Names, connotative and denotative meanings of words, symbols, genre, style, and culture all present obstacles for readers of a different culture with regard to the reception of a foreign literature. Although Broyles admits that "Latin American orthodoxies such as style, genre or other aesthetic norms perhaps also constitute reception barriers in some cases," she maintains that "the barriers to reception are mostly related to the disinterest and comprehension difficulties born of the confrontation with a world both foreign and not really considered worth knowing" (104-105).

This indictment of the Germans seems rather harsh, but it is probably a correct assessment. Several factors played a role in the earlier German unwillingness to experience Latin American literature. While it is true that Latin American literature was being well received in France[3] some time before the West Germans learned to appreciate it, we should keep in mind that the French and Spanish languages and cultures are more closely related and that a number of Latin American writers lived in France both as exiles and diplomats and spoke French with the Frenchmen. Personal contacts as well as the political, cultural, and literary climate were conducive to the writers living, publishing, and doing their own public relations there (Daus, Colloquiums-Protokoll 75). Several of those who lived in France for a period of time were Julio Cortázar (Argentina), Alejo Carpentier (Cuba), Antonio Cisneros (Peru), and Cristina Peri Rossi (Argentina). At least through the early 1970s, there simply were not that many Latin American writers living in West Germany, and there were few who could promote their own works in German to the Germans. A greater linguistic and cultural gap had to be bridged between Spanish America and Germany than between Spanish America and France.

Furthermore, the effort required to appreciate Spanish American literature proved to be too great for the Germans. When one examines the principal Spanish American works of the 1950s through the early 1970s, one finds such novels as *Pedro Páramo* (Juan Rulfo, Mexico), 1955; *Los ríos profundos* (José María Arguedas, Peru), 1958; *La muerte de Artemio Cruz* (Carlos Fuentes, Mexico), 1962; *Rayuela* (Julio Cortázar, Argentina) and *La ciudad y los perros* (Mario Vargas Llosa, Peru), 1963; *Tres tristes tigres* (Guillermo Cabrera Infante, Cuba) and *Cien años de soledad* [*Hundert Jahre Einsamkeit*], (Gabriel García Márquez, Colombia), 1967; and *Yo, el Supremo* (Augusto Roa Bastos, Paraguay), 1974. All of these novels could prove difficult for the unprepared reader. Those with fragmented narratives in one form or another include *Pedro Páramo*, *La muerte de Artemio Cruz*, *Rayuela*, *La ciudad y los perros*, *Tres tristes tigres*, and *Yo, el Supremo*. *Los ríos profundos* offers the uninitiated reader thematic difficulties of Peruvian White-Indian culture clash; and *Cien años de soledad* (*Hundert Jahre Einsamkeit*), as Hans-Joachim Müller explained in 1976, "ist sprachlich zwar vollkommen intakt, aber gerade aufgrund seiner barocken Fabulierfreude ist es apokalyptisch und voller beißender Aggressionen [...]" ("Rolle" 50). Regarding Latin American literature on the whole, he explains in the same article:

> Die neue Literatur Lateinamerikas versteht sich bewußt als antagonistischer Akt, der sich in seiner destruktiven Geste dem Zugriff politischer Ideologien entziehen will. Dementsprechend stellt sie in ihrer Mehrzahl nicht die Vielheit, sondern die Zerrissenheit einer dem lateinamerikanischen Denken nicht adäquaten Kultur in den Vordergrund. Die Texte sind heterogen und verwenden zumeist Collage-Techniken, was zu einer Auflösung von Form und Sprache der bisherigen Literatur führt. (49)

This difficult literature serves its purpose for Latin American culture; but Latin American literature of the '50s, '60s, and early '70s was indeed a "conscious antagonistic act," particularly for those who are not adequately prepared for the necessary deciphering processes. Obviously, the French were more sufficiently willing and prepared to receive Spanish American literature than the Germans. While Germans have had complicated literature in their heritage, for example, Expressionism, it was not adequate preparation for this Latin American literature, which presented the additional obstacle of being firmly embedded in the Latin American culture. Since the culture was physically and spiritually so far removed from the German culture, that two-fold gap could not be so easily bridged. Germans at that time were not yet ready to accept a literature from a culture which they did not esteem, a culture whose image in Germany tended to be negative.

3.2 The Image of Latin America in the 1960s and 1970s

The term "image" may be defined as "the total cognitive, affective, and evaluative structure of the behaviour unit" (Boulding 423). "Kurz gesagt, ist damit das subjektive Wissen von der Realität gemeint" (Wilke 80). By applying this definition, we can explore the subjective knowledge of the Latin American reality as perceived in West Germany prior to the 1980s.

What was the image of Latin America in the minds of the West Germans that caused them to be unreceptive to Latin American literature in the '60s and '70s? The following are four sets of images of Latin America in West Germany; I have retained the entire list of each so that the repetition of some of the images will reinforce the suggestion:

> 1) Armut, Unfähigkeit zur Selbsthilfe, Faulheit, Analphabeten, Revolutionen [...] Kaffee, Bananen, Sonne, Palmen, heiße Musik, hübsche Mädchen und [...] Karneval in Rio. (Helga Castellanos 55)

> 2) Kontinent der permanenten Revolten, des Terrors, der Putsche oder der Militärdiktaturen [...] oder als dem Kontinent der Reaktion, der Unterdrückung, der Folter, des Rückschritts und der Unfähigkeit. (Lorenz, "Bilder" 7)
>
> 3) Diktatoren, Putsche, Exotik, Staatsverschuldung, Ausbeutung der Indios, unbezwingbare Naturgewalten, astronomische Inflationsraten. (Strausfeld, "Lateinamerikanische" 928)
>
> 4) Man sucht in Lateinamerika das Exotische, nicht das Wesentliche, man sucht das Gewalttätige und Primitive mehr als den Geist [...], weil man meint, in Europa das Gruseln verlernt zu haben und ganz und gar Kulturmensch geworden zu sein, so daß man Gemütsbewegungen in der Ferne suchen muß. (Wagner de Reyna 47)

The fourth set of observations is particularly telling of both the Latin American outlook and the German perspective. Wagner de Reyna relates both what the Germans perceived of Latin America and what they failed to perceive.

The images of Latin America noted above are mostly negative and "fremd." The political aspect of the Latin American image is wholly negative and indicates no hope for any significant change. "Permanente Revolten" are not seen as producing consequential change. Economics fares no better in the image; "Armut," "Unfähigkeit zur Selbsthilfe," "Faulheit," etc. show no chance for improvement. The impressions of the way of life lie between depressing and utterly terrifying--with nothing to counterbalance this bleak image. Exoticism as a very distant "otherness" underlines the "Fremdheit." Indeed, when we consider that literature as a reflection of a culture and society and when we ponder the "antagonistic" feature of Latin American literature up to the mid '70s, why would the general German reading public have wanted to read this literature? Why were the West Germans specifically so unprepared to read and receive Spanish American literature? Was there really a dearth of acculturation processes and institutions between West Germany and Latin America? What accounts for this "Nichtexistenz" and "non-reception" of Latin American literature in the decades prior to the 1980s?

3.3 Lack of Preparation

If "the image is always in some sense a product of messages received in the past" (Boulding 423), then the messages as presented by various informative institutions must be received before being formulated into an image. In any given country, several social institutions play a very significant role in preparing the response to foreign literatures. Günter W. Lorenz tells us that

> Interesse an der Literatur einer Region kann man wohl dann erwarten, wenn der Leser--der doch nur in seltenen Fällen den literarischen Wert an sich sucht--dieser Region ein wenigstens grundsätzliches Interesse entgegenbringt. ("Krise" 99)

He goes on to illustrate his point with the interaction between tourism in Spain and Spanish literature in the early sixties. With tourism comes one kind of exposure. Another source of image formation is the media. Jürgen Wilke, professor of journalism, explains,

> Was die Bevölkerung, also die Rezipienten der Massenmedien angeht, so sind es deren Vorstellungen von Welt und Wirklichkeit, die durch die (Auslands-) Berichterstattung geformt und geprägt werden. Diesen Vorgang bzw. diese Wirkung bezeichnen wir als 'Imagebildung.' (8)

A third source is the educational system, the introduction of one culture to another in the schools and universities. Broyles assails the educational system and the mass media of the 1970s for their failure to expose West Germans to information regarding Latin America. Schools and universities, she shows, offered very little stimulus to develop "interest in, consciousness of or a responsive attitude toward the Latin American continent and its literature (87). Broyles furthermore found the mass media in their various forms created no basis for the public's formation of an informed view of Latin America, nor did the press foster the development of interest in Latin America (90). Broyles concludes:

> The virtual absence of all things Latin American from what could be called the collective education--involving those institutions of socialization discussed here--signifies its absence from reader consciousness. As such little or no basis exists in West Germany [in the 1970s] for the formation of reader interest in or for the transmission of Latin American literature. (92)

Wiese likewise evaluates the situation at German universities and finds the situation bleak but improving (*Die hispanoamerikanischen Boom-Romane* 95-6).

The literary preparation process of publisher and literary critic is yet another institution that failed to prepare the West German reading public for Latin American literature. As Ronald Daus stated in his 1976 article "Der deutsche Leser und seine Schwierigkeiten mit einer fremden Realität":

> Ratlosigkeit macht sich breit unter den deutschen Lateinamerika-Experten. Seit einigen Jahren spüren sie immer deutlicher einen Unwillen des Publikums, sich mit Büchern aus oder über Lateinamerika auseinanderzusetzen. Dieses Desinteresse ist nicht nur eine vage atmosphärische Wahrnehmung, es läßt sich auch--und so geschah es schon in mehreren Untersuchungen--mit schlüssigen Zahlen belegen. Die Erklärung, die deutsche Verleger, Leser und Kritiker hierfür liefern, treffen sich zumeist in einem Begriff: "Fremdheit." (53)

This "Fremdheit" deterred West German publishers from publishing Latin American works in the 1960s, while during the 1970s only occasional Latin American works were produced in West Germany. Gabriel García Márquez's *Hundert Jahre Einsamkeit* was published in 1970 by Kiepenheuer & Witsch Verlag; but in spite of the advanced printing in a newspaper before the publication of the novel, and in spite of approximately fifty favorable reviews written on the novel, Kiepenheuer & Witsch did not produce a second edition until 1979. By 1976 no major work by such noted Latin American writers as Juan Carlos Onetti, Felisberto Hernández, and Mario Benedetti (Uruguay); Fernando del Paso and Augustín Yáñez (Mexico); Antonio Skármeta (Chile); or Guillermo Cabrera Infante (Cuba), to name a few, had been translated into German (Reichardt "Bestandsaufnahme" 68). Since then all of these except Fernando del Paso and Yáñez have been translated into German. Publishers quoted in the '70s regarding the chances of Latin American literature on the West German book market confirm the problem of "Fremdheit." Broyles cites two publishers on this subject: In 1976 Heinrich-Maria Ledig-Rowohlt felt that "die lateinamerikanische Welt ist vom Geschichtlichen und Sozialen dem deutschen Leser zu fremd" (103), and the editor-in-chief of Hanser Verlag asserted that the

> USA ist dem deutschen Kulturkreis näher. Der lateinamerikanische Kulturkreis ist uns fremder. Lateinamerikanische Probleme sind uns nicht nah. [...] Ich meine aufgrund beobachtender Erfahrung scheint mir doch etwas daran zu sein, daß das eben eine ganz andere Welt ist. (Broyles 103)

Even Siegfried Unseld, head of Suhrkamp Verlag, wrote in a publishers' brochure in 1976:

> Die Einführung dieser Literatur ist im deutschen Sprachbereich bisher gescheitert. Die deutsche Öffentlichkeit, der deutsche Leser, ließ sich bisher wohl durch die Fremdartigkeit ihres Milieus und vor allem durch Unkenntnis der Geschichte und Gegenwart eines ganzen Kontinents nicht für die Annahme auch der bedeutendsten ins Deutsche übersetzten Werke gewinnen. (Introduction to the Suhrkamp Program brochure for the 1976 Frankfurt Bookfair)

Clearly, prior to 1976 most German publishers found little reason to produce Latin American works in translation for an audience that was not prepared to consume such a strange and difficult product.

> Auch die Verbrauchsgüterindustrie in der kapitalistischen Wirtschaft muß auf ein Mindestmaß von Übereinstimmung zwischen der Art der Ware und der Art des Konsumentenbedarfs sehen, sollen sich die Investitionen in Produktion und Werbung lohnen. [...] Es besteht eine gewisse Übereinstimmung zwischen [einem Buch] und der Erwartung, Mentalität und Ideologie (zumindest eines Teils) derer, die es so eifrig sich selbst und anderen zuführen. (von Bülow 9)

The West German *Erwartungshorizont*, the attitude and preparation, was not yet conducive to a reception, consumption, and understanding of Latin American literature widespread enough to make that literature worth the publishers' investment.

While German publishers were reluctant to produce that which the public was not prepared to read, the literary critics, for the most part, were not helping to prepare the German reading public for Latin American texts. It is the task of the critic to inform the reading public about an author and a literary work, to "prepare" the public, and to help the public form an opinion, an attitude. But during the 1960s and 1970s the German critic's own lack of a knowledgeable background--i.e., preparation--of Latin America frequently prevented him or her from understanding Latin American politics, culture, traditions, and literature as a whole. This, combined with the fact that West German critics had not dealt with Latin American works consistently but rather as individual works (Friedl Zapata 78), therefore prevented the work from being discussed within a continuous and comprehensive framework. The critic would then present an unenlightened assessment of a Latin American work, which in turn had the effect of misinforming or not fully informing the German public and thus negatively influencing reception. There were exceptions: Menén Desleal exculpates Stefan Baciu, Curt Meyer-Clason, Wolfgang Luchting, Günter Lorenz, K. A. Horst, and Gustav Siebenmann (Siebenmann is actually Swiss):

> Sonst jedoch führt die Unkenntnis der kulturellen Verhältnisse, Zusammenhänge, Traditionen zuwangsläufing dazu, daß die Unsicherheit des Kritikers den noch unsicheren potentiellen Leser abschreckt (qtd. in Reichardt, "Bestandsaufnahme" 65).

This unpreparedness on the part of the critic led then to arrogance when contemplating Latin America and its literature: "Das reine Unwissen steigert sich zur Arroganz" wrote Friedl Zapata (78), and there existed "bezeigte und bezeugte intellektuelle Arroganz gegenüber Lateinamerika und seinen Autoren" (Lorenz, "Krise" 100). This arrogance did nothing to ease the transition from literatures known to the Germans to a literature that was in truth "fremd." Friedl Zapata concludes by saying,

> Dieser Haltung ist es auch zuzuschreiben, daß es nie zu einer kontinuierlichen Darstellung der Literatur Lateinamerikas im deutschen Sprachraum gekommen ist, denn die Kritik erfüllt weder ihre Aufgabe als Informant, noch die als Vermittler, und daran wird sich wohl so schnell auch nichts ändern. (80)

Nevertheless, something did change. We will now turn to concrete proof that Spanish American novels did become successful in the 1980s, to the indications that the Germans have indeed become some of the greatest consumers of Spanish American literature, and to the changes that occurred to create an environment in which Germans in the 1980s would become some of the most avid readers of Spanish American literature.

3.4 Statistical Indications of Increased Reception

In order to show the increase in the number of translations from Spanish into German, I will begin the survey with information taken from *Buch und Buchhandel in Zahlen.* I have begun with 1978 rather than with 1980 to provide a clearer picture of the end of the 1970s as compared with the 1980s.

Within the category "Belletristik" or "Schöne Literatur," from 1978 to 1990 there is an increase from 22.1% (1978) to 42.6% (1990) of the title productions which are translations from other languages ("Anteile der Übersetzungen in Deutsch in den einzelnen Sachgebieten").[4] In 1990, 3,811 titles were translations from other languages into German within the category of "Belletristik" literature, equaling the 42.6% (*Buchhandel 1991*, Table 38, p. 62). Of those "Belletristik" works translated from other languages into German in 1990, 68.6% were translations from English, 12.3% from French, 3.3% from Russian, 3.3% from Spanish, and 2.9% from Italian (*Buchhandel 1991*, Table 37, p. 60). This would seem to indicate that translations from Spanish play a rather insignificant role in belletristic translations into German. However, the case of Spanish translations becomes more consequential when we examine the increase in translations from English, French, Russian, Italian, Spanish, and Swedish over a twelve-year period of 1978 to 1990. (See Table 1)

==

Table 1

Translations into German in the area of "Schöne Literatur"/"Belletristic" by title production and originating language.

Year/Total Number of Translations	*Ranking/ Language*	*Titles Produced*	*% of Translated Belletristic Titles*
1978 2,687	1 English	2017	75.1%
	2 French	296	11.0%
	3 Russian	88	3.3%
	4 Italian	46	1.7%
	5 Swedish	39	1.4%
	6 Spanish	37	1.4%

Year/Total Number of Translations	*Ranking/ Language*	*Titles Produced*	*% of Translated Belletristic Titles*
1980 2,705	1 English	1849	68.35%
	2 French	347	12.8%
	3 Russian	122	4.5%
	4 Italian	66	2.4%
	5 Swedish	56	2.1%
	6 Spanish	46	1.7%

Year/Total Number of Translations	*Ranking/ Language*	*Titles Produced*	*% of Translated Belletristic Titles*
1981 3,008	1 English	2127	70.7%
	2 French	386	12.8%
	3 Russian	91	3.0%
	4 Italian	72	2.4%
	5 Spanish	53	1.8%
	6 Swedish	49	1.6%

Year/Total Number of Translations	*Ranking/ Language*	*Titles Produced*	*% of Translated Belletristic Titles*
1982 2,894	1 English	2060	71.2%
	2 French	354	12.2%
	3 Russian	89	3.1%
	4 Italian	65	2.2%
	5 Spanish	54	1.9%
	6 Swedish	49	1.7%

Year/Total Number of Translations	*Ranking/ Language*	*Titles Produced*	*% of Translated Belletristic Titles*
1983 2,836	1 English	2021	71.3%
	2 French	327	11.5%
	3 Russian	74	2.6%
	4 Italian	74	2.6%
	5 Spanish	59	2.1%
	6 Swedish	41	1.4%

Year/Total Number of Translations	*Ranking/ Language*	*Titles Produced*	*% of Translated Belletristic Titles*
1985 2,562	1 English	1607	62.7%
	2 French	361	14.1%
	3 Russian	95	3.7%
	4 Italian	87	3.4%
	5 Spanish	71	2.8%
	6 Swedish	45	1.75%

Year/Total Number of Translations	*Ranking/ Language*	*Titles Produced*	*% of Translated Belletristic Titles*
1986 3,828	1 English	2825	73.8%
	2 French	389	10.2%
	3 Russian	99	2.6%
	4 Italian	98	2.6%
	5 Spanish	78	2.0%
	6 Swedish	62	1.6%

Year/Total Number of Translations	*Ranking/ Language*	*Titles Produced*	*% of Translated Belletristic Titles*
1987 4,343	1 English	3062	70.5%
	2 French	466	10.7%
	3 Russian	135	3.1%
	4 Italian	111	2.6%
	5 Spanish	106	2.4%
	6 Swedish	48	1.1%

Year/Total Number <u>*of Translations*</u>	*Ranking/* <u>*Language*</u>	*Titles* <u>*Produced*</u>	*% of Translated* <u>*Belletristic Titles*</u>
1989 3,210	1 English	2040	63.6%
	2 French	371	11.6%
	3 Russian	145	4.5%
	4 Italian	126	3.9%
	5 Spanish	124	3.9%
	6 Swedish	56	1.8%

Year/Total Number <u>*of Translations*</u>	*Ranking/* <u>*Language*</u>	*Titles* <u>*Produced*</u>	*% of Translated* <u>*Belletristic Titles*</u>
1990 3,811	1 English	2617	68.6%
	2 French	468	12.3%
	3 Russian	125	3.3%
	4 Spanish	124	3.3%
	5 Italian	111	2.6%
	6 Swedish	40	1.0%

Source: *Buch und Buchhandel in Zahlen 1979*, Table 12, p. 26; *1982*, Table 13, p. 29; *1984*, Table 13, p. 28; *1987*, Table 12, p. 28; *1988*, Table 10, p. 26; *1989/1990*, Table 10, p. 24; *1991*, Table 37, p 60.

Table 1 demonstrates several facts. First, we learn that the belletristic translations from Spanish into German increased from 37 to 124 in this twelve-year time frame, causing the ranking for Spanish to move from sixth to fourth (almost tied for third), which in itself in not very significant. More important is the percentage of increase in belletristic title production in translation from Spanish in relation to the percentage increase of works in translation from the other five major languages listed in Table 1. (See Table 2.) Publication of works translated from Spanish was up by far more than was publication of works from any other language, and even Italian--ranking second in percentage increase--trailed Spanish by approximately one hundred percentage points.

Table 2
Percent increase in belletristic title production in translation from originating language 1978 to 1990.

Originating Language	% Increase
Spanish	235.1%
Italian	141.3%
French	58.1%
Russian	42.1%
Average from all languages	41.8%
English	29.8%
Swedish	2.6%

Based on information in Table 2, using *Buch und Buchhandel in Zahlen* 1979-1991 as sources.

From the information in Table 2 it becomes clear that literature translated from Spanish into German has made more substantial gains in the literature market in Germany than literature from all other major languages. Translations from Spanish increased at five and a half times the average rate for all languages and at almost eight times the rate of translations from English. This is not to deprecate the importance of English, French, Russian, or Italian translations nor even to suggest that Spanish will one day surpass translations from those other languages. The purpose of this figure is to prove the increasing importance of literary translations from Spanish during the 1980s. Furthermore, it indicates that belletristic translations from Spanish (235.1% increase) increased at a faster rate than the increase in the total number of translations of "schöne Literatur" into German (41.8%).

Unfortunately, the available statistics do not provide information on two relevant points: 1) the total number of literary books produced, i.e., not just the number of titles produced but also the total number of copies of each single work of all translations produced and 2) the increase of literary translations from Spanish American as opposed to Peninsular Spanish. In order to come to a closer determination of these two aspects, we now turn to the figures of the Spanish American best sellers produced by the West German publishers. It should be noted that these figures are in round numbers. (See Table 3.)

Table 3

Numbers of Hardback Copies of the Spanish American Best Sellers in West Germany ("K & W" indicates Kiepenheuer & Witsch Verlag.)

Novel	Year Published	Publisher	Copies in German
Hundert Jahre Einsamkeit	1970	K & W	186,000
Chronik eines angekündigten Todes	1981	K & W	88,000
Geisterhaus	1984	Suhrkamp	556,000
Von Liebe und Schatten	1986	Suhrkamp	316,000
Liebe in den Zeiten der Cholera	1987	K & W	489,000
Mexikanischer Tango	1988	Suhrkamp	37,000
Eva Luna	1988	Suhrkamp	351,000
Lob der Stiefmutter	1989	Suhrkamp	101,000
General in seinem Labyrinth	1989	K & W	130,000
Geschichten der Eva Luna	1990	Suhrkamp	122,000
Geschichtenerzähler	1990	Suhrkamp	40,000

Source: *Verzeichnis der lieferbaren Bücher 1992 bis 1993 Suhrkamp Verlag* (August 1992) and Kiepenheuer & Witsch Verlag, sales figures (June 1992).[5]

In comparison to these figures, Siebenmann reported in his *Die neuere Literatur Lateinamerikas und ihre Rezeption im deutschen Sprachraum* (1972) that only 8000 copies of Mario Vargas Llosa's *Das grüne Haus* were printed when it was first published in 1968; and the delivery catalog of the second half of 1971 reported no second edition (76). In the same publication, Siebenmann offered the following figures for numbers of copies printed for the following Spanish American authors:

Asturias	*Legenden aus* Guatemala	23,000
	Der Herr Präsident	54,000 (3 Verleger)
Borges	*Labyrinthe*	37,000
Vargas Llosa	*Die Stadt und die Hunde*	29,000 (76)

It is interesting to compare the figure of 54,000 for Asturias's *Der Herr Präsident*, for which Asturias won the Nobel Prize for Literature in 1967, and the figures for García Márquez's *Hundert Jahre Einsamkeit*, for which he was cited when he won the Nobel Prize in 1982. Siebenmann tells us that

> haben wir Mitte 1971 beim Verleger [von *Hundert Jahre Einsamkeit*] nachgefragt und einen Absatz von 8000 Exemplaren seit

> dem Erscheinen (1970) festgestellt, was weit unter dem liegt, was angesichts des übrigen Auslandserfolges und der gegen 50 erschienenen Rezensionen im deutschen Sprachraum hätte erwartet werden dürfen. (76-77)

Clearly, we can see here evidence that in the 1980s more Spanish American novels were being translated and published in Germany than during the 1960s and 1970s. There is an obvious relationship between the number of copies of a book produced and the number of copies of a book sold: If there is more demand, there is more supply. But how can we learn about the demand for Spanish American novels? What will measure the demand?

From 1981 to 1991 four Spanish American novelists produced twelve works (when one includes García Márquez's non-fiction work *Abenteuer des Miguel Littín*) that have made the *Spiegel/Buchreport* Best Seller List: Six of these made the *Jahres-Bestseller* List (*Das Geisterhaus, Von Liebe und Schatten, Die Liebe in den Zeiten der Cholera, Abenteuer des Miguel Littín, Eva Luna,* and *General in seinem Labyrinth*). Indeed, Allende's *Geisterhaus* was on the yearly best seller lists for 1984, 1985, 1986, 1987, and 1988; her other two novels *Von Liebe und Schatten* and *Eva Luna* were each on the list for two years. García Márquez's *Liebe in den Zeiten der Cholera* made the lists for three years (1987, '88, and '89), and his *Abenteuer des Miguel Littín* and *General in seinem Labyrinth* for one year each, 1988 and 1990 respectively.[6]

The *Spiegel/Buchreport* weekly Best Seller Lists show us the pattern of increased occurrence, frequency, length of time, ranking, and number of Spanish American novels on the West German best seller list during the 1980s. It is important to note that no Spanish American novel appeared on the *Spiegel/Buchreport* Best Seller List during the 1970s, and no novel from Spain or Portugal was on the list during the 1970s or 1980s. Guatemalan Miguel Angel Asturias's being awarded the Nobel Prize for Literature in 1967 did not result in any of his works attaining best seller status in West Germany, while Gabriel García Márquez's *Hundert Jahre Einsamkeit* became a best seller only after he received the Nobel Prize in 1982. We find novels from Spanish America beginning to appear briefly on the list in 1981 and increasing in numbers, ranking, and length of time on the list through the 1980s and tapering off into 1991. (See the Spanish American Belletristic Literature on the *Spiegel/Buchreport* Best Seller List.)

SPANISH AMERICAN BELLETRISTIC LITERATURE ON THE SPIEGEL/BUCHREPORT HARDCOVER BEST SELLER LIST WITH MONTHLY RANKING[a]

BOOK TITLE	1981 JAN	FEB	MAR	APR	MAY	JUN	JUL	AUG	SEP	OCT	NOV	DEC
CHRONIK EINES ANGEKÜNDIGTEN TODES											9[b]	

BOOK TITLE	1982 JAN	FEB	MAR	APR	MAY	JUN	JUL	AUG	SEP	OCT	NOV	DEC
HUNDERT JAHRE EINSAMKEIT												7

BOOK TITLE	1983 JAN	FEB	MAR	APR	MAY	JUN	JUL	AUG	SEP	OCT	NOV	DEC
HUNDERT JAHRE EINSAMKEIT	7	8	8	10								

BOOK TITLE	1984 JAN	FEB	MAR	APR	MAY	JUN	JUL	AUG	SEP	OCT	NOV	DEC
GEISTERHAUS						10	8	3	3	3	1	1

BOOK TITLE	1985 JAN	FEB	MAR	APR	MAY	JUN	JUL	AUG	SEP	OCT	NOV	DEC
GEISTERHAUS	1	1	1	1	1	2	2	2	2	4	7	7

BOOK TITLE	1986 JAN	FEB	MAR	APR	MAY	JUN	JUL	AUG	SEP	OCT	NOV	DEC
GEISTERHAUS	8	3	4	4	5	4	4	4	4	5	6	4
VON LIEBE UND SCHATTEN							1	1	1	1	1	1

BOOK TITLE	1987 JAN	FEB	MAR	APR	MAY	JUN	JUL	AUG	SEP	OCT	NOV	DEC
GEISTERHAUS	9	6	5	10	8	9	7	6	8	11	10	14
VON LIEBE UND SCHATTEN	1	1	2	5	4	5	5	8	7	15[c]		
LIEBE IN DEN ZEITEN DER CHOLERA		4	1	1	1	1	1	1	1	1	1	11

BOOK TITLE	1988 JAN	FEB	MAR	APR	MAY	JUN	JUL	AUG	SEP	OCT	NOV	DEC
GEISTERHAUS	14	14	12	11	15	11	14	14	12	15		
LIEBE IN DEN ZEITEN DER CHOLERA	2	1	1	1	1	1	1	1	2	2	3	7
(ABENTEUER DES MIGUEL LITTIN)		15	8	5	7	9	11	13				
MEXIKANISCHER TANGO					12	15	13	8	8	14		
EVA LUNA								1[d]	1	1	1	1

BOOK TITLE	1989 JAN	FEB	MAR	APR	MAY	JUN	JUL	AUG	SEP	OCT	NOV	DEC
LIEBE IN DEN ZEITEN DER CHOLERA	7	8	9	13	14	15						
EVA LUNA	1	1	1	2	2	5	6	8	8	8	14	
LOB DER STIEFMUTTER								12	12	5	5	6
DER GENERAL IN SEINEM LABYRINTH												7

BOOK TITLE	1990 JAN	FEB	MAR	APR	MAY	JUN	JUL	AUG	SEP	OCT	NOV	DEC
LOB DER STIEFMUTTER	10	13	14									
DER GENERAL IN SEINEM LABYRINTH	5	4	5	6	12	15						
GESCHICHTEN DER EVA LUNA								6	5	3	6	7
GESCHICHTENERZÄHLER										14	15[e]	

BOOK TITLE	1991 JAN	FEB	MAR	APR	MAY	JUN	JUL	AUG	SEP	OCT	NOV	DEC
GESCHICHTEN DER EVA LUNA	7	13	15									

[a] The numbers represent the ranking of the book on the Spiegel/Buchreport Bestseller list for the first week the book appeared on the list in that month.

[b] Chronik eines angekündigten Todes was on the list for three weeks in November 1981.

[c] Prior to September 1987, the Spiegel Bestseller List ranked 10 books; since then 15 books have been ranked.

[d] Eva Luna displaced Liebe in den Zeiten der Cholera in the #1 position in the last two weeks of August 1988.

[e] Geschichtenerzähler was on the list for three weeks between 10 September and 8 October 1990.

3.5 Spanish American Novels and the Best Seller List

The implications of the best seller lists in relation to Spanish American novels are manifold. First, we should consider the overall picture of the increased number of translations from the Spanish language into German (Tables 3 and 4) together with the instances of Spanish American works on the best seller list in Germany and the lack of novels from Spain on the list. We can conjecture that a great number of the translations "from Spanish" do in fact come from Spanish America rather than from Spain. All of the best sellers translated from Spanish came from Spanish America. This fact shows that there were literary acceptance and active acculturation processes taking place through the literary medium in West Germany with regard specifically to Spanish America.

In focusing on the individual works on the best seller list, we find further implications. *Chronik eines angekündigten Todes* was the first of these novels to have made the best seller list, and it did so without any one single "drawing factor" (Nobel Prize, politics, a name already very well known, etc.). The reason it made the list must lie, then, in the actual qualities of the novel itself as well as in marketing and publicity in Germany.

Hundert Jahre Einsamkeit, in contrast, clearly needed the impetus of the Nobel Prize. First published in German in 1970, it was not on the list at any time during the 1970s but only made the list in the months immediately following García Márquez's being awarded the Nobel Prize in 1982. The fact that such a highly regarded work remained on the best seller list for four and a half months indicates that the Germans were "testing the water," attempting to try out Spanish American literature now that a respected international body had recognized the Latin American author. The notoriety of *Chronik* was most likely also a factor in the increased sales of *Hundert Jahre Einsamkeit*. The most significant implication of García Márquez's novels' (*Chronik eines angekündigten Todes* and *Hundert Jahre Einsamkeit*) best seller status was that the novels broke the ice and paved the way for later best-selling Latin American authors.

With Isabel Allende's *Geisterhaus*, the reception of Spanish American literature in West Germany moved into a new era; judging from the Spanish American works on the best seller list, the "trend" as such had actually begun. The author's name, or rather that of her uncle, was probably the initial attraction for German readers. Almost all of the reviews written on *Geisterhaus* mention her relationship to Salvador Allende. While Salvador Allende's name likely helped put *Geisterhaus* on the best seller list, Isabel's personal appeal (she has made several reading tours in West Germany) and the appeal of the novel itself sustained the book on the list and turned it into a "longseller." The longevity of the novel on the list implies a very real interest: the book was bought, read, discussed, recommended, given to others, and read further.

The "female factor"--the fact that the novel was written by a female author primarily about females for a largely female audience and promoted heavily by female booksellers--unquestionably aided in its distribution. The Latin American editor at Suhrkamp confirmed that two factors which contributed to the popularity of *Geisterhaus* were the fact that Allende is a woman and that most of the primary characters of *Geisterhaus* are women (Clara, Blanca, and Alba) (Dormagen, personal interview 18 May 1989).[7] He additionally discussed the role of females who work in bookstores and who talk with and recommend books to their customers. Furthermore, based on the largely female audience that attended her reading tour in West Germany in 1989 and on Allende's own comments on her German audiences (Allende, personal interview 3 June 1989), we can conjecture that women constitute a large portion of her reading public in West Germany. By the time her second novel, *Von Liebe und Schatten*, was published in Germany in 1986, the name "Allende" standing alone usually implied Isabel.

By 1986 Allende had established her circle of fans; her second novel immediately attained the number one position on the best seller list. Allende's fans bought and read *Von Liebe und Schatten* and kept it on the best seller list for one year and three months in spite of the much more critical reviews in newspapers and magazines than those written on *Geisterhaus*. Germans were now eagerly reading Latin American literature that dealt with Latin American subject matter. The preparation for reading this literature, whether preceding the publication of *Geisterhaus* or incorporated in the novel, proved adequate for the enthusiastic reception of Allende herself and also García Márquez Angeles Mastretta, and Vargas Llosa. While García Márquez had broken the ice for Spanish American literature in the early 1980s, Allende had made it fashionable in the mid and late '80s and early '90s.

Liebe in den Zeiten der Cholera (1987) was awaited with great anticipation and took only two weeks to be ranked Number 1 on the best seller list. It is the Spanish American novel that remained on the list second longest, second only to *Geisterhaus*. Like *Geisterhaus*, it had the characteristics needed to turn it into a "longseller."

The best seller status of Mastretta's *Mexikanischer Tango* (1988) shows us that Spanish American novels could now become popular even when the author's name was completely unknown and even though the novel deals with and takes place in the decades following the Revolution in Mexico, a time frame that is less known to Germans than Chile during the 1970s. In this case, the theme of female emancipation was probably instrumental to its success,[8] especially when viewed in connection with the same "female factor" that helped Allende.

As did *Von Liebe und Schatten*, *Eva Luna* (1988) jumped to the #1 position on the best seller list immediately after appearing in bookstores, again attesting to Allende's popularity. *Eva Luna* remained on the list for approximately the same length of time as *Von Liebe und Schatten*, and, again, in spite of numerous negative reviews.

With Vargas Llosa's *Lob der Stiefmutter* (1989) we find new elements for Spanish American literary success in West Germany. Besides the preparedness, which by now has enabled the perceived Spanish American sub-genre to become a trend in Germany, Germans find a novelist whose name was already known to a number of people in literary and political contexts and who wanted to be the elected president of Peru. With the words "erotic" (on the semi-transparent band around the book) and "Stiefmutter" on the cover, together with the enticing picture, the novel was alluring to the audience; and the novel's multimedia feature combining literature and painting reproductions is intriguing for the reader. Although the novel does not have a strong Latin American flavor, Germans are aware that the author is Latin American because of his name, the publicity he received from his candidacy, and from the words "Peruvian author" found almost without exception in advertising and reviews and on the cover of *Lob der Stiefmutter*. This confirms the fact that Latin American literature in the 1980s had not only become accepted, it was embraced by the Germans.

Following *Lob der Stiefmutter* was García Márquez's *General in seinem Labyrinth*. The book was considered very different from his earlier works; nevertheless, it remained a best seller for six months. By now, the German public had its set of expectations, what it anticipated in Spanish American literature and in works by García Márquez. I believe that part of the reason that *General in seinem Labyrinth* did not stay on the best seller list longer is that the novel significantly digressed from the German *Erwartungshorizont* for Latin American literature and novels by García Márquez.

Allende's *Geschichten der Eva Luna*, six and a half months on the best seller list, may have had the opposite problem from that of *General in seinem Labyrinth*. It was *too* similar to *Eva Luna* and offered its readers little that was new. The book had the additional disadvantage of being a work of short stories rather than a novel. Traditionally, books of short stories do not sell as well in Germany as do novels. The fact that it did become a best seller may be attributed to the Allende name, Suhrkamp as its publisher, and the German public's set of expectations.

Geschichtenerzähler by Mario Vargas Llosa appealed not only to Vargas Llosa fans and to Latin American enthusiasts but to some degree also to those Germans concerned about the impact of technology on life in general. On a more superficial level, the title "Geschichtenerzähler" surely attracted those Germans who simply wanted to read a good story. However, the nature of the work is complex: In its more esoteric and alien subject matter, it presents Indian mythology, many Indian names, and Indian outlook on life. These factors together with the theme may make the novel less accessible for the distant German audience. In a sense, *Geschichtenerzähler* and *General in seinem Labyrinth* approach some of the earlier Latin American novels like Colombian José Eustasio Rivera's *La vorágine*, Peruvian José María Arguedas's *Los ríos profundos*, and Cuban Alejo Carpentier's *Los pasos perdidos*, which were too psychologically and spiritually removed from the broad-based German public. Like *Chronik eines angekündigten Todes* at the beginning of the "Latin American trend," *Geschichtenerzähler* was a best seller for just three weeks. As with *General in seinem Labyrinth*, the German set of expectations had not been entirely fulfilled.

Disappointment in these last three Spanish American best sellers is reflected in their shorter tenure on the best seller list. This less overwhelming acclamation may signal an end to a "Latin American trend" per se, although individual works by the four Spanish American best-selling authors--and hopefully by others as well--will probably continue to attain success in Germany.

3.6 Change in Preparation

What prepared the Germans to receive this literature so warmly during the '80s?

Gabriel García Márquez said in an interview in 1988:

> Ja, das beste an diesem Buch [*Liebe in den Zeiten der Cholera*] ist für mich, daß es in Deutschland so viel Erfolg gehabt hat. Endlich habe ich die Deutschen erobert. Und ich glaube, das liegt am Thema Liebe. Ich weiß nicht warum, aber die Liebe scheint den Deutschen sehr am Herzen zu liegen. Merkwürdigerweise ist Frankreich das Land, wo ich möglicherweise die wenigsten Leser habe. [...] Mit meinem letzten Buch allerdings scheinen sich die Deutschen in besonderer Weise zu identifizieren.[9]

Isabel Allende expressed a similar view, paraphrased and translated by Michi Strausfeld:

> Das Herz der Deutschen ist eben romantisch, und deshalb fühlen sie sich den Themen [verbunden], die Isabel beschreibt, wo ja

> immer die Liebe eine sehr ausgeprägte Stellung hat, daß sie vielleicht deshalb den deutschen Leser so rühren.[10]

Allende's novels, in her own view, have had more impact in Germany than in most other countries in the world (Allende, personal interview). When asked how she drew this conclusion, she replied that she was basing it on the letters that she had received from her readers from all over the world.

Allende went on to explain that Germans are often seen as reserved and cold, but that she finds this to be a superficial judgment; she added that Germans are not really like that but rather that there is a real warmth in the German people. In her opinion, the German attention to her novels reflects a fresh encounter with latent emotions and feelings and an interest in the history and politics of Latin America. (Her comment on the latent emotions brings to mind the observations of Wagner de Reyna on the image of Latin America on the part of the Germans when he wrote that Germans search for *Gemütsbewegungen* in distant cultures.) Finally, she conveyed the idea that German novels of twenty years ago were intellectual novels written for the critics and not for the people and that one possible explanation for the popularity of her novels in West Germany is that her books are written for the people and not for the critics.

While García Márquez and Allende both suggest that the reason for their success in West Germany is rooted in the German heart, the reasons are far more complex and go much deeper. A whole constellation of events and factors prepared the Germans to accept and to esteem contemporary Spanish American novels. Eight events and movements led up to this changed mental climate; the factors intrinsic to the novels will be the subject of discussion in Part II as viewed in conjunction with the reviews written on these novels. The eight extrinsic catalysts are the these:

1. The first and principal turning point in preparing Germans for Spanish American literature of the 1980s came in 1976 when the theme of the Frankfurt Book Fair was "Latin American Literature--An Unknown Continent." The Book Fair focused attention on the unfamiliar literature from the "unknown continent." Nevertheless, not everything contributed to a harmonious transition from unknown to known. During the preparation in the year prior to the '76 Book Fair, the Fair Director was asked on numerous occasions: "Why Latin American and not another region that has more to offer for the book sector, the USA or the Soviet Union?" (Strausfeld, "Multiplikatoren" 1).

Mario Vargas Llosa, then the president of the International PEN Club, opened the Book Fair in English, to the displeasure of most of the listeners (Strausfeld, "Multiplikatoren" 3). Strausfeld says that other events were a "fiasco": The two discussion meetings that should have been the high points of the

Latin America Program were its low point on account of problems with translators and with discussion leaders ("Multiplikatoren" 6).

In spite of the problems encountered during the Book Fair, it was as a result of the Fair's focus that West German publishers took a greater interest in Latin American literature, and more of an effort was made to publish Latin American works. For the occasion of the '76 Book Fair, German publishers presented approximately 40 Latin American works.[11] In the years after the 1976 Book Fair, German publishers continued to publish Latin America works.

With the increased interest on the part of the publishers and the consequential augmentation in publication of Latin American works, critics were devoting more of their columns to Latin American literature. Besides literary reviews, critics became more interested in interviewing Latin American authors, and the interviews were then often published in newspapers and magazines. Almost all published interviews with Latin American writers date from after the 1976 Frankfurt Book Fair (Wiese, "La recepción" 51).

2. A second major impetus in the increased reception of Latin American literature was the Festival Horizonte in Berlin, 1982, in which music, theather, literature, film, and exhibits from Latin America were presented. Almost 170,000 people took part. The literary events, to which 35 Latin American authors were invited, took place over five days. The press releases conveyed the vitality, fantasy, and "Weltbedeutung" of Latin American literature. Strausfeld says that while the 1976 Frankfurt Book Fair focused attention on Latin American culture but perhaps left behind more likely negative remembrances and associations, the positive literary events at the 1982 Horizonte Festival could be termed a "break-through," a "new beginning" between Germans and Latin Americans ("Multiplikatoren" 11).

3. The third event that furthered the cause of Latin American literature in West Germany and the world was the awarding of the 1982 Nobel Prize for literature to Gabriel García Márquez. Obviously, the fact that García Márquez, a writer of prose rather than poetry, won the Nobel Prize made it easier for the German general public to become acquainted with his works and from that point other Latin American works.

4. The fourth contributing event was the awarding of the *Friedenspreis des Deutschen Buchhandels* in 1984 to Octavio Paz. This served a tri-fold function in regard to the reception of Latin American literature in Germany: First, for those who subsequently read his essays, the awarding of the prize functioned to introduce Germans to the Latin American political, economic, and cultural way of thinking. Second, for those who subsequently read his poetry for the first time, it helped function as an introduction to Latin American literature. Third, for those who did not go on to read his works but heard that he, a Latin

American, had received the prize, it functioned as a stamp of acceptability specifically for the German reader.

5. The fifth force in advancing the word about Latin American literature was the 1984 arrival of Isabel Allende on the German literary scene. If Spanish American literature had finally been recognized by German intellectuals through García Márquez and Octavio Paz, the "Allende phenomenon" was celebrated by the general public and the critics alike. Studies were done on the reasons behind her success:

> Ob es eine besondere Werbekampagne des Verlags gegeben habe (nein), was man gemanagt habe (nichts). Die Buchhändler waren begeistert von dem Roman [*Geisterhaus*], und die Empfehlung lief immer schneller weiter von Leser zu Leser, bevor überhaupt die ersten Rezensionen erschienen waren. (Strausfeld, "Multiplikatoren" 15)

As we have seen, *Geisterhaus* remained on the best seller list for four and a half years, and it was on the yearly best seller list for five. Nothing breeds success more than success.

While some publishers--including Suhrkamp's Latin American Program--had attempted to introduce the German market to Latin American literature in the 1960s and again in the 1970s, their success had been minimal. The solid popularity of Allende's *Geisterhaus* opened up the West German market to a situation where particular Latin American works were primed to be devoured by the broad based reading public.

> Viele Jahre lang mühte sich der Suhrkamp Verlag, lateinamerikanische Literatur unter die Leute zu bringen. Ein großes Geschäft war das nicht. Aber dann, unverhofft, verschönte Isabel Allende die Bilanz. Ihr Buch *Das Geisterhaus* wurde in der Bundesrepublik zum erfolgreichsten Roman des Jahres 1984.[12]

With Allende, the balance shifted.

6. The sixth catalyst is Suhrkamp Verlag's Latin American Program, begun in 1974. At that time the head of Suhrkamp, Siegfried Unseld, had decided to bring to the German reading public a Latin American literature program, not just of individual works, but modern, recently discovered writers as well as already established authors. This would be done within the framework of a continuous, systematic program. It was meant to be a "lebendiges" program, not academic, to bring this literature to Germans (Dormagen, personal interview 18 May 1989).

Suhrkamp Verlag and Insel Verlag had published individual Spanish writers such as García Lorca and Ramón Sender, but with the Latin American program, there came a shift of emphasis to the more distant continent and a more continuous and systematic program. Since then, Suhrkamp has established itself as a major publisher of quality Latin American and Peninsular Spanish literature. Among others, Suhrkamp is the publisher for Juan Carlos Onetti (Uruguay), Cabrera Infante (Cuba), Alejo Carpentier (Cuba), Julio Cortázar (Argentina), Manuel Puig (Argentina), Rosario Castellanos (Mexico), Octavio Paz (Mexico), César Vallejo (Peru), Felisberto Hernández (Uruguay), Horacio Quiroga (Uruguay), Mario Vargas Llosa (Peru), Isabel Allende (Chile), and Angeles Mastretta (Mexico), among others.

Suhrkamp's contribution to the spread of Latin American authors in West Germany in terms of quantity and quality should not be overlooked. The quality is sometimes viewed as originating from the author and sometimes as in fact stemming more from the Suhrkamp name on the novel than from the literary work itself. It is true that Suhrkamp has received criticism from various sources, generally from intellectuals, for having published Latin American novels which are considered below the level of quality expected from a novel published by Suhrkamp.[13] But since Suhrkamp has long been equated with quality literature, the fact that Suhrkamp published Allende, Mastretta, and Vargas Llosa (*Lob der Stiefmutter*) contributed to their novels being taken more seriously and receiving more critical attention than if their novels had been published by a less respected publisher.

Furthermore, a novel published by Suhrkamp is more likely to be reviewed in more newspapers and magazines--and in more prestigious ones--than is one by some of the smaller and less esteemed presses. Approximately 200 titles have been published within Suhrkamp's Latin American Program in the last fifteen years (Strausfeld, "Multiplikatoren" 16), and this aspect in the dissemination of Latin American literature in West Germany is significant.

7. The seventh event which helped acquaint Germans with Spanish American literature took place in Hamburg in 1986. Presented by the public authorities and taking place during the month of September, it was called "Iberoamericana" and included concerts, exhibits, films, and literature. The literary segment was offered in conjunction with the Ibero-Amerikanisches Institut of Hamburg, and Isabel Allende read to an audience in the sold out municipal theater.

8. The eighth and last impetus in the increased popularity of Latin American literature in West Germany in the last decade and even in the late 1970s were political events. The sojourn of Germans in exile to Latin America during the 1930s and 1940s may be considered as an early political preparatory step. When they returned to East and West Germany, some of them brought with

them the influence of the Spanish American culture, and some of the former exiles translated Spanish American works into German. These exiles did not have a strong impact on the reception of Spanish American literature in West Germany as such. However, they likely helped lay the foundations so that Germans were better prepared to receive Spanish American literature when other conditions later changed and became "ripe."

More pronounced were political events of the 1970s and '80s. The overthrow of Salvador Allende in 1973 had the further consequences of German sympathy toward Allende's liberal Chilean supporters and the exile of many Chileans who then went to West Germany. Broyles speculates that without the coup, Neruda and a number of other Latin American writers would probably not have "made a breakthrough in West Germany" (Broyles 220).[14]

The revolution in Nicaragua in 1979 added renewed hope for democratic civilian rule in Latin America. In South America over a decade ago, nine of the twelve independent republics were ruled by the military. Since 1979 those nine nations that have made the transition to an elected government are Argentina, Bolivia, Brazil, Chile, Ecuador, Paraguay, Peru, Uruguay, and Surinam. More recently, the candidacy of novelist Mario Vargas Llosa for president of Peru drew attention from the international press, including the press in West Germany. The majority of the reviews of his *Lob der Stiefmutter* mention his candidacy--often in the first paragraph.

Thus, the negative perception of Latin America as a continent of military dictatorships was replaced with the awareness that these countries are striving to do away with their dictatorships and are electing their governments: Change is possible despite economic stagnation and continued instability. This subject will be discussed in relation to the best-selling novels in Part II.

I concur with Strausfeld in her assessment that the most important points in the improvement of the reception of Latin American literature in West Germany may be listed as the Frankfurt Book Fair 1976, Horizonte 1982, the Nobel Prize to García Márquez 1982, the "Allende phenomenon" beginning 1984, and the Latin American Program at Suhrkamp Verlag ("Multiplikatoren" 16)--all of which were literary events. I would also add the sixth point of the political developments in Chile 1973, Nicaragua 1979, and the switch from military dictatorships to elected governments in so many Latin American countries as an indirect influence on reception. The increased reception may, therefore, be viewed primarily as a literary phenomenon.

3.7 The Image of Latin America in the 1980s

With the number of positive developments in the reception of Spanish American works in West Germany, it would seem plausible that the image of Latin America in Germany would have also taken a turn for the better. In the examination of the image formation of Latin America in West Germany during the late 1970s and 1980s, we find that more students were indeed learning Spanish. A 1989 article entitled "Spanish an bayerischen Gymnasien immer beliebter" in a Bavarian newspaper tells us:

> Spanisch wird als Unterrichtsfach immer beliebter. Die Zahl der Spanisch lernenden Schüler an bayerischen Gymnasien ist seit dem Schuljahr 1983/84 um 77 Prozent gestiegen. [...] An sieben Gymnasien sei Spanisch regulär dritte Fremdsprache.[15]

Also, the enrollment of students studying Spanish as their major subject in many university programs increased in West Germany during the 1980s (Janik, Kloepfer, Meyer-Minnemann; personal interviews), although, as Broyles points out, no distinction is usually made between Latin American and Peninsular programs. The exception to this would be the Ibero-Amerikanisches Institut of the Universität Hamburg, which also expanded. The educational institutions, then, have made strides in the acculturation process, but it is difficult to know to what degree.

Also difficult to gauge is the amount of tourist traffic travelling to Latin America; but again, indications are that more and more Germans, among the world's most traveled people, have been visiting Latin America more frequently (Ripken, personal interview). Direct contact with a foreign country is important in the acculturation process and therefore in image building.

The third institution of acculturation is the literary process: publishers willing to publish Spanish American works in translation, critics capable of offering informed and informative analyses on Spanish American works, and a reading public willing and prepared to encounter this literature. We have already seen the role of Suhrkamp Verlag and Kiepenheuer & Witsch in the production of key Spanish American texts in Germany. Today, a number of smaller publishers also produce translations of Spanish American works.[16] The critics will be examined more closely in the next chapter. The general reading public in West Germany has, in fact, become an eager consumer of a number of Spanish American novels.

Can cross-cultural reception of literature affect the image of a country? Jürgen Wilke answers this question for us:

> Das 'Image' eines Landes oder Kontinents dürfte aber auch durch andere Quellen mitbestimmt werden, nicht zuletzt durch die Literatur und die ihr eigene 'Bildlichkeit.' So könnte es durchaus sein, daß die ins Deutsche übersetzte Literatur Lateinamerikas--beispielsweise die in vergleichsweise hohen Auflagen verbreiteten Werke von Gabriel García Márquez--nicht weniger für das Bild Lateinamerikas bedeutet und gewirkt haben als die journalistische Berichterstattung (15).[17]

The media coverage of Latin America may have had less impact on Latin America's image formation in Germany than the literary processes. The amount of coverage in the media helping to shape the image of Latin America may still be relatively small: Winfried Schulz reports that a content analysis of West German media conducted in 1979 showed that the percentage of newspaper and television foreign reports dealing with Latin America was between 6.1% (ZDF) (television station) and 2.5% (*Bild*) (265-273). Between these figures lay the *Frankfurter Rundschau* with 5.4%, the *Süddeutsche Zeitung* with 5.1%, the Deutsche Presse-Agentur (dpa) with 4.7%, the *Frankfurter Allgemeine* with 4.4%, ARD (television station) 4.1%, and *Die Welt* with 4.0%. Schulz concludes that in Germany there was less coverage of events in Latin America than of those in Africa and Asia.

Hans Hübner disagrees with Schulz, saying,

> Insgesamt kann gesagt werden, daß--verglichen mit anderen europäischen Ländern, von den USA gar nicht zu reden--relativ viel Platz für Lateinamerika-Berichterstattung zur Verfügung steht

but adds that "[f]ür die große Mehrzahl der bundesdeutschen Zuschauer rangiert das Interesse für Lateinamerika und lateinamerikanische Themen ziemlich weit hinten" (75, 76). Furthermore, in a report presented in 1986, we learn that the different television stations do not have Latin America specialists, and that it sometimes happens that journalists who speak no Spanish or Portuguese and who have not previously worked with Latin America are sent to the continent since journalists are often sent on foreign assignments on a rotation basis so as not to lose contact with Germany and the viewers at home (Hans Hübner 81).

How Latin America is covered in the German media is even more telling than how much and who reports on it. Hans Hübner answers that Latin America is covered with 1) lack of objectivity, 2) ideological prejudice, 3) Eurocentricity, 4) an emphasis upon exoticism, 5) lack of continuity and 6) reporting with a preference for misery and poverty (86-90). One could also add "violence" to Hübner's last item. The end result is the "image" that Germans form as a result of their preparation through the media.

During a 1986 conference on the topic "Deutschland und Lateinamerika. Imagebildung und Informationslage," sets of Latin American "images" in Germany were presented. Interestingly, they differed little from the images of the 1970s presented earlier in this chapter. The only new element was the drug trade. In the following two sets of images of Latin America, we find a comprehensive view of the continent in the 1980s:

> 1) Umsturzversuche, Bürgerkriege, Guerillabewegungen, Schuldenprobleme, Wahlmanipulation usw. (Wilke 10)
>
> 2) [...] Projektion antiker Mythen; Utopie und verkehrte Welt; El Dorado; Degradierte Natur; Exotische, unbezwingbare Natur und Raum der Einsamkeit; [...] Barbaren [...]; Der Edle Wilde; Robinsonaden; Abenteuer; Land der unbegrenzten Möglichkeiten; Kontinent der Zukunft; Vision der Emigranten; Refugium für Verfolgte; Theologische Erneuerung; Dependenz; Soziale Revolution; Drogen und Drogenhandel; Verschwommene Identität; Kultureller Reichtum. (Siebenmann, "Bild Lateinamerikas" 20)[18]

We can plainly see that the image of Latin America in West Germany did not improved in the last decade. What had shifted was 1) the literary image and 2) the sense of hope that the negative political, social, and economic situation *can* change as already seen in the nine republics that converted from a military government to elected leaders since 1979. The potential and the hope for political change, and from this social and economic change, is, then, one aspect that has helped make West Germans of the 1980s perceive Latin America in a more favorable light.

The literary process of the more accessible novel coming out of Spanish America, the German publishers endorsing Latin American literature by producing the translations, and the critics offering more frequent and more positive or at least enlightened reviews of the novels all contributed to a greater readership of Spanish American novels in West Germany and to the Spanish American best seller as a market system. These factors, combined with the six primary extrinsic catalysts and the hope for political and social change in Latin America all led to better reception of this literature in Germany.

Notes

[1] I am indebted to Strausfeld for her permission to peruse this 1989 essay. It is forthcoming in *Begegnungen in 500 Jahren Lateinamerika und Deutschland*, Eds. D. Briesemeister, K. Kohut, G. Siebenmann. Frankfurt/M: Vervuert Verlag, 1993.

[2] The term "Third World" is indeed problematic. Wagner de Reyna takes Latin America's cultural, historical, and human connections as an indication of its belonging to the West rather than to the Third World. In contrast, Robert Holz at the University of Texas at Austin calls First World countries "those very wealthy, industrial, capitalist countries of the West, which include the U.S., Japan, Great Britain, France and Germany [...]" He refers to "a second echelon of countries which were kind of the Communist-bloc countries [...] and included [...] East Germany, Czechoslovakia, Romania, Bulgaria and the like." Based on economic criteria and Holz's definition, many countries of Latin America may be considered "Third World." (The *Austin American-Statesman* of Jan. 21, 1990: N. pag.)

[3] For French reception of Latin American works, see Sylvia Molloy, *La diffusion de la littérature hispano-américaine en France au XXe siècle* (Paris: Presses universitaires de France), 1972. Indeed, Claudia Wiese demonstrates that France influenced the German reception of Latin American "boom" literature due in part to its earlier engagement with this literature. See Wiese, *Die hispanoamerikanischen Boom-Romane in Deutschland*, 116.

[4] *Buch und Buchhandel in Zahlen 1979*, Chart 2, p. 24 and in same, *1991*, Table 38, p. 62. Frankfurt am Main: Buchhändler-Vereinigung GmbH, 1979 and 1991. All further references to this series will be noted in the text by *Buchhandel*, the year on the title page, the table number, and the page number, for example, *Buchhandel 1978*, Table 4, p. 16.

[5] This includes the 1970, 1979, and 1988 hardback editions of *Hundert Jahre Einsamkeit*. The figures from Kiepenheuer & Witsch are the sales figures, and the figures from Suhrkamp are print run counts.

[6] In 1988, the second year that 15 works are on the list as opposed to 10, *Geisterhaus* was #12 while *Abenteuer des Miguel Littín* was #14. In 1989 *Liebe in den Zeiten der Cholera* was #15. All of the other incidences of yearly best seller placement were in the top ten.

By contrast, only two French novels became yearly best sellers in West Germany during the time frame covered here: Marguerite Duras's *Der Liebhaber* (1985) and Benoîte Groult's *Salz auf unserer Haut* (1989-91).

Also, during the period from 1979 through 1991, the trade magazine *Publishers' Weekly* in the United States registered just four Spanish American novels on its best seller list: *Love in the Time of Cholera* (approximately 10 months from May 1988 to February 1989), *The General in His Labyrinth* (four months from September 1990 to February 1991), *In Praise of the Stepmother* (two weeks in November 1990), and *The Stories of Eva Luna* (two weeks in March and April 1991). It is interesting to note which novels were not on the list (earlier works by García Márquez and especially those by Allende) as well as the ranking achieved by those that were on the list. *Love in the Time of Cholera* was as high as #3, #4, and #5 for nine weeks; the remainder of the time it was lower. *The General in His Labyrinth* was in fourth and fifth places for three weeks and lower the rest of the time. *In Praise of the Stepmother* was ranked #15 both weeks on the list, and *The Stories of Eva Luna* were #14 and #15.

[7] Both Eckard Hooge and Monika López also discussed the importance of the female in selling books.

[8] The translator of *Mexikanischer Tango*, Monika López, believes the success of the book had to do with the fact that it is a novel "von einer Frau, von einer Frau geschrieben, und zwar mit scheinbar leichter Hand, ohne jeden Klageton. Dieser Klageton, der der europäischen Frauenliteratur bis vor kurzem noch anhaftete" [...] (letter, 14 May 1990).

[9] "Garcia [sic] Márquez: Liegt die Liebe den Deutschen so am Herzen?" *Die Welt* 11 January 1988: N. pag.

[10] Strausfeld, Sept. 1989 cassette-recorded interview for and in possession of this author.

[11] Strausfeld, "Multiplikatoren" 3 and Wiese, "La recepción" 50. Strausfeld reports, "Acht Verlage präsentierten aus Anlaß des Schwerpunktthemas insgesamt rund dreißig lateinamerikanische Novitäten," while Wiese states, "On the occasion of the first Frankfurt Book Fair with a central theme [1976], some 50 [Latin American] novels were translated."

[12] Ulrich Greiner, "Ein schnelles Buch," *Die Zeit* 25 July 1986: N. pag.

[13] See Jörg Drews, "Isabel Allende bei Suhrkamp," *Merkur. Deutsche Zeitschrift für europäisches Denken* Dec. 1986: 1069. See also Joachim Kaiser, "Die neue Lust am kulinarischen Roman," *Stern* 16 Feb. 1989: 71.

[14] As already indicated, some Spanish American writers had already been translated into German; for example, Neruda had been translated by Erich Arendt. Arendt's translations of Neruda that were published by Volk und Welt in East Germany were *Spanien im Herzen* (mit Stephan Hermlin), 1952; *Der Groß Gesang*, 1953; *Die Trauben und der Wind*, 1955; *Elementare Oden*, 1961; *Extravaganzenbrevier*, 1967; and *Memorial von Isla Negra*, 1976. Those published by Reclam in Leipzig were *20 Liebesgedichte*, 1958, and *Aufenthalt auf Erden*, 1973. Those that were published in West Germany include *Aufenthalt auf Erden*. Hamburg: Rowohlt, 1960; *Dichtungen I/II*. Neuwied: Luchterhand 1967; and *Viele sind wir*. Neuwied: Luchterhand, 1972. The fact of translations and that of a "breakthrough," however, are not synonymous.

[15] *Berchtesgadener Anzeiger*, 29 April 1989: N. pag.

[16] See *Quellen*. Ed. Gesellschaft zur Förderung der Literatur aus Afrika, Asien und Lateinamerika, Frankfurt/Main, 1990 or 1992.

[17] Compare Siebenmann, *Die neuere Literatur Lateinamerikas und ihre Rezeption im deutschen Sprachraum* (Berlin: Colloquium Verlag, 1972) with Siebenmann and Casetti, *Bibliographie der aus dem Spanischen, Portugiesischen und Katalanischen ins Deutsche übersetzten Literatur 1945-1983* (Tübingen: Max Niemeyer Verlag, 1985).

[18] See also Claudia Wiese, *Die hispanoamerikanischen Boom-Romane in Deutschland* 132.

Chapter 4

Stimuli to Buy Books and the Role of the Critic

Die Verpackung ist ebenso wichtig wie der Inhalt: Diese Binsenweisheit hat sich auch die Frankfurter Stadtbibliothek zu eigen gemacht. (Frankfurter Allgemeine Zeitung 5 Feb. 1987)

Es sei "wohl schon fast egal, was ich schreibe," meinte [der erfolgreiche belletristische Autor] Siegfried Lenz mit Recht [...] (Schnell, Die Literatur der Bundesrepublik 27)

Schlagt ihn tot, den Hund! Es ist ein Rezensent. (Goethe, "Rezensent" 1773)

What motivates West Germans to purchase certain books and not others? More specifically, what influenced Germans to buy particular Spanish American fiction during the 1980s and '90s when they had lagged behind other countries in Spanish American reception during the '60s and '70s?

The number of sources recommending books is varied, and there is no consensus on which sources are the most influential. I will introduce the diverse motivational factors and attempt to evaluate in general terms their effectiveness in convincing the buying public to purchase certain novels. The stimuli to be discussed are the author; the publisher; bookstore window advertising and displays; recommendations from family, friends, and booksellers; the best seller lists; radio and television; and reviews in newspapers and magazines.

4.1 Motivational Factors

Surveys have been conducted on the numerous motivational factors involved in book-buying; but I find that they are not applicable here, for they cover an earlier time frame, they attempt to assess in percentages the degree to which each factor influences book-buying, they do not compare similar factors, and they do not include all of the factors that I include.[1] Rather, I will explore all of the factors with the idea that it is frequently not just any one factor that influences people to buy but often a combination of factors, for example, a recommendation from a friend combined with seeing the book listed on the best seller list.

One of the strongest influences that makes people want to purchase books is the recommendation of family members and friends (Siebenmann, *Neuere Literatur* 41). This kind of recommendation may be viewed as a network either in limited circles--such as the few West Germans knowledgeable about Latin American literature in the 1960s--or extend to a very wide group--as seen in the network of female readers who discovered and spread the word about Allende's *Geisterhaus* and later García Márquez's *Liebe in den Zeiten der Cholera.*

A second persuasive drawing factor for buying a book is the author. Once the author has established himself or herself with a certain circle of readers, those readers generally know what they can expect from the writer and so continue to buy his or her books. The author's name is a marketable label affixed to the article, and his or her name brings a certain assurance of sales. Novelist Siegfried Lenz can serve as an example. The authors of an article entitled "Spiegel-Report über Bestseller und Bestseller-Macher. 'Wir haben uns alle total heiß gemacht'" (Nr. 41, 1973: 182-197) report that the name Lenz "hat sich im Bewußtsein bestimmter Käufer festgesetzt, was sich [...] in permanenten Absatzerfolgen der betreffenden Bücher äußert (182, qtd. in Lauterbach 170). As has already been shown, Werner Faulstich mentions the "Bestseller als Bestseller-Autor [...] Er selber ist die Ware [...]" (*Bestandsaufnahme* 24-25).

Also, when a photograph of the author is seen frequently, whether on his or her books, in newspaper or magazine articles, or in advertisements, a kind of brand-name identification results, which in turn promotes sales of the book (King 96). The photograph and resulting identification may have a further effect: "Die Illusion, teilzunehmen am Leben und Produzieren 'großer' Personen und in dieser Identifikation selbst 'reicher' zu werden, stiftet zusätzlich soziale Befriedung" (Raoul Hübner 116).

Photographs of Isabel Allende and Angeles Mastretta have been used particularly effectively in the promotion of their books. Allende's photographs appeared on the wrap-around strips on the novels themselves, in reviews of her novel, in advertisements in newspapers and magazines, and on posters promoting her readings.[2] Similarly, Mastretta's photograph was placed in newspaper and magazine reviews and in advertising for her novel. In both cases, the idea of reader identification combined with the "female factor" mentioned in Chapter 3 suggests an identification with Allende and Mastretta on the part of many West German female readers. In contrast, photographs of Gabriel García Márquez and Mario Vargas Llosa appear in reviews but less frequently in advertising.

One evident motivational force in relation to the author is the awarding of the Nobel Prize to that writer. It has already been shown that García Márquez's receiving the 1982 Nobel Prize was clearly a factor, if not the primary influence, in *Hundert Jahre Einsamkeit* becoming a best seller that year. It should be noted, however, that Germans do not automatically buy books by an author once he or she has received the Nobel Prize: Recent examples are the Nobel

Prize winners Naguib Mahfouz (Egypt, 1988), Camilo José Cela (Spain, 1989), and Octavio Paz (Mexico, 1990).

In her book *Best-Sellers by Design*, King describes the importance of the interaction between the author and publisher, the latter constituting a third stimulus (74-75). Siegfried Unseld at Suhrkamp Verlag sees the cooperation between author and publisher as integral:

> A literary publishing house does not build its reputation on individual books, especially not on best-sellers [...] The publishing program, as well as that program's scope, grows in accordance with the growth of its authors. The right admixture in the program is, of course, a matter of importance. (28)

Both Kiepenheuer & Witsch and Suhrkamp are prominent publishing houses in West Germany, and both have built their reputations on their authors. Suhrkamp is naturally pleased with the best sellers it has produced within its Latin American Program. But the Latin American editor emphasizes that he is very proud of the Latin American program as a whole, particularly its production of translations of such Spanish American writers as Onetti, Carpentier, and Cortázar. These authors are recognized as premier Spanish American writers even though their novels have not become best sellers in Germany.

Hohendahl maintains that it is in fact the publisher who, above all, is the determining factor in the success of a book (175). He names several responsibilities of the publisher that contribute to the possible success of a novel. Publishers, especially publishers such as Kiepenheuer & Witsch and Suhrkamp, know how to maximize marketing and professional promotion through marketing research; publicity; readings, personal appearances, and interviews with the author; and full utilization of the media market (175-176).

The publisher's marketing in the wide sense of the word has been discussed in Chapter 2, and its importance cannot be taken lightly. At least one survey on book-buying stimuli by the Börsenverein des Deutschen Buchhandels reports that a great portion of those people purchasing books had related the deciding factor as the diverse publicity campaign on the part of the publishers (Heller 484). This publicity begins with the design of the book jacket and the choice of the book jacket blurb and continues through the advertisements placed in newspapers and magazines according to the anticipated target readership. Unseld explains,

> Each individual step in the production of a book is important: the treatment of the manuscript, the watchful care along the way of

> transformation from manuscript to book, the book's exterior, its jacket, its typography, and the words used to announce the book. A book's exterior is an expression of its interior. [...] [T]he exterior must not only do justice to the interior, it must also be effective advertising, i.e., make the buyer decide to buy the book. In addition, it must please the author, do justice to his expectations, and yet at the same time be successful in the marketplace. (30)

All of the above are phases in the production of the best seller as a market system.

Two other components in the attempt to attract possible buyers deal with the bookstores themselves. Continuing with the concept of marketing, bookstore windows and displays, a fourth impetus, can emit an ambiance that can entice and direct a customer to certain kinds of books or books set in a certain geographical region or time. I observed several store front windows promoting books from and about Latin America. One window contained a sombrero, a guitar, sand, a miniature cardboard palm tree, a colorful Latin American print textile, and the various Latin American books the bookstore was promoting. While stereotypical, the store front window attracted the attention of passers-by.

Booksellers in the bookstores are a fifth valuable source of book recommendations. As was already intimated in an earlier chapter, customers ask personnel in bookstores to suggest books to them, usually books of a certain type. The more recent popularity of Latin American works and the corresponding familiarity of the booksellers with these works augment the Spanish American best seller sales. Like the situation of the best seller lists as an indicator and as a factor in book recommendation, the booksellers perform a two-fold role in the best seller system: selling and recommending.

Since the role of the best seller itself as a recommendation was discussed in Chapter 1, there is no need to go into detail here. However, it is worth reiterating the importance of the best seller list as a sixth source. Rollka maintains, "die Verkaufsförderung durch diese [...] Bestsellerliste [darf] nicht unterschätzt werden" (21). Furthermore, Lauterbach quotes the manager of a large bookstore in Hannover as saying,

> Die Bestsellerlisten sind notwendig, um dem Käufer eine Orientierung zu geben. Die Leute kommen mit den Bestsellerlisten in der Hand in den Laden. (138)

The increase of the *Spiegel* Best Seller List from ten books to fifteen in 1987 indicates that the influence of the best seller lists has actually grown during the 1980s, and the expectation is that this stimulus will be transferred to more books sold.

The influence of the electronic media, a seventh persuading force, has also gained importance since the 1960s. In one survey on the influences on book-buying, television and radio are ranked separately against the press, bookstore windows, publishers' advertising, brochures and catalogue mailings, and local community advertising (Rollka 128, 129). While television is reported to be more influential than radio, both are consequential ingredients in the diffusion of information on books.

The form this information takes will vary. Book reviews are carried on the radio, sometimes discussing one book in detail and sometimes several books in less detail. Occasionally, interviews are conducted with the authors, either as a segment of a regular program or occasionally as a program in its own right. None of the four authors covered in this study speaks German. García Márquez, Allende, and Vargas Llosa have been interviewed by West German television stations or have had programs on one of their books. In each case there was an interpreter from Spanish into German or from English into German or there was a German voice-over as the author spoke Spanish. Besides functioning as additional publicity, the more direct contact with the author, whether on radio or on television, would doubtlessly serve to enhance the viewer's identification with the writer and to make the novelist and his or her works more accessible, more real, to the potential reader.

The role of the critic and the newspaper and magazine review is integral to the best seller system, but their function as the eighth and final book-buying impetus is less defined. In West Germany, best sellers, both those of the upper echelon of literature and those considered higher quality *Unterhaltungsliteratur*, are reviewed, often for the purposes of "Verkaufsstimulanz" (Faulstich, *Bestandsaufnahme* 164).

However, it is often the case that a novel receives a great many favorable reviews without much effect on the sales; at the same time, a novel unfavorably reviewed can still become a best seller. Dieter Zimmer has written that the literary critic prevents no book from becoming a best seller, nor can he or she make one ("Die Herzen" 112-115, qtd. in Faulstich, *Bestandsaufnahme* 61). Others, such as Heinz B. Heller, concur with Zimmer's assessment. Heller illustrates this situation with references to critics' comments on reviews. He quotes Heinrich Vormweg's assessment that, in spite of the 1973 series of plausible negative reviews of Siegfried Lenz's *Das Vorbild*, sales continued to climb without interruption (483). Heller continues:

> [W]enn Klaus Ramm andererseits am Beispiel Herbert Achternbuschs detailliert ausführt, daß viele und nahezu ausschließlich

> positive Rezensionen folgenlos geblieben sind, dann bestätigen solche Beobachtungen das Ergebnis einer vom Börsenverein des Deutschen Buchhandels durchgeführten Umfrage. Danach erhält nur eine Minderheit der Buchkäufer seinen entscheidenden Kaufimpuls durch die Literaturkritik [...] (483-4)

While it is true that reviews do not "make or break" novels (or best sellers), they may in fact affect sales to some extent:

> Aber immerhin können die Urteile von Kritikern für die literarische Zukunft zumal jüngerer, noch nicht arrivierter Autoren mitentscheidend sein. Und ebenso gewiß können sie Absatzzahlen beeinflussen. (Schnell 47)

Most reviewers do include judgments ranging from denunciation to high praise. The real function of reviews is not to create a best seller or to prevent a novel from becoming a best seller, but rather to inform the public about a book, an author, an author's oeuvre. The review is an important source of a wide variety of information for the potential reader.[3]

As an information source, the critics' reviews perform an important social role in their interaction with the reading public. The reader's discourse with the critiques deepens his or her understanding of a work and often his or her insight into a body of works. The reader then forms an opinion based in part on the views of the critics. The reviews therefore possess an integrative function of social cohesiveness as a shared experience and common opinions.

The reviews are not only a source of information and opinions; they also serve as a valuable form of publicity. King describes such a situation in which one German author's novel, Hans Habe's *Das Netz*, was unfavorably critiqued by major critics while another's, Hildegard Knef's *Der geschenkte Gaul*, was favorably reviewed. Yet both became best sellers (King 99). In this example, King refers to both Hohendahl's analysis of Hans Habe's *Das Netz* in his essay "Promoter, Konsumenten und Kritiker" and to the group of scholars' investigation of Hildegard Knef's *Der geschenkte Gaul* in *Deutsche Bestseller--Deutsche Ideologie*, edited by Heinz Ludwig Arnold.

According to Hohendahl, "[...] ist der Fall Habe auch exemplarisch für die Möglichkeiten, auf die Institution Literaturkritik von außen Einfluß zu nehmen" (180). In 1967, two years before *Das Netz* was published, Habe entered into an alliance with the reactionary Springer newspaper empire. As a conservative, he reflected the views of Springer and acted as the group's spokesman; and the Springer group made certain that Habe's novel became known. Articles and reviews appeared in the *Hamburger Abendblatt*, the *Welt am Sonntag*, the

Berliner Morgenpost, and even in the *Bild-Zeitung*. All of the reviews in these publications were positive, but Habe's novel was unfavorably reviewed among the greater number of other major critics. Nevertheless, I would contend, with King, that the case of Habe's *Das Netz* is exemplary for critics' negative reviews not preventing a novel from becoming a best seller.

A parallel case can be found among the Spanish American novels: both García Márquez's *Liebe in den Zeiten der Cholera*, with laudatory reviews, and Allende's *Von Liebe und Schatten*, more negatively critiqued, became best sellers. It seems that it does not matter what the critics write but rather that they do indeed write something, thus creating publicity, whether intentionally or not (King 99).

Publicity as a side benefit of reviews, however, still does not necessarily help a novel, either by a German or a foreign author, to become a best seller. As in the case of Lenz and Achternbusch, an example of this situation may be seen in the case of the Spanish American novels. *Hundert Jahre Einsamkeit* had been favorably critiqued in approximately fifty reviews when it was published in West Germany in 1970. However, it did not become a best seller until twelve years later. In contrast, Allende's second, third, and fourth works, *Von Liebe und Schatten*, *Eva Luna*, and *Geschichten der Eva Luna* were reviewed more unfavorably than *Hundert Jahre Einsamkeit*, yet those critiques apparently had little negative effect on their sales or on their best seller status. We may conclude that the phenomenon of *Von Liebe und Schatten* and *Eva Luna* (and perhaps to a lesser degree *Geschichten der Eva Luna*) exemplifies the situation of the review as a source of information and publicity at a time when West Germans were already better prepared for Spanish American literature than they were in the early 1970s.

Schnell agrees that one of the most important sources of information for readers regarding contemporary literature is that of the feuilletons of leading political/cultural weekly publications (*Die Zeit*, *Der Spiegel*) as well as weekend feuilletons of important supraregional daily newspapers (*Süddeutsche Zeitung*, *Frankfurter Allgemeine Zeitung*, *Frankfurter Rundschau*) (47). These are considered among the most prestigious publications in West Germany. Schnell adds, "Hier schreiben professionelle Kritiker ebenso wie Fachwissenschaftler oder auch Schriftsteller" (47).

4.2 The Reviews and the Critics

Several elements must be taken into consideration in the discussion of using critiques from newspapers and magazines to study the reception, the image, and the dissemination of a foreign literature in West Germany. We must consider the advantages and disadvantages of an analysis of the reviews, the types of newspapers and magazines to be examined, and the general aesthetic criteria of the reviewing publications.

There are, of course, drawbacks in the analysis of the reviews of the Spanish American best sellers in West Germany. It is not always possible to obtain all of the critiques on a work; and even if that were possible, many are repetitions of the same critique under different titles. Reviews by the Deutsche Presse Agentur, often written by Christine Wischmann, are published, in part or full, by a number of newspapers. Some of the reviews are thorough analyses of a work's content, style, theme, and history; they may also provide information on the author and his or her other works. Others are very short and contain little more than a brief description of the work. In other words, the unequal quality of the reviews precludes consistent evaluation. A further difficulty is that, while the critic may be considered the "representative reader" (von Bülow 10), one must recognize that the critic's reactions cannot be considered always typical for a general reading population. It is the critic's job to be a reader. However, as a critic, he or she commonly develops a more refined sensitivity to literature since the critic is also usually trained to perform the task of book reviews.

Nevertheless, the benefits of analyzing reviews outweigh the disadvantages. Published literary criticism is essential in ascertaining the publicly accepted view of works and authors. In this case the works and authors are from Spanish America, so the role of the critic is even more important in this determination since it is the critic's task to inform the public about literature with which it is less familiar.

In dealing with reception aesthetics, critiques have an important function. Reception aesthetics concentrates on the role of the reader in the literary process. Critics are first readers before they become evaluators of literature (Jauß, *Literaturgeschichte* 169). The critics' reviews usually represent the only extant written body of reactions to a work. Another advantage to the examination of reviews is that critics justify their opinions with arguments and examples, providing indications of the critic's literary value system (Zeller 202). Furthermore, it is the task of the critic to develop a concretization of a literary work and to evaluate it according to the prevailing system of criteria. The professional critic's evaluation of Spanish American fiction brings about an encounter between the qualities of the works and the contemporary literary norms in West Germany.

Besides effecting the concretization of a work, the critic is vital in the diffusion of literature, in this instance Spanish American works of fiction. Critics respond to the Spanish American novels by analyzing the books and by formulating verbal images which are then passed on to the public. Reviewers are thus "opinion-makers" (Broyles 21) and "opinion-multipliers" (von Bülow 10) as they reflect the current social, literary, and ideological tendencies in a different culture and with a dissimilar set of norms from the culture in which the Spanish American novels were written.

Peter Glotz's book *Buchkritik in deutschen Zeitungen* provides insights into this aspect of the German literary market system. Glotz divided the newspapers he studied into three categories (supraregional, local, and group newspapers and magazines) and conducted a survey of the publications based on the categories. His purpose was to determine, among other things, the educational background of the culture editors, their average ages, their aesthetic criteria, their self-image, and their image of their readership.

Glotz found that, with the exception of the avoidance of those authors who had a connection to National Socialism, the political beliefs of the editors and of the novelists play only a small part in the reviews (Glotz 143). Thus the liberal politics of García Márquez (and his friendship with Fidel Castro) and the more conservative politics of Vargas Llosa did not affect their novels being reviewed in Germany. Vargas Llosa's presidential candidacy, referred to in most reviews, interested the critics, but it was almost always mentioned more as a side note that had little to do with the content of *Lob der Stiefmutter* or *Geschichtenerzähler*. A contrasting case is that of Allende. Politics--more likely that of her uncle than her own--probably contributed to an increased interest in her novels on the part of German critics than would have been the case had she not carried the Allende name. Most articles mention Salvador Allende, usually at the very beginning, and discuss the content of the novel, including Salvador Allende and Chile's political background.

Of particular interest to this study is Glotz's contention that a small group of newspapers predominate in literary criticism (13). This group includes supraregional publications, the cultural editors of which help define "good literature" in West Germany through a common but general "ästhetischen Normenkanon" (143). Of primary importance to these cultural editors is linguistic and structural innovation, while content is considered secondary if the author presented his or her material in an innovative manner (143).

Literature that does not meet the standards of literary quality as determined by these cultural editors is considered *Trivialliteratur*, and it is a matter of prestige that supraregional publications never review *Trivialliteratur* (Glotz 117, 118). Although a number of the reviews of Allende's second, third, and fourth works allude to trivial aspects of the books, the fact that the novels were critiqued in supraregional newspapers and magazines would indicate, by the critics' own definition, that her novels are not *Trivialliteatur*.[4]

Difficulties arise in classifying the numerous publications which publish literary critiques. Classification of newspapers and magazines done by other scholars varies from Glotz's categorization. Further complications present themselves, too, with publications that fall into two categories, such as *Christ und Welt* and *Rheinischer Merkur*, which are, according to Glotz's classification, group newspapers but which may be regarded more as supraregional newspapers in their cultural sections.

It is nevertheless advantageous to classify the media reviews in order to better conceptualize their readership and circulation. As a means of general orientation for this study, the newspapers, magazines, and radio broadcasts containing reviews used in this study[5] are categorized as follows:

SUPRAREGIONAL DAILY NEWSPAPERS

Frankfurter Allgemeine Zeitung
Frankfurter Rundschau
Süddeutsche Zeitung
Welt

SUPRAREGIONAL WEEKLY NEWSPAPERS AND MAGAZINES

Deutsches Allgemeines Sonntagsblatt
Deutsche Zeitung-Christ und Welt
Rheinischer Merkur
Spiegel
Welt am Sonntag
Zeit

REGIONAL/LOCAL NEWSPAPERS AND MAGAZINES (Daily, Weekly and Monthly)

Aachener Nachrichten
Aachener Volkszeitung
Abendzeitung, München
Alfelder Zeitung
Allgemeine Zeitung, Mainz
Augsburger Allgemeine Zeitung
Badische Zeitung
Berliner Morgenpost
Berliner Zeitung
Coolibri (Ruhrgebiet)
Darmstädter Echo
Deutsche Post, Frankfurt
Elmshorner Nachrichten
Esslinger Zeitung
Express, Köln
Fränkische Volksblatt
Fränkische Wochenzeitung
General-Anzeiger, Bonn
Gießener Anzeiger
Goslarsche Zeitung
Hamburger Abendblatt
Hamburger Anzeiger und Nachrichten
Hamburger Morgenpost
Hamburger Rundschau
Hannoversche Allgemeine Zeitung
Heilbronner Stimme
Harburger Anzeigen und Nachrichten
Hessische Allgemeine
Kieler Nachrichten
Kölner Illustrierte
Kölner Stadt Anzeiger
Kölnische Rundschau
Landeszeitung für Lüneburger Heide
Main-Echo
Main-Post, Würzburg

Mannheimer Morgen
Memory-Magazin/Kulturwelt Köln
Mittelbayrische Zeitung
Morgen, Berlin
Münchner Merkur
Münstersche Zeitung
Nürnberger Nachrichten
Nürnberger Zeitung
Neue Osnabrücker Zeitung
Neue Presse, Hannover
Neue Ruhr Zeitung
Neue Westfälische Zeitung
Offenburger Tageblatt
Pirmasenser Zeitung
Reutlinger General-Anzeiger
Rhein-Main Presse
Rhein-Main Zeitung
Rhein-Neckar, Heidelberg
Rheinpfalz, Ludwigshafen
Ruhr-Nachrichten, Dortmund
Saarbrücker Zeitung
Schwäbische Zeitung
Siegener Zeitung
Stadtblatt Osnabrück
Städtemagazin 'Plärrer', Nürnberg
Stuttgarter Nachrichten
Stuttgarter Zeitung
Südkurier
Südwest Presse, Ulm
Szene, Hamburg
Tagesspiegel, Berlin
Tageszeitung, Berlin
Treffpunkt Spectrum Kulturjournal
Trend für Würzburg
Umbruch, Zeitschrift für Kultur Frankfurt
Unser Bremen
Westfälischer Anzeiger
Westfalen Post
Wetzlarer Neue Zeitung
Wiesbadener Kurier
Wiesbadener Tagblatt
Woche, Regensburg
Wolfenbütteler Zeitung

GROUP AND ASSOCIATION/PROFESSIONAL NEWSPAPERS AND MAGAZINES

Beamtenbund
Deutsche Beamte
Deutsches Ärzteblatt
Diners Club Magazin
Frontal
Hessisches Ärzteblatt
Holzarbeiter Zeitung
Industrie Magazin
Karlsruher Steuerbrief
Ketchup
Kirchenzeitung für das Erzbistum Köln
Lutherische Monatshefte
Neue Ärztliche
Pflasterstrand (Frankfurt)
Playboy
Rote Blätter
Welt der Arbeit

BOOKDEALER NEWSPAPERS AND MAGAZINES

August News/ Augustin Buchhandlung
Bayreuther Kultur/ Markgrafen Buchhandlung
Börsenblatt
Buch Journal
Bücherei aktuell München St. Michaelsbund
Buchhändler heute
Buchmagazin

Buchreport
Bücherpick
Neue Bücherei

WOMEN'S NEWSPAPERS AND MAGAZINES

Bild der Frau
Brigitte
Cosmopolitan
Elle
Frau in Bonn
Frau und Mutter
Freundin
Für Sie
Journal für die Frau
Petra
Emma[6]

RADIO AND TELEVISION

Bayrischer Rundfunk
Hessischer Rundfunk
Norddeutscher Rundfunk

CULTURAL NEWSPAPERS AND MAGAZINES

Merkur
Westermann's

WEEKLY ILLUSTRATED MAGAZINES (*Illustrierte*)

Bunte
Stern

OTHER INFORMATION SERVICES

dpa (Deutsche Presse Agentur) news wire service
Einkaufzentrale für öffentliche Bibliotheken

In this chapter it has been shown that the different motivational factors in West German book-buying are family and acquaintances, the author, the publisher and the publisher's advertising, bookstore window displays, bookstore personnel, best seller lists, radio and television exposure, and reviews. The critiques serve the reading audience more as publicity and as a source of information than as serious recommendations to purchase or not to purchase a book. Although the reviews are not as influential in persuading the public to purchase books, their real value lies in their constituting an extant and researchable body of opinion-makers, opinion-disseminators, and mirrors of the prevailing system of literary criteria.

Part II of this study turns to characteristics of the Spanish American works that became best sellers in West Germany and to the reviews of the novels to learn what literary needs and expectations of West Germans the novels satisfy.

Notes

[1] See Gustav Siebenmann, *Die neuere Literatur* 40-41; Heinz B. Heller, "Literatur als Institution in der Bundesrepublik, *Tendenzen der deutschen Gegenwartsliteratur*, ed. Thomas Koebner, 2nd edition, 483-484; Bodo Rollka, *Vom Elend der Literaturkritik* 128-129, and Dagmar Hintzenberg, Siegfried J. Schmidt, and Reinhard Zobel, *Zum Literaturbegriff in der Bundesrepublik Deutschland*, 79.

[2] During Allende's readings, she would read a selection in Spanish and a native German speaker, frequently an actress, would then read that selection from the German translation. Sometimes there are simultaneous translations of a Spanish American author's reading, as was the case when Mario Vargas Llosa read from *El hablador* (*Geschichtenerzähler*) in Düsseldorf in 1992.

[3] See Friedl Zapata, "Die Rolle der Literaturkritik."

[4] For a sample of those reviews which refer to the tendency toward the "trivial" in *Von Liebe und Schatten*, *Eva Luna*, and *Geschichten der Eva Luna* see Eckhard Heftrich, "Naiv und pathetisch," *Frankfurter Allgemeine Zeitung* 26 July 1986: N. pag.; Jörg Drews, "Isabel Allende bei Suhrkamp" *Merkur* Dec. 1986: 1065-1069; Caroline Fetscher, "Von Junta-Terror und glühenden Küssen," *Der Spiegel* 29 (1986): 149-151; Günter W. Lorenz, "Liebeslust neben dem Massengrab," *Die Welt* 5 July 1986: N. pag.; Joachim Kaiser, "Schickes aus Chile," *Süddeutsche Zeitung* 8/9 Oct. 1988: 142; Heidrun Adler, "Isabels gesammelte Schludrigkeiten," *Die Welt* 3 Sept. 1988: N. pag.; Agnes Meinold, "Eva Luna oder Märchen für große Kinder," *Welt am Sonntag* 4 Dec. 1988: 69; Matthias Wegner, "Schwunghafter Wörterhandel," *Frankfurter Allgemeine Zeitung* 17 Oct. 1990; and Hans-Peter Klatt, "So also ist Südamerika," *Nürnberger Zeitung* 26 Oct. 1990. *Geschichten der Eva Luna* comes the closest to being *Trivialliteratur*. It was indeed reviewed in fewer publications, largely because the critics found nothing new in Allende's book of stories.

[5] This list is by no means a complete list of newspapers and magazines published in West Germany and radio stations broadcasting in the country. Nor does the list represent even all those publications and radio stations that have reviewed the Spanish American best-selling novels, but rather only those I used in my analysis. As mentioned earlier, many of the same critiques appear in various publications; in other circumstances the "review" is little more than a couple of sentences on the content of the novels.

[6] *Emma* is a critical women's liberation publication that should not be equated with traditional women's journals.

Part II

Aber in den letzten Jahren hat [Schriftsteller/in X] jedenfalls einen historischen und einen politischen Roman geschrieben, sich im Kriminalgenre versucht und mit einem erotischen Divertimento die Zeit vertrieben--und einen seltsamen Zwitter zwischen journalistischer Recherche und naiver Erzählung, politischem Essay und autobiographischer Episode vorgelegt [...] (Martin Halter, Badische Zeitung, 24 Aug. 1990)

In Part I, I utilized a neopositive approach to establish the cultural context in which the West Germans read Spanish American literature. There I determined the definition of the term "best seller" for the purposes of my anaysis and demonstrated the author's and publisher's roles in creating and influencing the circumstances of the best seller along with a discussion of the Spanish American best-selling novels in West Germany. Chapter 3 showed that the reception of Spanish American novels in West Germany from earlier decades through the 1980s and into the early '90s increased significantly and introduced the extrinsic factors involved in this augmentation. Finally, in Chapter 4 I examined both the motivational considerations in the purchase of books and the task of the critic as disseminator of information and reflector of current literary values. I described the critic's role as reader and as creator and disperser of opinions in the concretization of literary works.

In Part II, I turn to reception aesthetics in order to discuss common characteristics of the Spanish American best-selling novels in West Germany as reflected in the West German critics' observations. In the process, the intrinsic reasons why these Spanish American novels hold a particular interest for West Germans will come to light. The critiques of the Spanish American novels serve as a measure of reader response; through them, it is possible both to observe the expectations the Germans have when they read Spanish American novels and to consider the critics' views as opinion-makers and opinion-multipliers regarding these works.

The body of reviews examined represents a wide spectrum of West German newspapers, magazines, and radio programs--the selection ranging from the nationally circulated and more conservative *Die Welt* to the *Rote Blätter*, the student magazine of the Marxist student association Spartakus. The reviews and articles, approximately 450 in number, were gathered from the archives of Kiepenheuer & Witsch Verlag and Suhrkamp Verlag. The selection excludes repeated articles and reviews, as well as short ones simply restating content without any further commentary. Only those published in the West German printed press and on West German radio were chosen, not those appearing in Austrian, Swiss, or East German publications or on the radio in those countries. Furthermore, it is not the purpose of this investigation to present information taken from critical Hispanic literary journals, as these do not reflect how Spanish American fiction was received and perceived among the mass reading public in West Germany.

Part II documents the characteristics of the eight novels which contributed to Spanish American works being considered collectively in West Germany as if they were a sub-genre. I use the term "Spanish American sub-genre" to indicate strictly this West German perception of these novels. The qualities of this perceived sub-genre fulfill certain cross-cultural literary desires and expectations of the general German reading public, and they are not collectively encountered by West Germans in novels from other places. Spanish American narrative fiction is viewed in Part II through the reviews of German critics in their role in the concretization process. The Spanish American sub-genre attained sufficient popularity in West Germany as a result of these characteristics to become a best-selling sub-genre from 1981 to 1991.

Chapter 5

Politics, History, and Culture of Latin America

The works covered in my analysis reflect Latin American politics, sexual politics, history, and culture and as such possess a special appeal for the Germans. Political torture, kidnapping, and killing; military dictatorships; "machismo" and exploitation; and guerrilla and resistance movements are all associated with the Latin American image in Europe. In this chapter I also examine two other specifically German motifs, that of overcoming the past and that of collective guilt, in relation to the novels. First, however, we will review the way West Germans contemplate Latin American politics.

Latin America and its politics have a unique position in the consciousness of many Germans. America in general and more specifically Latin America has represented hope, a kind of "El Dorado" (Bamberg, personal interview; Siebenmann, "Bild Lateinamerikas" 20; Wiese, *Die hispanoamerikanischen Boom-Romane* 63) for Germans since the time of Columbus. As the United States developed as an international capitalistic force, Latin America became a primary land of utopian projection. Particularly since the student movement of 1968, Latin America has symbolized for many West Germans that concept of political change, of revolution, of an illusion that seemed impossible in Germany. Such revolutionary political change in Latin America assumed an *Ersatzerfüllung* for liberal-left Germans (Bamberg, personal interview). This is the perspective especially of the more politically aware of the generation of '68 and of the younger people in their early twenties during the '80s. As demonstrated in an earlier chapter, the generation of '68 looked to the earlier Cuban Revolution as a reflection of that potential and as a hope for a shift to the political left in Central and South America and elsewhere. Fidel Castro and Che Guevara became folk heroes of the left as Germany's revolutionary consciousness awakened.

The three years that the Marxist Salvador Allende held power in Chile brought further political awareness of Latin American capacity for change, and the military coup d'état in 1973 heightened sympathy for the left. During Pinochet's dictatorship, exiles from Chile took up residence in West Germany. This contact with a people with whom Germans have long had economic and cultural ties further contributed to understanding and to a desire to learn more of the Latin American political situation.

The Sandinista revolution in Nicaragua and the Ortega government provided additional testimony for the German left that the Latin American people desired movement away from right-wing dictatorships and toward the left. The potential for change was manifesting itself, and the West German left lauded the change.

At the other extreme from Castro/Allende/Ortega were Pinochet in Chile, Stroessner in Paraguay, and other military-run governments of Latin America. These governments strengthened the reactions in Germany against right-wing military governments and the brutality associated with their regimes in that part of the world. At the same time, they reinforced in those who opposed that conservative form of government the support for any movement away from the right.

Since actual positive social change in Latin America did not occur during the '60s and '70s, Latin American politics came to connote disillusionment. Finally, in the '80s the political circumstances in Latin America improved. The political message that the Germans were receiving from Latin America became one of optimism for political change without revolution, a concept that could be embraced by an even wider spectrum of West German society. This message was then reflected in the Spanish American works in West Germany and in their best seller status. Whether real or "luxuriöse Ersatzgefühle" (Meyer-Clason, "Möglichkeiten" 101), this awareness of Latin America's political situation combined with the hope for political change, and it was being fulfilled.

As discussed earlier, hope for Latin America was renewed in the late 1980s when elections in the hemisphere put democratic leaders into power and political, economic, and social reforms into effect. While the aforementioned events prior to the 1980s appealed more to the left, these later elections were probably welcomed by a wider range of the West German population, since the movement was less toward the left than away from the right-wing military dictatorships. This enabled more Germans to become acquainted with Latin American politics, if only peripherally or superficially.

5.1 Politics and Sexual Politics

In most of the Spanish American best sellers that I analyzed, politics plays a principal part, thus making a strong impression on the Germans and appealing to the general reading public. Providing the background material or playing a direct role in the plot of the novel, Latin American politics surfaces in *Geisterhaus, Von Liebe und Schatten, Eva Luna, Mexikanischer Tango, Hundert Jahre Einsamkeit,* and *General in seinem Labyrinth,* and to a lesser degree in *Geschichten der Eva Luna* and *Geschichtenerzähler.*

The political facet constitutes the backdrop for *Hundert Jahre Einsamkeit.* Günter W. Lorenz noted:

> In seiner [Oberst Aureliano Buendías] Person gewinnt die dritte Ebene Raum, die politisch-weltanschauliche, die García Márquez dadurch für Lateinamerika--nur für Lateinamerika?--auf eine Formel bringt, daß er den Oberst sagen läßt, in seinen Kriegen gehe es nicht mehr um Überzeugungen, sondern um den Besitz der Macht, und der einzige Unterschied zwischen Konservativen und Liberalen bestehe darin, daß sie sonntags verschiedene Messen besuchten: Das ist die brutale Reduzierung aller lateinamerikanischen Soziologie und Politologie auf zwei Metaphern.[1]

Germans are also drawn to the political commentary in *General in seinem Labyrinth*, where García Márquez demonstrated the relationship between the political past and present, as we see here:

> Dies war García Márquez's eigentlicher Ansatz: Noch zu Lebzeiten Bolívars begann die verhängnisvolle Ära der lateinamerikanischen Diktaturen, die bis heute nicht beendet ist.[2]

Nevertheless, it may have been difficult for the average readers to have understood that association unless they read one of the few reviews that made that connection. Still, politics was a feature of García Márquez's novels that the public came to expect.

Politics as a theme is conveyed even more poignantly in the works of Isabel Allende than in those of García Márquez. Her political connections are almost inseparable from the political situations and messages found in her novels. Almost every critique of *Geisterhaus* mentions her relationship to Salvador Allende; approximately half of those of *Von Liebe und Schatten* mention it, while a little less than half of those discussing *Eva Luna* refer to her uncle. Her connection to the ex-president and her account of his overthrow were very popular with the German public. As Jörg Drews wrote, "[...] gegenüber einer Autorin mit dem Namen Allende: da mußte man doch solidarisch sein!"[3] Suhrkamp Verlag used her kinship to Salvador Allende to promote *Geisterhaus*, and this information was then further related to the public in the critiques. Typical are these references:

> Die im Exil lebende Autorin, Nichte des 1973 beim Militärputsch ermordeten chilenischen Präsidenten [...][4]

> Das Geisterhaus, Erstlingswerk von Isabel Allende, der Nichte des 1973 umgekommenen Chilenischen Präsidenten, ist ein Buch, das man einfach gelesen haben sollte.[5]

Isabel Allende eventually established her own identity as a writer, and the critiques noted this fact while continuing to allude to Salvador Allende:

> Isabel Allende ist heute nicht mehr nur die literarisch noch unbekannte Nichte eines Mannes, der zum Mythos der politischen Linken wurde.[6]

> Allende. Seit ein paar Monaten denkt man bei diesem Namen nicht mehr allein an Salvador Allende [...][7]

Politics functions prominently in most of the works of Isabel Allende as the three novels treat the political awakening to resistance against a military dictatorship: Alba's in *Geisterhaus*, Irene's in *Von Liebe und Schatten*, and Eva's in *Eva Luna*. Most of the West German reviews of her novels focus on the political aspect of military dictatorships: terror, murder, torture, and violence associated with the abuse of political power as well as resistance against these forces. Also in her book of stories, themes related to dictatorships and political corruption include torture, bribery, power abuse, fraud, and abduction.

The main political events in *Geisterhaus* are the election and overthrow of Salvador Allende and the subsequent abuses of power by supporters of Pinochet, the "am besten bekannten und am meisten verhaßten Diktatur Lateinamerikas."[8] This episode in Chile's history is probably, of all the political events in Spanish America, the closest to the consciousness of West Germans. The regime of Pinochet is one with which the Germans have the closest contact through Chilean exiles in West Germany. If Pinochet was the most hated Latin American politician in Germany, Salvador Allende was among the most popular.

From titles and key phrases from some of the reviews of *Geisterhaus*, we learn to what extent the Germans are drawn to that time in Chilean history when Allende was overthrown and the effects that this political event had on the country:

Titles of reviews of *Geisterhaus*:

> "Die Spaltung des Landes"[9]
> "Episches Panorama des chilenischen Schicksals"[10]
> "Der Irrtum des Patriarchen. Politisches Buch"[11]
> "Den Haß überwinden"[12]
> "Prall von Geschichte. Faschismus in Chile als Thema eines Romans"[13]

From the text of the reviews:

> Hier wird die Politik, der rauhe südamerikanische politische Alltag erlebt, gelebt, erfühlt, beschrieben [...][14]
>
> [...], daß Isabel Allende ein (fast) unmögliches Unterfangen gelungen ist: Lebensgeschichte und politische Geschichte anschaulich zu verbinden.[15]
>
> In einem vier Generationen umfassenden, etwa von der Jahrhundertwende bis zum Militärputsch von 1973 reichenden Zeitraum ersteht ein Bild der chilenischen Oberschicht [...][16]

German critics focus on the political history of Chile in the 1970s, the division among the Chilean people caused by the election and overthrow of Allende, and the hatred that was felt on both sides of the political spectrum. These sentiments are to some degree reminiscent of German reactions resulting from the Nazi regime and World War II.

In *Von Liebe und Schatten*, the political awakening of the leading female character is a primary concentration of the critics. Although not explicitly stated in the novel, it is clear to Latin Americans and also to West Germans that the novel takes place during the dictatorship of Pinochet. Virtually all of the reviews of the novel mentioned the political aspect of the book. Based again on the review titles and phrases and on the length of time the novel spent on the best seller list, the theme of love hand in hand with underground political resistance attracted German interest.

A perusal of some of the titles and key phrases taken from the critiques of *Von Liebe und Schatten* accentuates the juxtaposition of love and political resistance, some more favorably than others:

Titles:

> "Diktatur und Widerstand"[17]
> "Erwachen zum Widerstand"[18]
> "Ein Paar zwischen Liebe und Politik"[19]
> "Die Liebe macht das Leben mit der Gewalt erträglich"[20]
> "Von Junta-Terror und glühenden Küssen"[21]

Text of Reviews:

> [...] ein Roman gegen den Terror der Militärjunta [...][22]
>
> [...] die Liebe beflügelt das ungleiche Paar zum entschiedenen Protest gegen die Diktatur.[23]

> [...] Isabel Allende's Darstellung der Liebe [ist] eine Parabel des Widerstandes gegen die Willkür eines Despotenstaates [...][24]

> [...] des Romans, in dessen Handlung zahlreiche Fakten von teilweise atemverschlagender Brutalität eingeschmolzen sind, nicht nur von dem Grauen der chilenischen Militärdiktatur einen gegen die üblichen Verdrängungsmechanismen resistenten Eindruck, sondern gibt auch etwas über den besonderen Fall Hinausgehendes zu verstehen: Wie Diktaturen dieser Art funktionieren, wie es vor allem in den Köpfen der Täter und Handlanger aussieht."[25]

Again, we note in the critiques the German admiration of resistance to a military dictatorship. The last review extends the meaning beyond the novel to "dictatorships of this kind" as the critic recognizes the insight offered in the novel into how dictatorships function from the perspective of those who wield power. Put into the context of post-World War II Germany, the German desire for identification with the forces of resistance against a military dictatorship but without total condemnation of those who operate within the military system becomes even more discernible.

Eva Luna also brings a constellation of characters from the resistance together to play a part in the attack on a prison which, again, undermines military rule. Most Germans would not have been aware of the fact that the novel takes place during a dictatorship in Venezuela since the country remains unnamed and since there are insufficient indicators in the novel to point to Venezuela for those who are, like most Germans, unfamiliar with the country.

What Germans did realize was that this was another novel by the Spanish American best-selling author Allende and that it also played against a similar political background. The perceived Spanish American sub-genre feature helped to catapult *Eva Luna* onto the best seller list as soon as it became available for the public. Here politics took a less central stance in the titles of reviews yet was often incorporated into the discussion of the novel:

Text from reviews:

> [...] ein wichtiges Buch, das [...] viel über Politik und Gesellschaft Chiles [sic] ausagt.[26]

> Und noch eine Wiederholung: Deutlich wie in den vorangegangenen Romanen sympathisiert Isabel Allende mit Vertretern der politischen Linken und von Minderheiten.[27]

> Die Botschaft: Liebe, Phantasie und Versöhnung siegen über die Gewalt.[28]

> Einen schwächlichen Eindruck machen, wie schon in dem Roman 'Von Liebe und Schatten,' vor allem die politischen Bezüge.[29]

From these and other reviews of *Eva Luna*, we see that Germans recognized that Allende's use of the political backdrop is not meant to be a penetrating analysis of the political events in Venezuela but to produce more suspense of the sort found in *A Thousand and One Nights*: Eva Luna as a counterpart of Scheherazade is not just a story-teller but rather uses her ability to tell stories to change the anticipated behavior of those exerting power over others. This is obvious in the quote from *A Thousand and One Nights* that Allende uses to begin her novel (7) and from the following critique:

> Schon als Kind wird Eva Luna, eine Märchenerzählerin wie Scheherazade, mit Menschen und Situationen fertig, indem sie Geschichten erfindet, spannende, träumerische, parabelhafte, unheimliche.[30]

Although Allende was criticized in some reviews for the superficiality of the political references, it may be that most average German readers were not looking for more in-depth analyses. It becomes clear that the prevalent political component of Allende's novels, even though considered superficial and weak by some German critics, is one that draws Germans to the novels. In *Geschichten der Eva Luna* the political feature plays a much smaller role, and fewer critics refer to the general political theme. Rather, they simply mention the "Caudillo," "Diktator," "Patriarch," "Gewalt," "politischer Terror," and "Revolutionär." Still, one reviewer of the book remarks,

> "Politisches bleibt nicht ausgespart, das ist Isabel Allende ihrer Gemeinde schuldig. Sie beherrscht das einschlägige Problemprogramm [...][31]

By 1990, the public had come to expect "das Politische" from Allende's writing.

The reviews display constant identification with one particular theme of the political focus: the condemnation of and call for active opposition to military dictatorships. At the same time, Germans appreciate the understanding with which Allende portrays those of the conservative right. The primary agents of resistance in Allende's novels are the guerrilla and the revolutionary. A scan of the reviews shows that these figures do not escape the imagination of the German.

Geisterhaus:

> Alba, die Erzählerin, die ihren Geliebten aus der Guerilla im Haus ihres konservativen Großvaters versteckt hatte [...][32]

Von Liebe und Schatten:

> Francisco begeht nicht den Fehler Gustavos, "den Geheimdienst zu unterschätzen." Schließlich ist er der Sohn revolutionärer Eltern, [...] Irene hingegen entstammt der privilegierten Schicht [...][33]

Eva Luna:

> Eva Luna trifft, erwachsen geworden, den ehemaligen Jugendbandenchef wieder, der bald nach dem Beispiel von Castro und Guevara den Guerillakrieg in den Bergen organisiert.[34]

> Diese Guerilleros! Sie sind jung, idealistisch, opferbereit. "Monatelang hungrig, durstig, ständig durchnäßt, ruhelos, schmutzig, schmerzgeplagt, . . ." Kurz: echte Kerle, die alles für ihr Volk tun.[35]

As indicated in many critiques, the idealized figures of the revolutionary and the guerrilla join forces with the principal female character--in *Geisterhaus* and *Von Liebe und Schatten* she is of the bourgeois class, and in *Eva Luna* the character has ascended from the lower class to the middle class--to sabotage the brutal military government. The result is a happy ending to each of the love stories which joins, marries as it were, the bourgeois and the revolutionary, and the two mutually legitimize each other. With a good conscience West Germans could read the novels uniting both of these usually antagonistic and diametrically opposed groups, hence conveying a very positive message for the reader.

Love and political awakening are also woven together in Angeles Mastretta's *Mexikanischer Tango* as politics and sexual politics form the basis for the relationship between Catalina and her husband Andrés. *Mexikanischer Tango*'s description of the political mechanism in post-revolutionary Mexico paints a pessimistic picture of the macho politics with its flagrant corruption, violence, and subjugation of women. Furthermore, these abuses show no sign of changing. The German reviews exploit the interest that the German public has in political power and sexual politics. Titles of many reviews capitalize on this interplay of power, politics, and sexual politics:

> "Mexikanischer Tango der Macht, Korruption und Frauen"[36]
> "Politik und Liebe--Angeles Mastretta 'Mexikanischer Tango'"[37]
> "Die Macht der Machos"[38]
> "Die ideale Frau für den Macho"[39]
> "Starke Frauen, harte Männer und viel Sex"[40]

From the titles alone we encounter the recurring theme of "Woman versus Man ('Macho')" in the political setting. The novel itself is a condemnation and a critique of the macho culture as manifested in both politics and sexual politics, the macho way of thinking being associated in Germany with Latin American culture. Catalina recognizes her plight as a female in that culture and seeks to establish her own identity. We can speculate that this theme, reflected in the titles of the reviews, intrigued the German readers, especially the women and those involved in the strong feminist movement in Germany.

Sexual politics and machismo are also consistent subjects in reviews and in titles of reviews of Allende's novels, particularly in those of *Geisterhaus*:

> [...] Esteban Trueba, Großgrundbesitzer und ein "Macho," der zahllose uneheliche Kinder von den Töchtern seiner Landarbeiter hat.[41]

> Die wirklichen Helden der Chilenin sind Frauen. Isabel Allende sagt, warum: "Gewiß, die Frauen, viele Frauen, bewegen sich im *Geisterhaus* um einen selbstherrlichen und herrschsüchtigen Mann herum.[42]

> "Ein Macho im Gespensterhaus"[43]

The concept of machismo is also a, if not the, prominent theme of García Márquez's *Chronik eines angekündigten Todes*, and the majority of the reviews discuss the meaning of the word and its consequences in the novel:

Titles:

> "Mord aus Machismo"[44]

> "Die Sache der Ehre: Márquez: Eine südamerikanische Parabel von kollektiver Schuld"[45]

Text from the reviews:

> [...] eine andere Thematik, indem er auf die Frage, was er am meisten verabscheue, antwortet: den Machismo (lateinamerikanische Ausformung des Männlichkeitswahnes), den er aber auch bei Frauen finde. [...] Während sie die Moral hochhielten, übten die Männer den praktischen Machismo in der alltäglichen Frauenunterdrückung aus [...][46]

> Zwei Motive stehen im Mittelpunkt der Novelle: zum einen die rigiden Vorstellungen von Moral und Ehre (und die daraus entstehenden Racheakte), [...] Zum anderen wird aber hier die Frage der Schuld gestellt.[47]

> Soweit ist es eine Geschichte über den Machismo und die Gewalttätigkeit in der karibischen Heimat des Autors. Doch das eigentliche Thema des Romans ist gar nicht das machistische Verbrechen und seine Motive. Das eigentliche Thema ist das Verhalten der Mitbürger angesichts des Verbrechens.[48]

Germans thus applaud García Márquez's theme of denouncing the machismo honor code that compels men to kill against their will and that maintains the oppressed state of women. Sexual politics and machismo are also found in other novels of García Márquez and Vargas Llosa, but the message moves away from the idea of sexual politics and in the direction of purer eroticism, which I will discuss in the chapter on exoticism.

Lastly, Vargas Llosa's *Lob der Stiefmutter* exhibits one aspect of sexual politics as Alfonso clearly uses sex to manipulate his step-mother--and his father. There is clear separation of sexual politics and politics per se. Although the book is not considered a political novel, at least two German critics did find a political message:

> Insofern ist selbst der Koitus als Augenblick des höchsten Egoismus ein politischer Akt: Sexuelle Freiheit geht auf Kosten der gesellschaftlichen Phantasie.[49]

> Tragisch oder glücklich (wohl beides in einem): *politisch* ist dieses kultivierte Erotikon schließlich dort, [...] In anderen Worten: "Wir sind heilig und obsessiv geworden," wobei der Erotiker der erogenen Zonen zur Spekulation kommt: "Mein Körper ist das sonst Unmögliche: die egalitäre Gesellschaft." So reichen Politik & Ideologie noch ins "unschuldigste" Erotikon hinein.[50]

The concept of the association of the body with society and the need for a clean, pure, and healthy "body"/"society" here suggests that some Germans perceive in the novel a message beyond that which the book carried in Latin America.[51] Indeed, the aforementioned quotes from German reviews indicate that the political feature is so associated with the Spanish American novel that even in the most apolitical Spanish American work, Germans search for a political message.

5.2 History

The history of Latin America that is combined with fiction in these Spanish American works holds a particular interest for Germans, especially when the historical event is either one to which Germans can relate or one in which Germans take a personal interest. History and real events form the basis or the background for *Chronik eines angekündigten Todes*, *Hundert Jahre Einsamkeit*, *Geisterhaus*, *Von Liebe und Schatten*, *Mexikanischer Tango*, *General in seinem Labyrinth*, and *Geschichtenerzähler*.

The history of a family as representative of the history of a country or of the South American continent is the basis of both *Hundert Jahre Einsamkeit* and *Geisterhaus*, and the reviews of these novels convey this to the German public:

> *Hundert Jahre Einsamkeit*:
>
> Im Mikrokosmos Macondo [...] konzentriert sich die tragische Geschichte Lateinamerikas und das Schicksal seiner Menschen.[52]
>
> *Geisterhaus*:
>
> In vier Generationen vollzieht sich der Aufstieg und Fall einer Familie, der einhergeht mit Chiles Sturz in die Barbarei.[53]

The microcosmic and mythic worlds in *Hundert Jahre Einsamkeit* and *Geisterhaus* presented a very palatable, concise, and entertaining way for the Germans to learn about Latin American history.

The actual historical aspect is frequently mentioned in the articles and critiques of *Hundert Jahre Einsamkeit* and *Geisterhaus*, as exemplified above. Two instances of such references to the historical context of *Mexikanischer Tango* are these:

> Aber die Autorin geht noch weiter, auch die Geschichte Mexikos seit der Revolution (1910-1917), bisher unerschöpfliche Quelle öffentlichen Lamentierens über versäumte Chancen, ist Angeles

> Mastretta ein geradezu amüsanter Schauplatz--für Mord und Totschlag.[54]

> Sie erzählt ein Stück mexikanischer Geschichte vom Ende der zwanziger, bis in die Mitte der vierziger Jahre.[55]

Furthermore, several of the critiques apprised the readers that real events form the basis for *Chronik eines angekündigten Todes* and *Von Liebe und Schatten*. These discussions of the novels serve as samples of such critiques:

> *Chronik eines angekündigten Todes*:
> Der Chronik liegt, wie García Márquez betont, ein rund dreißig Jahre zurückliegendes reales Geschehen zugrunde. (Zwillingsbrüder, die sich in den Mördern wiederzuerkennen glauben, haben ihn auf eine halbe Million Dollar Schadensersatz verklagt.)[56]

> *Von Liebe und Schatten*:
> [...] die Aufdeckung von Massenexekutionen und Massengräbern im Chile Pinochets [...] benutzt sie als Story.[57]

The fact that a story is based on a real event in Latin America may create more interest for the reader, especially so if it is known that a real lawsuit or some other public controversy is involved in the publication.

While some of the novels have their basis on a real incident, *General in seinem Labyrinth* is itself history clothed in fiction. The German reviews note not only the historical interest, but some also remark on the difficulties that the German readers have in comprehending this more unfamiliar time period in Latin American history:

> Bolívar ist herzulande nicht viel mehr als ein fremder Name, mit dem sich keine reale [...] Vorstellung verbindet. [...]
> [...] Dieses Buch [...] erzählt freilich nicht nur die Geschichte der letzten Reise oder des ganzen Lebens von Bolívar, es erzählt auch, wovon es nie spricht: die Geschichte Lateinamerikas nach Bolívar, von ihm vielleicht in falsche Bahnen gelenkt, weil es die richtige Bahn womöglich gar nicht geben konnte.[58]

> Auch wenn also viele biographische und historische Details nur schwer verständlich sind -- die große Márquez-Gemeinde in Deutschland hat diesen [...] Roman freudig aufgenommen [...][59]

The first critic speaks directly about history and alludes to politics, while both acknowledge the fact that German readers may have difficulty with the Latin American historical details, due in part to their lack of knowledge about a time, place, and personage in Latin America that is too obscure for them.

Naturally, ties with European history have more meaning for the German reading public. One critic brings together *Geschichten der Eva Luna* and European/German history in the list of the story subjects, beginning with "Historische Tatsachen wie Vertreibung jüdischer Bürger aus Europa."[60] Real occurrences in German history also colored German perception of the Spanish American works. In reviews of a couple of the Spanish American novels, particular words and phrases seem to emanate from the German post-war situation when they describe a quality of the Spanish American novels. These phrases in titles and in texts reflect a heightened sense of the corresponding German experience:

Geisterhaus:

> "Auch Bewältigung der Vergangenheit"[61]
>
> "Vergangenheitsbewältigung in prallvollem literarischen Gewand"[62]
>
> Die Vergangenheitsbewältigung besteht darin, sich zu erinnern.[63]
>
> [...] ein Epos voller Sinnlichkeit, Stolz, Geburt, Tod, Gewalt und politischer Vergangenheitsbewältigung [...][64]
>
> Die Generationenfolge der Familie del Valle, beginnend im materiellen Nichts und endend in der geistigen Verzweiflung, dem Versuch, Entsetzen durch erkannte (nicht durch beklagte) Vergangenheit zu bewältigen, wird so zum Register historischer Prozesse, weiß Gott nicht nur Chiles. Die Fähigkeit der Schriftstellerin, Schuld auf beiden Seiten zu erkennen, Verständnis auch für den Gegner aufzubringen, sich von ideologischen Vorhaben abzusetzen, ihr Buch unter das Regime geschichtlicher Logik zu stellen--das gibt diesem Werk seine literarische und seine menschliche Bedeutung, das verleiht ihm [...] so etwas wie ein Postulat der Hoffnung.[65]

The West German people's need for self-reflection, for coming to terms with their own past, and overcoming the Nazi past allows them to see a meaning in these Spanish American works with which readers in other cultures would not be as likely to identify. The additional ability of Allende to show understanding for the conservative opponents in her novels signals another comforting message, besides that of hope, especially to the Germans. This helps to answer the question of why these particular novels were better received in West Germany than in many other countries.

As we have already seen, reviews of *Chronik eines angekündigten Todes* presented earlier in this chapter in the section on machismo intimated that Germans perceive a second theme of the novel beyond the antiquated honor code in sexual politics. Phrases found in the reviews address this other theme in *Chronik*; they also bring to mind World War II Germany in that they deal with the concept of collective guilt. Sample phrases vary slightly, but the notion remains consistent:

> Alle delegieren die Verantwortung an andere und beruhigen damit ihr Gewissen.[66]

> Der Mord ist in letzter Konsequenz die Tat des Dorfes, der Gemeinschaft, von Männern und Frauen [...][67]

> Denn dies ist eine Parabel über die Mitschuld der anderen, die wissen, aber nicht wissen wollen, die sehen, aber nicht sehen wollen.[68]

More poignant and directly referring to the German situation are these analyses of *Chronik*:

> Die Banalität des Bösen ist spätestens seit den Tagen des Naziregimes eins unserer bleibenden ganz großen Probleme: das Böse ohne Bösewichter, getan von normalen Menschen, die sich sogar besonders tugendkaft [sic] vorkommen, und zugelassen von der übrigen Bevölkerung, die aus irgendwelchen ganz hervorragenden Gründen untätig zusieht.[69]

> Kolumbien unterscheidet sich da nicht von Deutschland. Es braucht nicht mehr als die Übereinkunft, daß dort, wo jeder ein Verführer zu sein hat, der denunzierte Verführer sterben muß, damit alle anderen Verführer sich entsühnt glauben, oder die Übereinkunft, daß die Juden schuld an den menschenverachtenden Praktiken des Kapitalismus seien und deswegen ermordet werden müssen, damit die anderen weiterhin im Kapitalismus leben können--und alle, aber auch alle, sehen dem Mord, von dem

> sie wissen, daß er nicht begangen werden darf, teilnahmslos zu. Nachher waren sie alle nicht schuld, konnten sie alle nicht verhindern, was geschehen ist.[70]

These critics relate the events of *Chronik eines angekündigten Todes* directly to the Nazi regime and condemn what they consider an inherent German problem as a result of that regime: that perfectly normal and otherwise virtuous people are allowed to commit a murderous act while the rest of the population watches without acting to prevent it; that those who committed the act are denounced and have to die so that the remainder of the people believes itself forgiven for its part in the crime; and that afterward no one is guilty.

5.3 Culture

During the 1980s the Latin American culture, so different from the German culture, aroused the German curiosity as it had not in prior decades. Latin America had become more accessible to Germans as a result of more travel to that continent and more information available to Germans. With changes in the political climate and with Germans more willing to learn about the region, Spanish American culture became less forbidding and in fact appealing.

The cultural features of *Chronik eines angekündigten Todes*, *Mexikanischer Tango*, *Liebe in den Zeiten der Cholera*, and *Geschichten der Eva Luna* acquaint Germans with life in Latin America in earlier decades, to offer them scenes, whether typical and ordinary or unusual and extraordinary, of the cultural life of Latin America. *Geisterhaus*, *Von Liebe und Schatten*, *Chronik eines angekündigten Todes*, and *Mexikanischer Tango* all deal with a way of life which is "in Lateinamerika alltägliches Thema: die Gewalt, die unser tägliches Brot ist," as García Márquez has said.[71] In *Liebe in den Zeiten der Cholera*, the reader leaves behind violence and encounters a feature more like an old photo album with images of people moving though life without extraordinary events as part of their regular diet. Everyday life, love, and waiting for love are the simple themes of the book; and the reviews and their titles reflect the interest in these themes:

Titles:

"Das Leben leben gelernt durch die Liebe"[72]
"Eine Liebes- und Lebensschule"[73]

Text from the reviews:

> 51 Jahre, neun Monate und vier Tage vergehen bis der Gatte hoch in den Achtzigern stirbt. Da wirbt der Junge wieder um sie. Die Haare sind ihm ausgefallen, die Zähne hat er verloren, am Stock muß er gehen.[74]

> Eine gar nicht so kleine Kultur- und Sittengeschichte der Karibik von der Mitte des neunzehnten Jahrhunderts ist darüber entstanden [...] Unterrichtet jedoch werden wir auch über die Eröffnung und den Betrieb der Maultier- Straßenbahn, über die Entwicklung der Karibischen Flußschiffahrtskompanie, über das Telegraphensystem, den ersten Fesselballon, das erste Elektrizitätswerk, das erste Kino, die ersten Privattelephone und Schreibmaschinen.[75]

This novel is a less complicated and less violent encounter with Latin American culture for the Germans. It offers a culture different from their own, yet at the same time ordinary people with whom Germans can identify.

In *Hundert Jahre Einsamkeit* politics, history, and culture combine to constitute the essence of the Latin American experience:

> In diesem "Märchenbuch" erschließen sich denn auch grundlegende Erkenntnisse zur politischen und sozialen Situation des Halbkontinents. [...]
>
> [...] Historisch belegte Fakten über die nordamerikanische Bananengesellschaft in Kolumbien werden--eingekleidet in phantastische, erschreckende und gespenstische Details--aus der Sicht der Einwohner des tropischen Dorfes Macondo wiedergegeben.[76]

The combination of Latin American political, social, and historical situations with the element of fantasy reminiscent of the German fairy tale constituted a very rich and insightful work for the Germans.

The interest in Latin American culture and history, even though late-blooming, may have been assisted by the cultural and intellectual closeness (Ripkin, personal interview) that Europeans feel for Latin Americans. In spite of U.S. influence in Latin America since 1945, Latin America is still perceived in Europe as an offspring of Europe which has maintained a European-based or European superimposed culture to a large extent. From the European perspective, Latin America differs from most other countries and continents and especially from other "Third World" cultures exactly in that it has this European heritage.

This European cultural heritage is sometimes mentioned directly in the critiques. In discussions of *Geisterhaus*, we find the following:

> [...] Figuren im *Geisterhaus* denken und fühlen noch nach europäischen Vorstellungen [...][77]

> Denn Isabel Allende erzählt [...] konventionell und gleichsam europäisch.[78]

> "Isabel Allendes 'Buddenbrooks made in Chile'"[79]

This last review title alludes to Thomas Mann's highly regarded novel *Buddenbrooks*, written at the turn of the century, and thus links the content of Allende's book with a recognized German work.

In the above examples, the references to the European heritage are explicit. They aid the German reader in making that transition from the so-called "European" culture and literature to those of Spanish America. In contrast, at least one reviewer of García Márquez's *General in seinem Labyrinth* believes on the one hand that the novel was very European while recognizing that the European readers would have difficulties with it:

> [...] García Márquez hat gewissermaßen sein europäischstes, sein am wenigsten lateinamerikanisches Buch geschrieben. Paradoxerweise dürfte es dasjenige von seinen Hauptwerken sein, das in Europa am wenigsten Freunde finden wird.[80]

The book remains remote for German readers; there seem to be too many cultural obstacles to be overcome.

Nevertheless, politics, history, and culture in general do figure prominently in most of these Spanish American novels. It is natural that authors write about their homelands (or adopted homelands). These works would likely not be considered in Latin America to contain any special common characteristics to set them apart from other novels. However, the Spanish American setting, when read in the German context, comes to constitute a markedly different type of novel from others read in Germany and therefore contributes to these books being viewed as distinct. The military dictatorships, machismo, and resulting violence and exploitation are associated with the image of Latin America in West Germany. The corresponding resistance, guerrilla, and feminist movements are hailed in Germany with optimism that the status quo can change--indeed, is changing--in that distant continent.

Far removed from the Latin American setting, the Germans also see, though perhaps sometimes on a more subconscious level, parallels between the military governments and the Nazi regime. The Latin American people's resistance to those governments as reflected in the novels studied here can account in part for the special affinity the Germans feel for these novels. This helps to explain why these works achieved a popularity in Germany beyond that in most other non-Spanish speaking countries.

Therefore, Latin American politics, history, and culture are demonstrated here to distinguish these works from others in West Germany and as such to constitute collectively one characteristic of the Spanish American sub-genre as perceived in West Germany.

Notes

[1] Günter W. Lorenz, "*Hundert Jahre Einsamkeit*," *Die Welt* 25 Feb. 1970: 21.

[2] Jan-Barra Hentschel, "Von Freiheit, Ruhm und Resignation," *Marburger Anzeiger und Nachrichten* 24 Feb. 1990: N. pag. The reviews for all of the novels were copied from those in the archives of the German publishers Kiepenheuer & Witsch Verlag and Suhrkamp Verlag, and the page numbers rarely appear on the individual articles. Bibliographic information for all reviews is given to the full extent known to me.

[3] Jörg Drews, "Isabel Allende bei Suhrkamp," *Merkur* Dec. 1986: 1068. Future references to this review will be noted as: Drews, "Allende bei Suhrkamp."

[4] "Isabel Allende. Das Geisterhaus," *Deutsche Post* 5 Sept. 1984.

[5] "Das Geisterhaus," *Der Beamtenbund* 4 (1986): 21.

[6] Walter Haubrich, "Wo die Wirklichkeit phantastische Züge annimmt," *Frankfurter Allgemeine Zeitung* 26 Jan. 1985. Future references to this review will be noted as: Haubrich, "Wirklichkeit."

[7] "Liebe, Familiengeschichten, Agenten . . . ," *Freundin* 27 Feb. or Mar. 1985.

[8] Haubrich, "Wirklichkeit."

[9] Robert Meßmer, *Badische Zeitung* Freiburg 18/19 Aug. 1984.

[10] *Gießener Anzeiger* 5 April 1984.

[11] Jürgen Walter, *Plärrer*, Nürnberg, June 1984.

[12] Albert von Schirnding, "Erwachen zum Widerstand," *Süddeutsche Zeitung* 26/27 July 1986. Future references to this review will be noted as: von Schirnding, "Erwachen."

[13] Ulrich Aghte, *Welt der Arbeit* 3 May 1984.

[14] "Das Geisterhaus," *Der Beamtenbund* April 1986: 21.

[15] W. Martin Lüdke, "Der Zauber des Ungeheuerlichen," *Die Zeit* 17 Aug. 1984.

[16] Herbert Lindenberger, "Unseliger Kontinent," *Stuttgarter Zeitung* 27 Oct. 1984.

[17] Klaus Schwidrowski, *Hamburger Rundschau* 4 Sept. 1986.

[18] von Schirnding, "Erwachen."

[19] *Für Sie* 13 Aug. 1986.

[20] *Mittelbayerische Zeitung* 3 Oct. 1986.

[21] Caroline Fetscher, *Der Spiegel* 29 (1986): 149-51.

[22] Fetscher, 149.

[23] Hannelore Schlaffer, "Alles nur ein Puppentheater," *Stuttgarter Zeitung* 16 Aug. 1986.

[24] Sulamith Aparre, "Hoffnung auf Harmonie," *Nürnberger Zeitung* 2 Aug. 1986.

[25] von Schirnding, "Erwachen."

[26] Dieter Hurcks, "Hannovers Buchhändler sagen, was sie selbst am liebsten lesen," *Neue Presse* Hannover 16 Dec. 1988.

[27] "Isabel Allende wiederholt sich," *Kölner Stadt-Anzeiger* 16 Sept. 1988.

[28] Ulli Langenbrinck, *Deutsche Volkszeitung* 7 Oct. 1988.

[29] "Verfolgt vom Fluch des Geisterhauses," *Gießener Anzeiger* 6 Sept. 1988.

[30] Effi Horn, "Isabel Allende erzählte ihre prallen Geschichten," *Münchener Merkur* 2 Sept. 1988.

[31] Alfred Brugger, "Eine Lust zu lesen," *Hessische Allgemeine Zeitung* 15 Sept. 1990.

[32] Wolfram Schütte, "Töchter vieler Vergewaltigungen," *Frankfurter Rundschau* 28 April 1984.

[33] Eckhard Heftrich, "Naiv und pathetisch," *Frankfurt Allgemeine Zeitung* 26 July 1988.

[34] "Herzen anrühren," *Spiegel* 5 Sept. 1988: 208.

[35] Martin Ebel, "Wenn die Gartenlaube im Urlaub steht," *Badische Zeitung* 24 Aug. 1988.

[36] Sybille Fertsch-Demuth, *Main-Post* Würzburg 11/12 June 1988.

[37] Christiane Rasche, *Die Tageszeitung* Berlin 29 April 1988.

[38] Alfred Brugger, *Hessische Allgemeine* 23 July 1988.

[39] Jens Jessen, *Frankfurt Allegemeine Zeitung* 14 Mar. 1988: 28.

[40] Verena Auffermann, *Frankfurter Rundschau* 26 Mar. 1988. Future references to this review will be noted as: Auffermann, "Starke Frauen."

[41] Holger Schlodder, "Die Erben büßen für die Ahnen," *Darmstädter Echo* 24 Mar. 1984. Future references to this review will be noted as: Schlodder, "Die Erben."

[42] Haubrich, "Wirklichkeit."

[43] Gert Ueding, "Ein Macho im Gespensterhaus," *Frankfurter Allgemeine* 14 July 1984.

[44] Wolf Scheller, *Rhein-Neckar-Zeitung* 11 Jan. 1982: 26.

[45] Franz Gary, *Nürnberger Nachrichten* 22 Dec. 1981.

[46] Tom Königs, "Eine Novelle macht Furore," *Frankfurter Rundschau* 27 July 1981. Future references to this review will be noted as: Königs, "Eine Novelle."

[47] Christian Huther, "Sterben als Höhepunkt des Lebens," *Main-Echo* 11/12 Oct. 1986.

[48] Dieter E. Zimmer, "Autopsie an Frau Ananke," *Die Zeit* 16 Oct. 1981. Future references to this review will be noted as: Zimmer, "Autopsie."

[49] Martin Halter, "Süßlich parfümierte Liebesspiele zu dritt," *Saarbrücker Zeitung* 4 Jan. 1990.

[50] Wolfram Schütte, "Ein bravouröses Kunststück über alles & nichts," *Frankfurter Rundschau* 5 Aug. 1989: ZB4.

[51] Vargas Llosa is quoted in *Spiegel* as saying: "Es war wie eine große Befreiung, als ich das Buch schrieb. Als fiele all diese klebrige politische Alltäglichkeit von mir ab, weil ich in eine reine Phantasiewelt eintauchte, in eine im Grunde egoistische und persönliche Welt.

Sicher, auch die Politik kann ihre begeisternden Momente haben. Aber nie so intim, so privat." *Spiegel* 14 Aug. 1989: 170.

[52] Walter Haubrich, "*Hundert Jahre Einsamkeit*," *Frankfurt Allgemeine Zeitung* 8 May 1971. Future references to this review will be noted as: Haubrich, "*Hundert Jahre Einsamkeit.*"

[53] Thomas Schreiner, "Sturz in die Barbarei," *Nürnberger Zeitung* 13 April 1985.

[54] Christine Wischmann, "Wie man die Geister der Toten mit Singen fernhält," Deutsche Presse Agentur (dpa) 18 April 1988.

[55] Auffermann, "Starke Frauen."

[56] Rosemarie Bollinger, "Der Mörder stand um fünf Uhr auf," *Deutsches Allgemeines Sonntagsblatt* 18 Oct. 1981. Future references to this review will be noted as: Bollinger, "Der Mörder."

[57] Drews, "Allende bei Suhrkamp," 1066.

[58] Walter Boehlich, "Das Buch des Grauens," *Spiegel* 27 Nov. 1989.

[59] Hans F. Nöhbauer, "Der Held im Labyrinth der verlorenen Träume," *Welt am Sonntag* 8 Apr. 1990.

[60] Wilfriede Eichler, "Haß, Gewalt und Leidenschaft," *Der Morgen* (Berlin), 31 Dec. 1990/1 Jan. 1991.

[61] *Münstersche Zeitung* 5 [Month unknown] 1984.

[62] *Siegener Zeitung* 21 Dec. 1985.

[63] Runa Fecher, "Literatur aus Südamerika Chile," *Umbruch* Oct./Nov. 1984.

[64] *Rote Blätter* April 1984.

[65] Günther W. Lorenz, "Absage an die Verzweiflung," *Die Welt* 14 July 1984.

[66] Martha Christine Körling, "Schuld und Verantwortung im Klima der Gewalt," *Berliner Morgenpost* 22 Oct. 1981: 11.

[67] Bollinger, "Der Mörder."

[68] Christian Huther, "Sterben als Höhepunkt des Lebens," *Main-Echo* 11/12 Oct. 1986.

[69] Zimmer, "Autopsie."

[70] Walter Boehlich, "Fuenteovejuna in der Karibik," *Der Spiegel* 3 Aug. 1981: 134.

[71] Königs, "Eine Novelle."

[72] Hilke Prillmann, *Welt am Sonntag* 29 Mar. 1987.

[73] Leonore Schwartz, *General-Anzeiger* Bonn 18/19 July 1987.

[74] "Gabriel Garcia Marques [sic]. Revoluzzer des Herzens." *Bild der Frau* 23 Feb. 1987.

[75] Jochen Hieber, "Der Hymnus der absoluten Liebe," *Frankfurter Allgemeine Zeitung* 31 Jan. 1987.

[76] Haubrich, "*Hundert Jahre Einsamkeit.*"

[77] Haubrich, "Wirklichkeit."

[78] Schlodder, "Die Erben."

[79] *Siegener Zeitung* 21 Dec. 1985. Thomas Mann's *Buddenbrooks* is the chronicle over four generations of the decay of a patrician family in Lübeck. The process of decay expresses itself in the family's business fortunes, physical characteristics, and psychological makeup of the sons of each generation. The family declines and terminates with the death of fifteen-year old Hanno, the last of the Buddenbrook males.

Other allusions specifically to *Buddenbrooks* are also found in other critiques of *Geisterhaus*. See Gert Ueding, "Ein Macho im Gespensterhaus," *Frankfurter Allegemeine Zeitung* 14 July 1984; "Buchhandel und Presse äußern sich zu '*Das Geisterhaus*,' *Börsenblatt* 26 June 1984: 4317; and Lorenz Tomerius, "Unerschöpfliche Phantasie," *Industriemagazin* Nov. 1984. A number of other critics refer more generally to the European tradition of the rise and fall of the multigenerational family as representative of a country's history in their reviews of both *Geisterhaus* and *Hundert Jahre Einsamkeit*.

[80] Wolfgang Kunath, "Ein verbitterte Held," *Stuttgarter Zeitung* 9 Mar. 1990.

Chapter 6

Exoticism

Perhaps the most obvious characteristic of the German reception of the Spanish American novel is the appeal of the exotic. The search for the exotic in literature unquestionably plays a part in the popularity of Latin American fiction in West Germany. There is a legitimate interest as a kind of "Wahrnehmung, die die deutschen Leser in der Welt suchen" (Janik, personal interview).

The term "exoticism" is used here to mean "a state or quality of being exotic," with "exotic" taken to mean "foreign, introduced from a foreign country; unfamiliar" (*Webster's Unabridged Dictionary*). It will be understood that these terms refer to German perception of Latin America and its literature and not that the Spanish American authors deliberately enhanced the foreignness of their settings.

The desire for the exotic is seen in connection with the longing for a concrete unknown reality, the desire for novels of realist escapism (Ripken, personal interview): those which are exotic, which bring a distant reality to the world of the reader. However, the exotic quality should not be too exotic, distant, different, or strange. A certain degree of familiarity must exist for the reader to be able to decode and apprehend the exotic message of the text. Intellectual readers are usually better prepared and therefore more willing to decipher a more exotic text than are average readers, those who constitute the majority of best seller readers. This fact indicates that there was likely a shift in the nature of the exotic element found in Spanish American novels as perceived by the Germans for these novels to have become so successful in West Germany in the 1980s.

Prior to the late 1970s and 1980s, Latin America was too exotic and too different in its culture and its literature for the average West German reader to bridge that necessary gap to understand the message conveyed in its novels. During the '70s and '80s, Latin America became much more reachable: Through travel to South America (Ripken, personal interview) and through exiles living in Germany, through cultural exchanges and coverage of the changing political scene in Latin America, there resulted an increased contact with Spanish American culture. As the Spanish American novels themselves began being written in a less complicated style, the literature became more accessible to West Germans. Latin America, since it is reflected in its literature, then also became less foreign, strange, forbidding, and "threatening" to the Germans.

The concept of exoticism that Latin America represented for Germans as an utterly bizarre and very remote reality had diminished. Rather, a closer and less formidable, yet still different, reality had come into play and allowed Germans to discover and to want to comprehend that other reality. This variation of the perceived exoticism of the Spanish American novels became one factor in helping these novels to achieve wide popularity in Germany during the 1980s. Latin American exoticism came to mean for Germans a tropical place with warm sunshine; palm trees along a coast and tropical forests; extreme forms of nature; bright colors in nature and dress; Latin American peoples, i.e., that mixture of European, Indian, and African ethnicities; particular music and dances; and the eroticism of a macho culture.

The exotic element in the Spanish American novels enabled the German reader to encounter people, situations, and forms of nature alien to the ordinary German reader but still conceivable. Evidence that exoticism played a specific role in the reception of these works in West Germany is seen in the dust jackets, particularly those of Gabriel García Márquez's novels. *Chronik eines angekündigten Todes* offered the German reader a palm tree, suggesting a warm tropical breeze. The second jacket of *Hundert Jahre Einsamkeit*, which appeared in 1979, displayed a Latin American town with men in native clothing; and the jackets of the most recent edition, published in 1988, of *Liebe in den Zeiten der Cholera*, and of *General in seinem Labyrinth* place the reader in the tropics with lush vegetation, colorful flowers and birds, blue water, and a hammock.

Other novels present different kinds of exoticism for the German reader. In the title of Angeles Mastretta's *Mexikanischer Tango*, Germans find a distant place; rhythm, movement, and lasciviousness; and a suggestive Latin American dance. The tango dancers on the dust jacket enhance the sensations conveyed in the title. The book jacket of Vargas Llosa's *Geschichtenerzähler* develops the idea of exoticism as a distant people: an Indian's face hidden behind a mask of feathers.

The German critiques of the Spanish American novels confirm the attraction to the exotic. Titles of the reviews that most explicitly associate the exotic feature with Latin America and the Spanish American novels are these:

Hundert Jahre Einsamkeit:

"Exotische Familien-Saga"[1]
"Tropische Saga"[2]
"Tropische Familien-Saga"[3]
"Tropische Familienchronik"[4]
"Tornado bläst das Dorf der Guerillas weg"[5]

We observe here the frequency with which the above mentioned titles, all published in 1970, make direct reference to the "exotic" and "tropical" nature of the book, while in the last the "tornado" and the "Dorf der Guerillas" are slightly more marginal to exoticism. We can infer from the titles of the reviews of *Hundert Jahre Einsamkeit* that the terms "exotic" and "tropical" were the more frequent association Germans had with Latin America in the early 1970s. That earlier arbitrary attribution to Latin America's image of an exoticism that was "too" exotic, different, removed, threatening, and incomprehensible may help explain why *Hundert Jahre Einsamkeit* did not become a best seller in the early '70s.

It was not the terms of exoticism themselves, though, but rather the strange Latin American culture and literature which were conjured up through these terms and which were as yet still too different for the Germans. This "differentness" contributed to Germans' lack of interest in that literature in the early '70s:

> Daß [*Hundert Jahre Einsamkeit*] in der guten Übersetzung von Curt Meyer-Clason bei uns noch nicht so bekanntgeworden ist, wie er es verdient, mag an dem recht geringen Interesse der Deutschen an Lateinamerika liegen oder an der im Vergleich zu anderen Ländern noch provinziellen literarischen Information in Deutschland.[6]

Scanning titles of articles and reviews that were written during the 1980s and that dealt with exoticism explicitly or peripherally yields a wider selection of exotic images:

Chronik eines angekündigten Todes:
"Nach dem Hochzeits-Fiasko ein Mord im Karibik-Dorf"[7]

Eva Luna:
"Exotisches Märchen"[8]

Mexikanischer Tango:
"Tango in der mörderischen Macho-Welt"[9]
"Roman aus Mexiko: Musik im Blut"[10]
"Gesellschaftstanz auf dem Vulkan der mexikanischen Revolution"[11]
"Generalsfrau im Dschungel der Politik"[12]

Geschichten der Eva Luna:
"Exotisches Sofakissen"[13]

Geschichtenerzähler:

"Sprung in den Dschungel"[14]
"Urwaldszenen"[15]
"Indianische Phantasie"[16]

The later titles of critiques used the vague expression "exotic" itself less frequently. Instead, they concentrated on specific characteristics related to the work or on a specific form of Latin American exoticism (macho, volcano, jungle and "Urwald," tango, "Musik im Blut," Indians) corresponding to the theme of the book. The explicit images elicited a more concrete and comprehensible but still unknown reality.

The transition from the incomprehensible and inaccessible Latin American exoticism perceived in the 1970s to the less distant enticing exoticism of the 1980s is best illustrated in the following descriptions of *Hundert Jahre Einsamkeit* (1970), *Chronik eines angekündigten Todes* (1981), *Geisterhaus* (1984), and *Mexikanischer Tango* (1988) taken from West German reviews:

Hundert Jahre Einsamkeit:

[...] eine tropische Vegetation und Fauna, Sümpfe, Urwald und die unzugängliche Sierra; die blutige Auseinandersetzung zwischen den traditionellen Parteien, [...]; Bürgerkriege [...] Nun mußte die lateinamerikanische Wirklichkeit einer europäischen Kamera schon immer phantastisch, fiebrig und deliriumhaft vorkommen.[17]

Phantastisch wie die wuchernde Natur, rätselhaft, maßlos, überhitzt, voller Spuk und Zauber, erfüllt von Mythen, Mysterien und Mystifikationen ist die Welt der tropischen Breiten Lateinamerikas, und kein Erzähler hat ihre Magie, ihre wunderbare Wirklichkeit eindringlicher beschworen als der Kolumbianer Gabriel García Márquez in der tragisch-grotesken Saga vom hundertjährigen Aufstieg und Fall des Bananen-Dorfs Macondo.[18]

Chronik eines angekündigten Todes:

García Márquez ist nicht mehr nur der Beschwörer magischer (weil exotisch ferner) Welten, über die wir nur lustvoll zu staunen brauchen. Mit seinem enormen Kunstverstand führt uns der Dichter hier eine Welt vor, in der wir alle Betroffene und Mitspieler sind.[19]

Geisterhaus:

> Nur formal läßt sich diese chilenische Familienchronik mit europäischen Vorbildern vergleichen. Denn die Erzählung exponiert eine Wirklichkeit, die uns Europäern nicht nur fremd vorkommen und fremd bleiben, sondern vor allem "unwirklich" erscheinen muß: lateinamerikanische Realität.[20]

Mexikanischer Tango:

> Wie die Allende ist Angeles Mastretta eine virtuose Erzählerin, die ihre Leser in die reizvolle und spannungsgeladene Welt Lateinamerikas entführt.[21]

Geschichten der Eva Luna (about *Geisterhaus*):

> Allzu verführerisch erschien der exotisch parfümierte Zauber einer Erzählkunst, die den nordischen Trübsinn auf so unterhaltsame Weise vertrieb [...][22]

In the first two reviews, there is an overall tone of the formidable and inaccessible character of Latin American nature, magic, fantasy, and reality. In the discussion of *Chronik eines angekündigten Todes*, we learn that there has been a shift away from García Márquez's being associated almost exclusively with exotic magic realism. With *Chronik*, the critic has the impression of the inclusion of the reader in the collective "Mitspieler" feature of the novel. The critique of *Geisterhaus* identifies the strangeness of Latin American reality but in connection with a structure familiar to European readers: that of the multi-generational family chronicle. The success of the novel in Germany, in spite of strange and unreal reality mentioned in the article, gives testimony to the fact that the Latin American reality, while remaining *fremd*, is no longer too distant or incomprehensible. The review of *Mexikanischer Tango* confirms the attraction that Latin American literature held for German readers by the end of the 1980s. The exoticism ascribed to Latin America had by this time assumed a positive "differentness." Finally, the last critic, in looking back at *Geisterhaus* while writing in 1990, recognizes the "exotic" of Allende's narrative fiction as having had a magnetic attraction.

The exoticism perceived by Germans in the '80s takes on a number of manifestations in the reviews of the Spanish American novels. It is generally related to one form or another of spiritualism, the occult, and folklore; magic and magic realism; non-European populations (Indian, Arabic, African, gauchos); nature and the tropical atmosphere; and eroticism.

Taking for granted that reality and magic, spiritualism, and the occult can coexist without mutually nullifying one another is a feature that has been most associated with Latin American literature for several decades. What has changed is the increased willingness of the German reader to accept the matter-of-factness of magic realism. As was noted in Chapter 3, in decades prior to the 1980s there were too many obstacles between the average German reader and comprehension of the Spanish American text; and magic realism was viewed as one of those obstacles. Since Spanish American culture and literature have become more accessible, Germans seem to be more favorably disposed towards dealing with magic realism, spiritualism, and Spanish American folklore than they were in the early 1970s:

Hundert Jahre Einsamkeit:

> Und eine besondere Schwäche hat Márquez fürs Okkulte. Teppiche heben sich in die Lüfte, Geister rumpeln, Remedios verduftet per Levitation: Márquez macht Unglaubliches glaubhaft durch die Selbstverständlichkeit, mit der er es in die Fülle von Realistischem einschmuggelt.[23]

In this case, the average West German reader of 1970 was not yet prepared to accept the "credible unbelievable" (magic realism), one impediment to German best seller status. Some readers, in fact, were only prepared to read *Hundert Jahre Einsamkeit* after having read *Geisterhaus* (Flad, personal interview 13 Feb. 1989). The strange spirits, the fantastic, and the supernatural of the more accessible *Geisterhaus* enabled some readers of the '80s to then accept those features in *Hundert Jahre Einsamkeit*.

Geisterhaus:

> Manch europäischer Leser schreckt vor den spiritistischen Szenen im *Geisterhaus* zurück. Doch viele Lateinamerikaner--so die Antwort der Autorin--erleben ihre ohnehin oft absurde Realität als magisch mit all den Vorahnungen, Totenerscheinungen und sonstigen übernatürlichen Ereignissen und Fähigkeiten.[24]

> *Das Geisterhaus* mag aus mancherlei Gründen den europäischen Lesern gefallen haben. An das enge Nebeneinander einer phantastisch-magischen Welt und sehr aktueller, teilweiser kraß realistischer Ereignisse haben sich die Leser lateinamerikanischer Literatur schon gewöhnt.[25]

> [*Geisterhaus*] ist ein Buch [...] voll prallen Lebens, [...] ein ergreifender, manchmal erschreckender Hinblick [...] in eine [lateinamerikanische] Welt.[26]

> So begreift man beim Lesen die Eigenart und Problematik dieses Landes und seines Kontinents[,] nicht nur die starke Präsenz des Übernatürlichen.[27]

As these reviews indicate, Germans do not consider themselves alone in their "fear" of the spirits. Indeed, they suggest that Germans (and Europeans) perceive spirits differently from most Spanish Americans, for many of whom they are a part of life.

The way spirits are understood in Spanish America is tied to the native Indian and African heritage of the Latin Americans, and this heritage creates for the German reader a culture and people distinct from his or her own. Yet there are sufficient similarities to European culture to make these novels comprehensible and at the same time different for the European reader. In the novel *Eva Luna*, Eva's parents, a foundling of unknown origin and an Indian with yellow eyes, conjure up distant peoples for German readers:

> Seine Heldin bewährt sich wie ihre Vorgängerinnen in Allendes Werk. Auch sie erhält ihr besonderes Stigma durch 'exotische Herkunft und Vorgeschichte.[28]

People of different origins living on a distant continent hold a certain fascination for Germans, for those readers in a country like Germany where the people are relatively homogenous. Besides Eva Luna's own Indian father and mother of unknown origin, a mulatto cook, a black "grandmother," an Arab, and an Austrian who grew up during the Nazi regime figure prominently in her life and are mentioned in the majority of the critiques. In *Geschichtenerzähler* the Indians themselves are principle characters. However, while readers learn intimate details about their way of life, the Indians remain a nameless group. Individual personalities, except for that of Tasurinchi, do not come through.

A different--and curious--aspect of the exotic people of Latin America, as the Germans perceived them, is found in the following laudatory critique of Brazilian Jorge Amado's *Tocaia Grande* and Colombian Gabriel García Márquez's *Liebe in den Zeiten der Cholera*:

> Doch die beiden bekannten Erfolgsschriftsteller sind nur zwei von etlichen hervorragenden lateinamerikanischen Autoren, von Gauchos, die da auf uns zukommen.[29]

The mention of the "gaucho" in this context demonstrates the strong West German association of the exotic gaucho figure with the whole Latin American continent and culture.

Even more attractive to Germans are the, for them, exotic forms of nature and the tropical ambiance they exude for Central Europeans. Even the sun takes on an exotic connotation in a cloudy country like Germany. The photograph of Allende sitting in the sun, which was used on later book jackets (and on the cover of the paperback edition) and in the advertising of *Geisterhaus*, somehow transmits a very different atmosphere from that of Germany. In a critique of Mastretta's *Mexikanischer Tango*, the sun is combined with spirits to also relate a unique mood:

> Die Geister der Toten verblassen schnell unter der Sonne Mexikos.[30]

Usually, however, there is greater fascination with the more intense forms of nature. We have already encountered the jungle, the volcano, and the tornado in the titles of reviews of *Mexikanischer Tango* and *Hundert Jahre Einsamkeit*, but the interest extends beyond that. The exotic milieu is further conveyed in tactile, visual, and olfactory images in the reviews of the Spanish American novels:

Geisterhaus:

> Man [...] denkt an die Beschreibung des großen Erdbebens, wo der Boden fast auch unter dem Stuhl des Lesers zu wackeln scheint [...][31]

Eva Luna:

> Man [...] darf simple, wirklichkeitsnahe Wortwechsel genießen, in einer subtropischen Atmosphäre [...][32]
>
> Mit dicken Tupfern aus Schweiß, Sperma, Blut wird südamerikanisches Ambiente koloriert.[33]

Chronik eines angekündigten Todes:

> Ungemein kraftvoll ist diese Geschichte von Blut und Gewalt erzählt, in einer Prosa, die fiebrige Hitze und die Exotik der Karibik mit der nüchternen Präzision eines Gerichtsprotokolls verbindet.[34]

General in seinem Labyrinth:

> Die feuchtschwüle Stimmung der Urwälder mit [...] dem Warnschrei eines bunden Kakadus [...][35]

Liebe in den Zeiten der Cholera:

> Ein Roman voller Glücksangebote wie ein duftender Tropen-Nachmittag [...][36]
>
> [Der Roman] hat die ganze Epoche vor und nach der Jahrhundertwende und die karibische Weltgegend dazu aufgebaut, hingezaubert mit ihren Düften, Moden, Allüren, alles echt bis in den letzten schmiedeeisernen Schnörkel und Affenschrei, so bezaubernd echt wie nur Kulissen wirken können [...][37]
>
> Alles ist durchdrungen von den schweren Düften der Tropen, leuchtet in den grellen Farben einer exotischen Welt, liegt heiß und schwül unter dem drückenden Himmel der Karibik.[38]

Clearly, by the end of the 1980s, the exotic aura of Latin America was no longer perceived as an atmosphere that deterred the German reader from enjoying Latin American literature. Rather, exoticism became--particularly when the reader is in a colder, more overcast North European country--an ambiance to be experienced, to be visualized, heard, felt, smelled, and enjoyed in the reader's imagination. This sentiment was transmitted both in the novels and in the wording of the critiques of the novels.

In a review of Mastretta's *Mexikanischer Tango*, the author translates Latin American exoticism into eroticism:

> Neben [lateinamerikanischen] Salsarhythmen, Tangoatmosphäre und dementsprechender provozierend erotischer Mode leistet auch die Literatur ihren Tribut.[39]

Eroticism is also seen in connection with Latin America. The erotic nature of *Mexikanischer Tango* is a product of the nature of the tango and its corresponding theme in the novel, and a majority of critiques mention the erotic tone of the book. One example is the following:

> Andrés Ascencio ist die extreme Ausgeburt desjenigen Charakters, den die Emanzipation der westlichen Zivilisation in Grund und Boden gestampft hat, ein Super-Macho hoch Sex, ein hinreißender Schuft [...] voller Kraft und Gelächter, strotzend von der Erotik seines Willens zur Macht, der ein Unwille zur Unterordnung ist.[40]

Here we notice the association of machismo, an inherently Latin American trait in the eyes of Germans, with eroticism and power. Similarly, two reviews of *General in seinem Labyrinth* connect the erotic with power:

> Da zeigt sich der Erzähler von der Erotik der Macht.[41]

> Die Erotik der Macht [...] erweckt in den durch seine Liebe "Befreiten" keine Gefolgschaft.[42]

Although some of the other novels are less erotic, several critiques mention the erotic aspect of Allende's *Eva Luna*; and references to eroticism are found in reviews of *Hundert Jahre Einsamkeit*, *Geisterhaus*, and *Von Liebe und Schatten*, although less frequently so.

The most obviously erotic of the Spanish American works to have achieved best seller status in Germany are Mario Vargas Llosa's *Lob der Stiefmutter* and Isabel Allende's *Geschichten der Eva Luna*. Most of its reviews note the erotic nature of *Geschichten der Eva Luna*, exemplified in the following review title and excerpt:

> "Leidenschaft, Erotik und Humor--Geschichten, die das Leben schrieb"[43]

> Eine Art erotische Kunstmärchen für Erwachsene sind [Allendes] *Geschichten der Eva Luna*.[44]

More critical is this review title:

> "Feuchte Pobacken"[45]

The critics writing about *Lob der Stiefmutter* are more positive than those of *Geschichten der Eva Luna*. The advertising and the reviews focus on the erotic nature of *Stiefmutter* coupled with the Peruvian nationality of the author. On the wrap-around strip on the book appear the words "Der erotische Roman des großen peruanischen Schriftstellers." The reviews are often at least as explicit:

Review title and subtitle:

> "Zelebrierte Erotik. Vargas Llosas 'Lob der Stiefmutter'"[46]

Review subtitle:

> "Der peruanische Präsidentschaftskandidat Vargas Llosa als Erotiker"[47]

First paragraph of review:

> Seine literarischen Frivolitäten machen Mario Vargas Llosa im Wahlkampf um das Amt des peruanischen Staatspräsidenten, für das er nominiert wurde, gelegentlich zu schaffen. [...] Sein neuer Roman jedenfalls behandelt das Thema von Eros und Kunst mit einer Intensität und Ausschließlichkeit wie keines seiner Bücher zuvor.[48]

The erotic theme of the novel is clearly viewed in connection with the Peruvian origin of the author. It is also stated both in the work and in most of the reviews that the family lives in Peru. Beyond that, there is nothing in the novel which ties it to an exotic setting.

This is not to suggest that eroticism is viewed as an exclusively Latin American phenomenon but merely that there does exist a certain association between eroticism and the hot, steamy, tropical--and thus exotic--nature associated with Latin America in the minds of German readers. Eroticism may suggest to the German reader, then, a component tied to Latin America, one which he or she may expect to find in a Spanish American novel.

Exoticism is thus integrally connected with the West German concept of the sub-genre of the Spanish American novel. The exotic nature of Latin America became less strange and distant for Germans in the late 1970s and 1980s, yet the Latin American reality remained very different from the European experience. Taking into consideration the greater number of Spanish American works of fiction that were read from 1981 to '91 in Germany, we can infer that the more frequent contact with the literature also helped to make the exotic elements in it more familiar, less *fremd*. Spanish American exoticism consequently offered the reader in Germany that "concrete unknown reality" (Ripken, personal interview) to which he or she could escape from the colder and more industrialized way of life in Germany. Latin American exoticism is, then, a feature closely associated with the "Spanish American sub-genre" as perceived in West Germany and one that German readers expect to find in that literature.

Notes

[1] Wilfried Hierse, *Nürnberger Nachrichten* 29 Aug. 1970.

[2] *Spiegel* 30 Mar. 1970.

[3] Karl Krolow, *Süddeutsche Zeitung* 18 July 1970.

[4] Georg Rudolf Lind, *Stuttgarter Zeitung* 18 Apr. 1970.

[5] Harald Gröhler, "Tornado bläst das Dorf der Guerillas weg," *Kölner Stadt-Anzeiger* 9 May 1970. Future references to this review will be noted as: Gröhler, "Tornado."

[6] Walter Haubrich, "*Hundert Jahre Einsamkeit*," *Frankfurt Allgemeine Zeitung* 8 May 1971.

[7] Elisabeth Boetticher, *Welt am Sonntag* 13 Sept. 1981.

[8] Elisabeth Zeitler, *Städtemagazin Plärrer* No. 9 (1988).

[9] Bernhard Lassahn, *Szene* Hamburg Aug. 1988.

[10] *Fuldaer Zeitung* 13 Feb. 1989: 17.

[11] Edith Ibscher, *Frankfurter Neue Presse* 7 July 1988.

[12] Miriam Zink, *Welt am Sonntag* 18 Sept. 1988.

[13] Christine Wischmann, *Darmstädter Echo* 25 Aug. 1990.

[14] Hanspeter Brode, *Frankfurter Allgemeine Zeitung* 16 Mar. 1991.

[15] Wilfried F. Schoeller, *Die Zeit*, 5 Oct. 1990.

[16] *Elle* Jan. 1990.

[17] Hugo Loetscher, "Wo die Wirklichkeit schon übertreibt," *Die Zeit* 15 May 1970: 20-21.

[18] "Mutmaßungen über Gabo," *Spiegel* 6 July 1981: 150.

[19] Martha Christine Körling, "Schuld und Verantwortung im Klima der Gewalt," *Berliner Morgenpost* 22 Oct. 1981: 11.

[20] Martin Lüdke, "Der Zauber des Ungeheuerlichen," *Die Zeit* 17 Aug. 1984.

[21] Marion Rathmann, "Catalina tanzt den mexikanischen Tango," *Wetzlarer Neue Zeitung* 13 Aug. 1988.

[22] Matthias Wegner, "Schunghafter Wörterhandel," *Frankfurter Allgemeine Zeitung* 17 Oct. 1990: 34.

[23] Gröhler, "Tornado."

[24] Adriane Thomalla, "Eine Frau beschreibt Frauen," *Allgemeine Zeitung* Mainz 31 Dec. 1984.

[25] Walter Haubrich, "Wo die Wirklichkeit phantastische Züge annimmt," *Frankfurt Allgemeine Zeitung* 26. Jan. 1985.

[26] Heinz G. Konsalik, "Bücher für den Weihnachtstisch," Bayrische Rundfunk 23 Dec. 1984.

[27] Herbert Lindenberger, "Unseliger Kontinent," *Stuttgarter Zeitung* 27 Oct. 1984. Future references to this review will be noted as: Lindenberger, "Unseliger."

[28] "Isabel Allende wiederholt sich," *Kölner Stadt-Anzeiger* 16 Sept. 1988.

[29] Manfred Schmidt, "Subtile Erotik," *Playboy* Sept. 1987.

[30] Günther Engels, "Die freche Göre und der Macho," *Kölner Rundschau* 18 March 1988.

[31] Lindenberger, "Unseliger."

[32] Joachim Kaiser, "Schickes aus Chile," *Süddeutsche Zeitung* 8/9 Oct. 1988: 142.

[33] Christiaan L. Hart Nibbrig, "Fastfood mit Suchtgefahr," *Die Zeit* 7 Oct. 1988.

[34] Günther Engels, "Die verlorene Ehre der Angela Vicario," *Kölnische Rundschau* 25 Nov. 1981.

[35] Walter Gallasch, "Die Kälte der Einsamkeit," *Nürnberger Nachrichten* 16/17 Dec. 1989.

[36] "Das Glück braucht Zeit," *Aachener Volkszeitung* 28 Feb. 1987.

[37] Reinhard Baumgart, "Eine schöne Bescherung," *Die Zeit* 1 May 1987.

[38] Karsten Garscha, "Buch der Woche," Hessischer Rundfunk 5 Apr. 1987.

[39] Ennelyn Schmidt, "Warten auf den Tod," *Stadtblatt Osnabrück* Oct. 1988.

[40] Ariane Barth, "Geliebt und begraben," *Der Spiegel* 15 Aug. 1988.

[41] Andrea Köhler, "Chronik eines Seite für Seite angekündigten Todes," *Badische Zeitung* Freiburg 26 Feb. 1990.

[42] Wilfried F. Schoeller, "Gabriel García Márquez in seinem Labyrinth," *Süddeutsche Zeitung* 7 Dec. 1989.

[43] *Für Sie* 12 Sept. 1990.

[44] Toni Meissner, "Die Witwe greift sich den Räuber," *Abendzeitung* 7 Jan. 1991: 8.

[45] *Der Spiegel* 13 Aug. 1990: 173.

[46] Jan Schulz-Ojala, *Der Tagesspiegel* 24 Sept. 1989.

[47] Wolfram Schütte, "Ein bravouröses Kunststück über alles & nichts," *Frankfurter Rundschau* 5 Aug. 1989: ZB 4.

[48] Hanspeter Brode, "Eine Bereicherung des Ehelebens," *Frankfurter Allgemeine Zeitung* 16 Sept. 1989.

Chapter 7

A Return to Story-Telling

In contrast to many of the works of the Latin American "boom" of the 1960s, the Spanish American best sellers of the 1980s and early '90s reflected a return to basic story-telling and a more accessible, traditional style. This traditional style was often viewed by West German newspaper and magazine critics as part of the European heritage to which the Germans could more easily relate. The German reviews of these best-selling novels of the '80s reflect a fascination with the overlapping of the perceived Spanish American sub-genre with detective-type novels, the family sagas, fairy tales, and love stories. All four of the writers--García Márquez, Allende, Mastretta, and Vargas Llosa--have had careers in journalism. A journalistic quality, i.e., a more direct and concrete manner of "reporting" events, is discernible in most of the works. Above all, the language, structure, and style, which are considered to be particular to and consistent in the Spanish American novels, attract the German reader.

The fact that Spanish American fiction became more accessible and less of an "antagonistic act" (Hans-Joachim Müller, "Rolle" 49) in the 1980s certainly enabled the general reading public in Germany to change its perception of Spanish American literature. This in turn contributed to the Germans being able to comprehend Latin American culture and literature and to understand the messages conveyed in the works.

While maintaining the very distinctive Spanish American character and subject matter, these works of fiction are written using techniques and content seen in Germany as part of the European tradition. As discussed earlier, Germans regard Latin America as having a European heritage. The German critics often related the novels from that distant South American continent to a work already known to Germans, frequently mentioning either directly or indirectly a European genre, author, or work that may in some way be similar to the Spanish American novel. This initial encounter with a Spanish American novel, described in terms of a well-known European work, enabled the German reader to understand the South American book more easily.

"Every writer creates his own precursors," Argentine author Jorge Luis Borges once wrote about Franz Kafka. In the case of those Spanish American works that became popular in West Germany during the 1980s and at the beginning of the '90s, the Germans were able to relate the structure, the content, or the theme to European "precursors" while they recognized the special Spanish American quality that they could find only in the Spanish American works.

Interestingly, Kafka himself influenced not only Borges and García Márquez but also other Latin American authors. German critics recognize the link:

> Review title of Vargas Llosa's *Geschichtenerzähler*:
> "Kafka am Amazonas"[1]

> Review of García Márquez's *General in seinem Labyrinth*:
> Den Einfluß Franz Kafkas auf sein Werk sieht er [García Márquez] heute stärker als früher, vor allem das Lateinamerikanische in Kafka ziehe ihn an.[2]

Kafka himself plays a role in Spanish American writing and in the German view of its European heritage. His story "The Metamorphosis" is incorporated into Vargas Llosa's *Geschichtenerzähler* in theme and name: Saúl's parrot is called Gregor Samsa, and the "Geschichtenerzähler" tells the story of "Tasurinchi-Gregor's" transformation into an insect. One German critic sees a further connection between Mario Vargas Llosa, Franz Kafka, and Gabriel García Márquez:

> Fragen wird man sich dürfen, ob Vargas Llosas Versuch, Sául [sic] als authentischen Nachfolger der alten Tradition der Geschichtenerzähler zu verstehen, nicht auch eine verdeckte Anerkenntnis der poetischen Meisterschaft Gabriel García Márquez' ist. War doch, wie für Saul der Papagei namens Gregor Samsa sein Totemtier wurde, für den Kolumbianer die erste Begegnung mit Kafkas "Verwandlung" [...] die Initialzündung für die eignene poetisch-literarische Kreativität. Kafka hat "Gabo" [Gabo is García Márquez's nickname] zum Geschichtenerzähler verwandelt.[3]

Whether or not Vargas Llosa intended Kafka to symbolize García Márquez's impetus to become a writer, Kafka's influence on García Márquez and on Vargas Llosa is clear and direct.

Germans also found ties to other European fiction, associations that were less recognized by critics in other countries. Sometimes the title, and occasionally the text, of the critique make the initial connection between the Spanish American works and specific European books:

> *Geisterhaus*:
> "Isabel Allendes 'Buddenbrooks made in Chile'"[4]

Chronik eines angekündigten Todes:
"Die verlorene Ehre der Angela Vicario"[5]

"Mutmaßungen über Gabo"[6]

Geschichtenerzähler:
"Mutmaßungen über Sául [sic]"[7]

Liebe in den Zeiten der Cholera:
"Der Name der Liebe"[8]

The titles and text of these reviews relate each of the Spanish American works back to German novels: Thomas Mann's *Buddenbrooks* (1901), Uwe Johnson's *Mutmaßungen über Jakob* (1959), Heinrich Böll's *Die verlorene Ehre der Katharina Blum* (1974); and to the international best seller from Italy, Umberto Eco's *Der Name der Rose* (1980, German 1982), respectively. Most educated Germans are aware of the content, style, and structure of these European novels and are therefore more likely to have a general idea of those aspects in the corresponding Spanish American novel. The exception to this would be *Die Liebe in den Zeiten der Cholera*, which has little in common with *Der Name der Rose*. In this case it may be that the review title was chosen to associate "love" in García Márquez's novel title with "rose" in the title of another popular book that had been on the best seller list for a long period of time.

In the reviews, the novels are associated with the more general European genres and traditions as follows: *Hundert Jahre Einsamkeit* and *Das Geisterhaus* are each a multigenerational saga of the rise and fall of a family reflecting the course of a nation. *Chronik eines angekündigten Todes* is associated with the German *Novelle*[9]; *Chronik*, *Von Liebe und Schatten*, and a couple of stories in *Geschichten der Eva Luna* are seen as detective-type novels. *Hundert Jahre Einsamkeit*, *Eva Luna*, and *Geschichten der Eva Luna* are referred to in the tradition of the German *Märchen* (fairy tale); and *Eva Luna* is identified with the Spanish picaresque novel or its German *Schelmenroman* variant. *Mexikanischer Tango* is linked to the theme of female search for identification. *Die Liebe in den Zeiten der Cholera* is seen as a love story in the European nineteenth-century tradition, while *Lob der Stiefmutter* is compared to novels from fin-de-siècle Europe and European baroque and rococo novels. *General in seinem Labyrinth* is an historical biography, and *Geschichtenerzähler* is naturally coupled with Kafka's "Die Verwandlung." Thus all of the best sellers studied here are discussed in the German reviews as relating to familiar European genres and themes.

In the chapter on exoticism, we noted titles of reviews of *Hundert Jahre Einsamkeit* connecting the exotic setting with the European family saga genre (e.g., "Exotische Familien-Saga"). The following is exemplary of this European genre as a precursor of Allende's *Geisterhaus*:

> Familiengeschichten über mehrere Generationen hinweg werden bei uns immer noch gern gelesen, ganz gleich, wo sie herkommen. Große Familien, reich an Persönlichkeiten, die in der Geschichte ihrer Länder einflußreich sind, wie es sie früher in Europa gab, finden sich heute noch in Lateinamerika.[10]

While *Hundert Jahre Einsamkeit* and *Geisterhaus* were seen in the family saga tradition, several German critics viewed *Chronik eines angekündigten Todes* as a *Novelle*:

> Nicht nur wegen des Umfangs würde man das Werk im deutschen Sprachraum als Novelle bezeichnen. Die Handlung ist von einem einzigen Ereignis bestimmt: dem Tod Santiago Nasars, [...] Auch die strenge Einheitlichkeit von Zeit und Schauplatz ist die der deutschen Novelle.[11]

Numerous critiques discussed both the family history aspect of *Geisterhaus* and *Hundert Jahre Einsamkeit* and the *Novelle* feature of *Chronik*. However, Walter Haubrich, author of the two above-cited reviews and the upcoming review of *Hundert Jahre Einsamkeit*, describes these novels more directly in specifically European and German terms.

Describing *Chronik* in terms of a German *Novelle* and *Hundert Jahre Einsamkeit*, *Eva Luna*, and *Geschichten der Eva Luna* as *Märchen* is also an indication of the return to story-telling. Reviews of these three best sellers refer the reader back to the German tradition of the *Märchen*:

Hundert Jahre Einsamkeit:

> In diesem "Märchenbuch" erschließen sich denn auch grundlegende Erkenntnisse zur politischen und sozialen Situation des Halbkontinents.[12]

Eva Luna:

> Muntere Märchen, wie das Leben so spielt.[13]
>
> (Review Title:) "*Eva Luna* oder Märchen für große Kinder"[14]

Geschichten der Eva Luna:

> Eva Luna dagegen erzählt die Märchen ihrem Liebhaber [...][15]

The five reviews mentioned above, representative of a number of others, all take the works from the distant South American continent and put them in a context the Germans can more readily identify. This association aided German readers in their introduction to the best sellers.

The ease with which Germans could read Spanish American novels of the 1980s was not only due to the association with the European "precursors" but also to the actual accessible structure of the works. German novelist Uwe Timm expressed in his article "Zwischen Unterhaltung und Aufklärung" that the author with a political message who is concerned with efficient communication with his or her audience should reject the aesthetic standards equating quality literature with exclusivity and should aim to create literature with a wider appeal. He maintains that popular novels are successful, not only because of the essentially traditional, accessible narrative techniques employed, but also because of their content,

> in denen geschickt systemkonforme Wünsche mit solchen, die einem echten Bedürfnis entspringen, kombiniert werden. [...] Reproduziert wird eine anheimelnde Unmittelbarkeit. (79-90)

Although I have already suggested that the intensity of the political message of the Spanish American novels in question varies, most writers want to reach their greatest potential audience. García Márquez has asserted that "was ihn einzig interessiere, das sei die 'Kommunikation mit dem Leser,' mit einem möglichst großen Publikum. [...]"[16] We can see a correspondence between the greater accessibility of these Spanish American novels and the process of West Germans learning about Spanish American politics, history, culture, and people through literature. There was a return to story-telling within a framework that did not require the reader to fit together innumerable pieces of a complex puzzle in the correct chronological order or to decipher a code known almost exclusively to Spanish Americans. Besides a more linear construction, the less complicated language and style of the novels contributed to the readability of the works.

In a critique of *Liebe in den Zeiten der Cholera*, Andreas Graf writes about the return to story-telling:

> Es war einmal Mode unter europäischen Intellektuellen, vom Ende des Erzählens (der Musik, des Romans, der Kunst, des Gedichts)

> zu faseln. Dieser Roman könnte ein Beleg sein für das Ende des Endes.[17]

This "end to the end of story-telling" began in South America in the 1970s and continued in the 1980s and early '90s. Dieter Janik has said about Latin American literature, "Die Kraft der Darstellung ist überzeugend" (personal interview). Many reviews comment on the "poetische Erzählweise" and "kraftvolle poetische Sprache" of the Spanish American novels. Similarly, the greater accessibility of the works themselves is noted repeatedly in terms such as "ein munter zu lesendes Buch," "ein leicht zu lesender Roman," "Ihr [Mastretta's] Stil ist leicht lesbar und humorvoll," and "leserfreundlich."

The German reviews of the Spanish American novels note the progressive turning away from the more complex style and construction typical of Spanish American novels of the 1950s and '60s toward the more accessible style of the '70s and especially of the '80s and early '90s. Most of the Spanish American best sellers retain a fairly linear structure. The exceptions, *Chronik eines angekündigten Todes*, *General in seinem Labyrinth*, and *Geschichtenerzähler* are nevertheless lucid in their construction. *Geschichtenerzähler* is slightly less clear due to the alien and supernatural narratives of the "Geschichtenerzähler."

Beginning with *Hundert Jahre Einsamkeit* we find references not only to the fact that the novels become more readable, but also that they develop a certain style in the language.

Hundert Jahre Einsamkeit:

> Sprache und Struktur des Romans sind leicht zugänglich, von einer allerdings recht hinterhältigen und trügerischen Einfachheit.[18]

Chronik eines angekündigten Todes:

> Die Sprache des kolumbianischen Erzählers, frei von barocken Elementen, ist noch einfacher und gleichzeitig subtiler geworden.[19]

Walter Haubrich, the author of both critiques, recognizes that García Márquez's language and structure had been fairly complex, or "baroque" as he and others have described it, in his earlier works. Haubrich believes that with *Hundert Jahre Einsamkeit* and particularly *Chronik eines angekündigten Todes*, García Márquez's language had indeed become simpler and therefore easier to read. More specifically, a number of critics describe the preciseness, exactness, and descriptive nature of the prose used in the Spanish American works:

Chronik eines angekündigten Todes:

> Die Geschichte selbst wird [...] präzis und objektiv referiert [...][20]

Geisterhaus:

> Erstaunlicher scheint mir aber noch die epische Souveränität des Blicks dieser Erzählerin zu sein, die Genauigkeit und Leuchtkraft ihrer Prosa.[21]
>
> In kraftvoller poetischer Sprache stellt die Autorin den Lesern zahlreiche Angehörige der Familie Trueba [...] vor [...][22]

Von Liebe und Schatten:

> Was in *Liebe und Schatten* außer der wieder sehr dichten, anschaulichen und leidenschaftlichen Sprache auffällt, ist eine Art epischer Gerechtigkeit.[23]

Eva Luna:

> Dem Leser kommt es vor, als kenne er die verschiedenen Personen von Angesicht zu Angesicht, so illustrativ ist die Sprache der Darstellung [...][24]

Liebe in den Zeiten der Cholera:

> [...] [der] Roman, der nicht die geringsten Anleihen an avantgardistische Techniken macht, [ist] ganz und gar konventionell geschrieben [...][25]

Lob der Stiefmutter:

> Brillant formuliert das Ganze, gewürzt mit Ironie. Bildern, Metaphern, Erzähltricks halten den Leser in Atem.[26]

General in seinem Labyrinth:

> Er [Garcia Márquez] sucht, lange nach dem präzisen Wort, der treffenden Formulierung.[27]

Geschichten der Eva Luna:

> [...] sie [Allende] schildert Komik und Tragik des Alltags präzise und detailgenau.[28]

Another element of accessibility is the documentary and journalistic nature of most of the Spanish American best sellers. *Hundert Jahre Einsamkeit*,

Geisterhaus, Mexikanischer Tango, and *General in seinem Labyrinth* chronicled historical events, while *Von Liebe und Schatten, Chronik eines angekündigten Todes,* and *Geschichtenerzähler* are based on real occurrences. In every case, the structure of the novel mirrors the factual preciseness of a documentary or chronicle. The German appreciation of this aspect is illustrated in a critique of *Chronik eines angekündigten Todes*:

> Denn der Chronist, der das Konkrete scheinbar genau rekonstuieren, der durch Ratio Ordnung in den Schrecken, in das Gefühlschaos bringen will, der Uhrzeiten pedantisch genau angibt und nie vergißt zu erwähnen, wer wo was ihm gegenüber geäußert hat.[29]

The reviews are evidence of the greater accessibility called for by Uwe Timm, even though the authors do not necessarily wish to convey a political message. The accessibility then created a wider appeal through the less complex narrative techniques and descriptive language. These allowed the German reader--and readers elsewhere--to understand the cultural, political, and historical codes of the novels better and to sense the immediacy that would not be found otherwise. The messages of these works transmitted more meaning for Germans than they would have had they been written with less accessible narrative techniques.

Besides being more accessible, these Spanish American novels were written in a way that could sustain interest in the story. The critics acknowledge the suspenseful narrative style in the works, often even using similar terms:

Hundert Jahre Einsamkeit:

> [García Márquez'] Angriff vollzog sich mittels erzählerischer Handlung, die den Leser nur selten zu Atem kommen läßt.[30]

Chronik eines angekündigten Todes:

> [...] ein atemberaubender Spannungsbogen, höchst kunstvoll und raffiniert gewölbt vom ersten bis zum letzten Satz.[31]

Liebe in den Zeiten der Cholera:

> [...] nach dem atemberaubenden Beginn, [...] nach dem frühen Ende auf Seite 509 bleibt der Leser erschrocken wie ein jäh verlassener Liebhaber zurück.[32]

General in seinem Labyrinth:

> Und dennoch entsteht Spannung, wächst von Kapitel zu Kapitel das, was wir Atmosphäre nennen.[33]

Geisterhaus:

> Amüsant und unterhaltsam, spannend informativ, überzeugend und dramatisch [...][34]

Von Liebe und Schatten:

> Ein Buch, das vom Anfang bis zur letzten Seite spannend und erregend ist.[35]

Eva Luna:

> Elf spannungsgeladene Kapitel [...][36]

Geschichten der Eva Luna:

> Isabel Allende erzählt ihre 23 Geschichten fesselnd, spannend und rund.[37]

Mexikanischer Tango:

> [...] ist Angeles Mastretta eine virtuose Erzählerin, die ihre Leser in die reizvolle und spannungsgeladene Welt Lateinamerikas entführt.[38]

Lob der Stiefmutter:

> Lakonisch erzählt, erreicht die Spannung des Buches ihren Höhepunkt im Kapitel "Die schlechten Wörter" [...][39]

Geschichtenerzähler:

> So löst sich schließlich der spannende Kern dieses Romans. [...] Der Roman [...] ist in seinen realistischen Abschnitten überaus spannend.[40]

"Breath-taking" "suspense" held the reader's attention as he or she read the Spanish American best sellers. The consistency with which critics describe Spanish American works shows the fulfilled expectation that came to be associated in West Germany with Spanish American fiction of the '80s and early '90s. This feature is thus one that contributed to these novels being perceived as if they constituted a separate sub-genre.

Another quality that drew West German readers to the Spanish American novels was the element of humor. "Wir Deutsche sind zu ernst. Wir haben Angst vor Humor," said the head of InterNationes Hans Joachim Wulschner, while translator Maria Bamberg reflected that "Die Deutschen sind traurig" (personal interviews). Nevertheless, German readers do enjoy humor in the books they read, particularly those from Spanish America:

Chronik eines angekündigten Todes:

> [...] García Márquez' Humor, seiner sanften Ironie und seiner Vorliebe für die Groteske [...][41]

General in seinem Labyrinth:

> Denn García Márquez' Libertador ist [...] auch: humorvoll, träumerisch, stolz [...][42]

Geisterhaus:

> [...] voller Witz, Humor, Ironie und der Phantasie einer Südamerikanerin, die noch nicht durch die Massenmedien genormt ist.[43]

Eva Luna:

> [...] Geschichten [...], die staunen lassen über diese Quelle der Erzählkunst voll [...] Humor, Witz und Musikalität.[44]

Geschichten der Eva Luna:

> Aber es gibt kein falsches Pathos, stattdessen Witz und humorig-sarkastischen Hintersinn.[45]

Lob der Stiefmutter:

> Mario Vargas Llosa erzählt diese bitterböse Tragikomödie mit hintersinnigem Witz.[46]

Mexikanischer Tango:

> Und doch ist der Roman zugleich ein Bolero, denn er ist voller Humor, erfüllt von Leidenschaften und Phantasien.[47]

Although humor is not always translatable across cultural and linguistic boundries, the Spanish American humor in these best sellers is sufficiently international for it to appeal to the Germans.

Finally, we find in reviews of several of the Spanish American novels frequent mention of hope for positive changes in politics and society and a romantic happy ending. These sentiments are frequently found in the last two sentences of the reviews, making the message more poignant. The following are illustrative of such optimism found in critiques of *Geisterhaus*, *Von Liebe und Schatten*, *Eva Luna*, *Liebe in den Zeiten der Cholera*, and even occasionally in those of *Lob der Stiefmutter*:

Geisterhaus:

> Und trotzdem steht am Ende die Hoffnung. Die Hoffnung, daß auch in Chile die Zeiten wieder anders werden.[48]

Liebe in den Zeiten der Cholera:

> Jetzt, in *Die Liebe in den Zeiten der Cholera*, überwindet die Liebe alle Hindernisse und gelangt zum glücklichen, zum märchenhaft glücklichen Ende.[49]

Lob der Stiefmutter:

> Eine amour à trois, genauer: à quatre offenbart sich da, und sie mündet auch noch nach tragischer Klimax in ein geradezu durchtriebenes Happy-End.[50]

The optimism for positive political change in all of Allende's works gives hope to the reader for Chile and also for other countries. Allende's novels parallel the political message with love stories, and the love stories likewise come to a happy ending. García Márquez's love story with a happy ending transmits a positive message not only about love but also about life in general.

While the Spanish American best sellers on the whole did create and then affirm the German set of expectations, we should take note of the disappointment in *General in seinem Labyrinth* and *Geschichtenerzähler* expressed in some of the reviews. Although some critics found the novels "spannend," and filled with descriptive language, other critics recorded either their own disappointment or their acknowledgment that the reading public would be disappointed since the novels did not confirm the expectations:

Geschichtenerzähler:

> Doch die Story ist allzu glatt [...] über weite Strecken liest sich der Roman wie eine Aufbereitung biographischer Details des peruanischen Autors.[51]

The title of the novel--*The Storyteller*--would have drawn German readers to the book with the impression of just that: story telling. However, the more complex nature of the theme, the Indian vocabulary and narrative passages, and the long seemingly autobiographical chapters likely disillusioned the readers, thus accounting for its tenure of just three weeks on the best seller list.

General in seinem Labyrinth also apparently did not live up to expectations. Critics mention expected features the reader might interpret as lacking in the novel and the resulting decreased interest it would hold. Exemplary is this comment:

> [E]s fällt fast auf jeder Seite leicht, das Buch aus der Hand zu legen, die Lektüre zu unterbrechen.[52]

Walter Boehlich's review of the book discusses the author as genre--and resulting reader expectations:

> Autoren wecken Erwartungen bei ihren Lesern. Sie schreiben, heißt es, ja doch immer nur dasselbe Buch, in immer neuen Variationen; und weil das geglaubt wird, besteht die Trägheit darauf, in jedem neuen Buch wiederzufinden, worin die alten einen eingeübt hatten. [...] Das geht nun schlecht bei dem Buch über Simón Bolívar. [...] Sein Fehler scheint zu sein, daß es eben nicht das Buch ist, das alle erwartet hatten: kein richtiger Roman, aber auch keine richtige Biographie. [...] Was neun von zehn Lesern nicht missen wollen, die oberflächliche Spannung, fehlt diesem Werk.[53]

Boehlich recognizes that a number of readers will be disappointed in the book exactly because it does not fulfill the German *Erwartungshorizont.*

From the evidence presented in this chapter, the return to story-telling and the greater accessibility of the Spanish American best sellers progressively increased German interest in these works during the '80s. The German characterization of the "Ende des Erzählens" and "Tod der Literatur" (Ploetz, personal interview) indicated that many found German writing since the 1960s to be too sterile, too subjective, and unreadable (Pracht-Fitzell, personal interview).

The Spanish American novel of the 1980s had returned to more conventional and less avant-garde narrative techniques, combining suspense and humor with vividness of description and often concluding with optimistic hope for political change and a romantic happy ending. Germans were then able to see aspects of familiar German and European novels, usually belonging to the respected canon of literature, in the Spanish American works. In spite of the overlapping into European literature, the observed features mentioned above became closely associated in West Germany during the '80s with the contemporary literature of the perceived Spanish American sub-genre.

Notes

[1] "Kafka am Amazons," *Der Spiegel* 17 Sept. 1990.

[2] Walter Haubrich, "Demokratie ohne Wahlen?" *Frankfurter Allgemeine Zeitung* 22 Mar. 1990.

[3] Nikolaus Markgraf, "Aber das Vorbild bleibt fern," *Frankfurter Rundschau* 28 Aug. 1990. Future references to this review will be listed under: Markgraf, "Aber das Vorbild."

[4] *Siegener Zeitung* 21 Dec. 1985.

[5] Günther Engels, *Kölnische Rundschau* 25 Nov. 1981. Heinrich Böll's novel *Die verlorene Ehre der Katharina Blum* shares with *Chronik* the theme of "honor," but in a very different sense of the word from that in *Chronik*. In *Katharina Blum*, the "lost honor" refers to Katharina's demise through the overzealous efforts of the press to report "news." Future references to this review will be noted as: Engels, "Die verlorene Ehre."

[6] *Der Spiegel* 6 July 1981. The title is suggestive of Uwe Johnson's *Mutmaßungen über Jakob*, in which Johnson employs a montage of rapidly shifting points of view and time perspectives to piece together the events surrounding the mysterious death of Jakob, an East German train dispatcher. Jakob is the object of speculation indirectly from several points of view but never directly perceived. The title of the *Spiegel* review has thus cleverly related the article on *Chronik eines angekündigten Todes*--its structure and content--as well as the occasionally elusive Gabriel García Márquez to a German work known to most of the better educated reading public.

[7] Markgraf, "Aber das Vorbild."

[8] W. Christian Schmitt, *Saarbrücker Zeitung* 6 Mar. 1987.

[9] The *Novelle* is considered to be a genre much cultivated in the German-speaking countries during the nineteenth- and twentieth-centuries. It refers to realistic fiction of medium length between that of a short story and a novel; it generally describes an unusual but real event and often has a clear turning point (*Wendepunkt*) from which it unexpectedly takes a completely different direction. Each *Novelle* should have an official symbol (*Dingsymbol*) that signals the decisive stations of the plot.

[10] Walter Haubrich, "Wo die Wirklichkeit phantastische Züge annimmt," *Frankfurter Allgemeine Zeitung* 26 Jan. 1985.

[11] Walter Haubrich, "*Chronik eines angekündigten Todes*," *Frankfurter Allgemeine Zeitung* 10 June 1981. Future references to this review will be noted as: Haubrich, "*Chronik*."

[12] Walter Haubrich, "*Hundert Jahre Einsamkeit*," *Frankfurter Allgemeine Zeitung* 9 May 1971. Future references to this review will be noted as: Haubrich, "*Hundert*."

[13] Joachim Kaiser, "Schickes aus Chile," *Süddeutsche Zeitung* 8/9 Oct. 1988.

[14] Agnes Meinold, *Welt am Sonntag* 4 Dec. 1988.

[15] Ursula Schramm, "Schwüle Märchen von Liebe und Leidenschaft," *Die Rheinpfalz*, No date (Postdate 11 Oct. 1990).

[16] "Mutmaßungen über Gabo," *Spiegel* 6 July 1981: 153.

[17] Andreas Graf, "Der Anfang vom Ende des Endes," *Kölner Illustrierte* Mar. 1987.

[18] Haubrich, "*Hundert.*"

[19] Haubrich, "*Chronik.*"

[20] Christian Huther, "Sterben als Höhepunkt des Lebens," *Main-Echo* 11/12 Oct. 1986.

[21] Wolfram Schütte, "Töchter vieler Vergewaltigungen," *Frankfurter Rundschau* 28 Apr. 1984.

[22] Günther Mayer, "Isabel Allende, *Das Geisterhaus*," *Holzarbeiter-Zeitung* Mar. 1985.

[23] Geno Hartlaub, "Der Schritt ins Freie," *Deutsches Allgemeines Sonntagsblatt* 13 July 1986.

[24] Elisabeth Zeitler, "Exotisches Märchen," *Städtemagazin 'Plärrer'* 9 (1988). Future references to this review will be noted as: Zeitler, "Exotisches Märchen."

[25] Jochen Hieber, "Der Hymnus der absoluten Liebe," *Frankfurter Allgemeine Zeitung* 31 Jan. 1987.

[26] Adelheid Omiotek, "Eros oder Politik?" *Wiesbadener Kurier* 12 Oct. 1989.

[27] Walter Haubrich, "Der General in seinem Labyrinth," *Frankfurter Allgemeine Zeitung* 20 April 1989. Future references to this review will be noted as: Haubrich, "General."

[28] "Scheherazade geht der Atem aus," *Augsburger Allgemeine Zeitung* (day unknown) Oct. 1990.

[29] Rosemarie Bollinger, "Der Mörder stand um fünf Uhr auf," *Deutsches Allgemeines Sonntagsblatt* 18 Oct. 1981. Future references to this review will be noted as: Bollinger, "Der Mörder."

[30] Karl Krolow, "Tropische Familien-Saga," *Süddeutsche Zeitung* 18 July 1970.

[31] Engels, "Die verlorene Ehre."

[32] "Das Glück braucht Zeit," *Aachener Volkszeitung* 28 Feb. 1987.

[33] Walter Gallasch, "Die Kälte der Einsamkeit," *Nürnberger Nachtrichten* 16/17 Dec. 1989.

[34] Horst Schuler, "Meine Bücher des Jahres '84," *Hamburger Abendblatt* 7 Dec. 1984.

[35] "Die neue Allende," *Bayreuther Kultur- und Bücherzeitung der Markgrafen Buchhandlung* July 1986.

[36] Zeitler, "Exotisches Märchen."

[37] Sabine Lennartz, "Die kleine Schwester der Eva Luna," *Südkurier* 3 Nov. 1990.

[38] Marion Rathmann, "Catalina tanzt den mexikanischen Tango," *Wetzlarer Neue Zeitung* 13 Aug. 1988.

[39] Rainer Traub, "Das tödliche Risiko des Schriftstellers," *Der Spiegel* 14 Aug. 1988.

[40] Hanspeter Brode, "Sprung in den Dschungel," *Frankfurter Allgemeine Zeitung* 16 Mar. 1991.

[41] Bollinger, "Der Mörder."

[42] Ciro Krauthausen, "Im Labyrinth der Macht," *Tageszeitung* Berlin 10 May 1989.

[43] Hilke Holika, "Familiensaga--Nationalepos--Frauenroman," *Hamburger Rundschau* 13 Dec. 1984.

[44] Effi Horn, "Isabel Allende erzählte ihre prallen Geschichten," *Münchner Merkur* 2 Sept. 1988.

[45] Helene Schreiber, "Die Worteverkäuferin," *Rheinischer Merkur* 5 Oct. 1990.

[46] Bernd Lubowski, "Bitterböse Tragikomödie um die Sinneslust," *Berliner Morgenpost* 24 Sept. 1989: 43.

[47] Sybille Brantl, "Wilder Tango auf glattem Parkett," *Cosmopolitan* 4 (1988).

[48] Thomas Schreiner, "Sturz in die Barbarei," *Nürnberger Zeitung* 13 April 1985.

[49] Karsten Garscha, "Buch der Woche," Hessischer Rundfunk 5 Apr. 1987.

[50] Jan Schulz-Ojala, "Zelebrierte Erotik," *Der Tagesspiegel* 24 Sept. 1989.

[51] Charlotte Bernau, "'Stürmische Wolke stößt an den Baum'--der magische Realismus," *Berliner Zeitung* 15/16 June 1991.

[52] Haubrich, "General."

[53] Walter Boehlich, "Das Buch des Grauens," *Der Spiegel* 27 Nov. 1989.

Chapter 8

Polarity, Vitality, Humanity

The contrast between the way of life in West Germany and that in Latin America is substantial. Germany is a very highly industrialized and socialized country, while many countries in Latin America have agrarian-based economies with extremes in income levels. As a result, great differences ensue in the people, their way of thinking, and their outlook on the world, all of which are reflected in their respective literatures.

The German way of life is considered by many Germans to be based on relative homogeneity and harmony compared with that in Latin America. "Alles ist begehbar," and "versichert" in Germany (Dieter Janik, personal interview). As a result, life in Germany is relatively without conflict and risk. In contrast, life in most Latin American countries is seen in Germany as one of polarity, of extremes in people, classes, and nature. Through reports of the news media, Germans receive the message that there is a daily close association with death and therefore a greater appreciation and celebration of life. Consequently, Germans regard Latin American people and situations as changing from very serious to lighthearted much more quickly and with greater frequency than in Germany (Janik, personal interview).

The respective literatures reflect the way in which Germans and Latin Americans react to their way of life. Literature from West Germany and from Spanish America during the last two decades therefore presents a number of contrasts. In the years prior to Latin American literature's becoming popular in West Germany, German literature was characterized to a large degree by politics, subjectivism, and the look inward. During the 1960s and early '70s, there was a tendency toward literary experiments and committed political literature, often rejecting aesthetics in favor of conveying a political message. This "zunehmende Politisierung" (Schonauer 257) created a literature that often lacked accessibility and therefore failed to appeal to the general public. In the later '70s political questions were substantially replaced by treatments of existential and psychological problems (Bangerter 8). In the 1980s, literature magnified the subjectivism and focused on problems of alienation, confusion, and fear with consistent themes of insanity, death, surrender, injury, distance, desolation, coldness, and a "distinct farewell to hope" (Bangerter 9). Bangerter further describes German literature of the '80s as follows:

> Representations of the present often depict contemporary man as a wounded, injured, disabled creature who exists in a world near-

> ing collapse. Distrust and inability to communicate are major characteristics of a life full of crisis, falseness, and hostility. [...] Stress is placed on the individual's lack of influence upon institutions such as government. The response to these conditions is a literature that seeks for escape into alternate worlds. (9-10)

It is interesting to note that the German writers of this time react against their society with a despairing and hopeless turn inward. Unlike society, which is depicted as an "harmonious" and relatively struggle-free society, the life of the individual is depicted as fraught with crisis and conflict in literature.

In contrast to Allende's message of optimism for political change, German literature reflects frustration with one's inability to influence the government. Jürgen Dormagen said in a personal interview that, at the time that Spanish American novels were becoming best sellers, German literature was "anemic," somewhat inflexible, and without passion (18 May 1989). He qualified his statement by saying that it is difficult simply to classify "*the* German literature" and "*the* Latin American literature." While I acknowledge the difficulties of generalizations, one must nevertheless recognize that there are trends in literature that vary country to country and from one language to another at any given time.

Many German readers of the 1980s were thus looking for literary diversion that did not deal with the cold world of urban reality, a mundane reality of supermarkets, the office, insurance, and so forth (Dormagen, personal interview 18 May 1989). What Germans found in Spanish American literature of the 1980s and '90s was quite different. They discovered a literature that is "vital, blutvoll, lebendig" (Bamberg, personal interview), "saftig, kraftvoll" (Wullschner, personal interview), and "spontan" (Janik, personal interview); they saw it as being filled with vitality, color, and emotions, usually set against a background with political and social--rather than individual--conflicts and struggles. When asked what was so different about the South American culture and its authors and what made both so attractive to the European, Dr. Barbara Osterkamp replied,

> Das Rohe und Unvermittelte; die Tatsache, daß dort das Leben noch direkt und authentisch wirkt.
>
> Der blasse Stadtneurotiker berauscht sich an den satten Farben. Der Bewohner des Elfenbeinturms genießt die Gewalt der Gefühle [...][1]

8.1 Polarity and Extremes

Allende has said in response to the comparison of her writing with that of García Márquez, "Schließlich leben wir beide in einer Welt gewaltiger Kontraste."[2] These contrasts give rise to powerful feelings, emotions, passions, and dreams, which then surface in Spanish American literature. German reviews concur with Allende's analysis linking these emotions to the popularity of her books in Germany:

> Isabel Allende hat wohl gar nicht so unrecht, wenn sie den Erfolg ihrer Bücher in Deutschland vor allem der Tatsache zuschreibt, daß sie von Gefühlen spricht.[3]

Throughout the reviews of the Spanish American best sellers, we find repeated references to extremes in the emotion-producing conditions of Latin American life:

Chronik eines angekündigten Todes:

> Leben und Tod sind Verwandte [...][4]

Geisterhaus:

> [...] ein Hinblick in eine Welt, in der Reichtum und Armut, Elend und Glanz, Verzweiflung und Freude eng nebeneinander wohnen.[5]

Eva Luna:

> [...] zwischen Diktatur und Demokratie sammeln sich um Eva Luna Typen gegensätzlichster Art vom geliebten Guerillero bis zum höchsten, um sie werbenden Vertreter der Staatsmacht, von der irren Mulattin bis zur liebevollen Oma-Negerin, vom fürsorglichen Transsexuellen bis zum gütigen, mit einer Hasenscharte geschlagenen Araber Riad Halabi.[6]

Geschichten der Eva Luna:

> Leidenschaft ist angesagt in diesen Geschichten. Heftige Gemütsbewegungen, Haß, Gewalttätigkeit werden begleitet von Zärtlichkeit, Erbarmen, Aufopferung und Nachdenklichkeit.[7]

Germans view Latin America to be a place where one easily encounters extremes in the form of life and death, riches and poverty, doubt and joy, dictatorship and democracy, guerrillas and powerful military personnel. In the

Spanish American texts, the juxtaposition of the contrastive elements has the effect of evoking corresponding emotions in the texts and in the German reader:

> *Mexikanischer Tango*:
>
> Ein [...] Wechselbad der Gefühle garantieren Catalina und Andrés [...] und die Könnerschaft der Autorin [...][8]
>
> *Von Liebe und Schatten*:
>
> Da mischen sich Ernst und unfreiwillige Komik [...][9]
>
> *Eva Luna*:
>
> *Eva Luna* ist für mich der witzigste und tragischste [...] Roman [...][10]
>
> *Liebe in den Zeiten der Cholera*:
>
> Mit ihm, mit dem traurig komischen Todessturz des Doktors Urbino auf der Jagd nach einem Papagei hat der Roman eingesetzt.[11]
>
> *General in seinem Labyrinth*:
>
> Die Augen voller Panik sehen den ungeheuerlichen Unterschied zwischen Realität und Fiktion, alles is Glanz, Schein, und Widerspruch. Eben das pulsiert in dem ganzen Stil des Romans, nicht nur in seinen unendlichen Gegenüberstellung von Gegesätzen auf allen Ausdrucksebenen, sondern auch in den Charakteren und Handlungen der Personen unter sich.[12]

The representative comments in reviews listed above reflect that aspect of Latin American life found less frequently in Germany: the close relationship between life and death, the comic and the serious, the witty and the tragic, reality and fiction. German critics were able to find polarities even in a novel as subdued and even-keeled as *Lob der Stiefmutter*:

> Ein Labyrinth um Liebe und Haß, um Schönheit und Häßlichkeit[13]
>
> [...] aber aus dem wachsenden Erbleichen des Vaters über des Sohnes Besinnungsaufsatz wird uns das ganze tragisch-(&)komische Ausmaß der stiefmütterlichen Zuneigung zum angeheirateten Eleven indirekt [...][14]

Even here the two diametrically opposed emotions of love and hate and the tragic and the comic are associated with the Spanish American novel.

8.2 Vitality, Color, and Spontaneity

The polarity perceived by Germans had the effect of also creating an appreciation for life reflected in vitality, color, and spontaneity. This is seen in the reviews in the frequent mention of "Vitalität, Fülle, und Farbigkeit" of Latin American literature (Dormagen, personal interview, 18 May 1989). The vibrancy of these novels is emphasized in the reviews, where the critics celebrate this vitality, abundance, liveliness, and color. The colorfulness of Spanish American life and its depiction in the novels is consistently noted by German critics:

> *Hundert Jahre Einsamkeit*:
>
> [...] um [...] ihm [dem Roman] unablässig Fülle, Farbe, Unterhaltung, Amüsement und Tragik mitzugeben [...][15]
>
> *Eva Luna*:
>
> Mit farbigen Worten und Wendungen voller Lebendigkeit malt die Literatin Bilderbögen und Portraits.[16]
>
> *General in seinem Labyrinth*:
>
> Das verspricht einiges an prallem Leben, Farbe und Fabulierkunst.[17]
>
> *General in seinem Labyrinth* ist ein spannender historischer Roman mit aktuellem Zeitbezug, [...] mit schönen Beschreibungen, farbigen Bildern und lebendigen Schilderungen, einfühlsame, ruhige Erzählung.[18]
>
> *Geschichten der Eva Luna*:
>
> Ein farbiges Bild Südamerikas entsteht [...][19]
>
> *Geisterhaus*:
>
> Ein wirklich großer, überaus faszinierender Roman, ein Bild mit kräftigen Farben.[20]

> Isabell [sic] Allende [...] erzählt diese Geschichte mit der den lateinamerikanischen Werken eigenen Farbigkeit und Lebendigeit [sic].[21]

Mexikanischer Tango:

> Mexiko! Da erwartet man donnerndes Leben, in einer Farbigkeit, wie man sie bei uns gar nicht kennt![22]

As seen above, the vibrancy of the colorful Latin American way of life as Germans perceive it to be is often combined with vivacity (*Lebendigkeit*), and both characteristics are thus obviously appreciated by the German readers. The consistency with which numerous forms of the expression *Farben* appear in the reviews is accompanied by a tendency for the reviewer to describe the novel as he would a painting. The critic is relating the written word in terms of the more concrete visual medium; the German concept of the Spanish American "farbige Realität" is one Germans are more likely to have seen in pictures and paintings than one they can relate to personally. The last two critiques are also evidence that Germans view colorfulness and vivacity in connection with Latin America and Latin American literature but not with Germany.

Even more than to color, Germans respond to the perceived *Lebendigkeit* and vitality in the Spanish American novels. Evidence that German critics found these qualities in *Geisterhaus, Eva Luna, General in seinem Labyrinth*, and *Mexikanischer Tango* was presented above. Critiques of other novels also reflect this appreciation:

Chronik eines angekündigten Todes:

> Ungemein kraftvoll ist diese Geschichte. [...] Eine Gesellschaft wird lebendig [...][23]

Von Liebe und Schatten:

> [...] [Allendes] Bücher, herzlich und lebensprall [...][24]

Liebe in den Zeiten der Cholera:

> Sehr vernünftig, höchst romantisch, tödlich und vital beendet Márquez den Roman, um damit noch einmal, als Sphinx und als Faun, auf höchster Höhe über allen Gegensätzen zu thronen.[25]

Lob der Stiefmutter:

> Mario Vargas Llosas neuer vitaler Roman. [...] Llosa läßt (mit den im Buch abgebildeten Gemälden) gierige Vitalität und Suche nach

der unmittelbaren Leidenschaft asynchron zur Geschichte verlaufen.[26]

In the above, we discover frequent variations on the expressions "lebendig" and "vital," indicating that this is a recurring aspect of these and other Spanish American novels to which German critics and readers are drawn. The review of *Liebe in den Zeiten der Cholera* attributes the vitality of García Márquez's writing to the concept of polarity, or antithesis, in his joining of "tödlich und vital" and his reference "auf höchster Höhe über allen Gegensätzen." The earlier review of *General in seinem Labyrinth* similarly discusses García Márquez's "unendlichen Gegenüberstellung von Gegensätzen."

Coupled with the notions of Latin American colorfulness, vivacity, and vitality are those of spontaneity and humanity. Heinrich Böll once wrote: "There exists in this land a fear known previously only in times of great epidemics: a fear of spontaneity, or naiveté" (312). Böll links spontaneity and naiveté with impulsive honesty and expressing one's emotions, all of which are viewed as anti-social behavior in Germany. German society's insistence on one's conformity to social conventions contrasts radically with the spontaneity in Latin American society and literature as Germans perceive it in the Spanish American best sellers. A critique of *Von Liebe und Schatten* comments on European society as an extension of German society:

> Jene "endlose Geschichte von Schmerz, Blut und Liebe" [...] das mögen wir halt manchmal doch gar zu gerne lesen, wir reflektierten, unspontanen, so gar nicht mehr instinktsicheren Europäer.[27]

Jörg Drews, the writer of this pronouncement, relates what many Germans consider to be their contemporary state of being. Although Drews's article is highly critical of Isabel Allende and particularly of *Von Liebe und Schatten*, he recognizes how the reflective and unspontaneous general European reading public could be drawn to qualities in Allende's writing. While Germans, as Europeans, consider themselves very reflective and premeditative, they praise the spontaneity that they perceive in Spanish American literature:

Hundert Jahre Einsamkeit:

> Die Schranken des konventionellen Realismus sind selten so spontan und überzeugend durchbrochen worden.[28]

Liebe in den Zeiten der Cholera:

> Und tatsächlich ist Márquez genau diese Quadratur des Kreises gelungen. Sie sieht über lange Strecken sogar so mühelos und spontan aus.[29]

The critics thus associate spontaneity with García Márquez's writing and how he ostensibly breaks through what they consider conventional literary lines. We observe here the reflection of a society in its literature, both in the perceived unrestrained and instinctive Spanish American life and literature and in the restrictive and reflective West German way of life and literature.

The final component that combines the feelings of vitality and spontaneity as a result of polarity in Latin American life is the phenomenon of the diverse natural occurrences in South America as perceived by Germans. Nature has already been discussed in the chapter on exoticism. Nevertheless, the emphasis on the extremes found in nature is worth noting in addition to its role as an element of exoticism.

The German reader encountered forces of nature and of *Urnatur* (tropical heat, earthquakes, deserts, jungles) without the "risk" perceived in earlier Spanish American works in which nature sometimes became the central "character" and in fact triumphed over human characters.[30] The various forms of nature in Latin America as represented in the Spanish American novels of the 1980s allowed the German reader to experience the adventure of going from a safe environment to one of moderate "risks." These encounters with extreme and different forms of nature are ones that fulfill certain needs of adventure, of experiencing the unknown, of vicarious risks for the West German reader, who lives in a relatively peril-free society.

Also of note is the German interest in the juxtaposition of nature and the technological worlds:

Geschichtenerzähler:

> Der im Einverständnis mit der Natur lebende Primative ist sogar Gegenbild für den von der Technik gejagten Großstadtmenschen [...][31]

> Welchen Platz lassen wir dem ganz anderen, wie es sich in der Welt der "Primitiven" zeigt und entzieht, in unserer "modernen" Gesellschaft?[32]

Geschichten der Eva Luna:

> [...] ist Lateinamerika nicht nur in europäischen, sondern auch in lateinamerikanischen Augen [...] der Schauplatz dieses unentweg-

> ten Ringens von Barbarei und Zivilisation, wie Simón Bolívar sagte, oder von Rückschrittlichkeit und Modernität, wie Entwicklungstheoretiker unserer Tage formulieren würden. Natürlich hat dieser Gegensatz lateinamerikanische Schriftsteller in seinen Bann geschlagen, und mit ihnen auch europäische Leser, wie der Siegeszug lateinamerikanischer Literatur auf dem hiesigen Buchmarkt beweist.[33]

In this review of *Geschichten der Eva Luna*, the critic links the writing of Isabel Allende, the theme of Vargas Llosa's *Geschichtenerzähler*, and the protagonist of Spanish American history in García Márquez's *General in seinem Labyrinth* to give one explanation for the success of Latin American literature in Germany.

8.3 Humanity

A comparable situation exists in the German attitude toward humanity, *Menschlichkeit*. The frequent references to *Menschlichkeit, Menschenkenntniss, menschlich*, etc. in the reviews of the Spanish American works indicate a felt loss of the human element in West Germany's highly industrialized, urban, capitalistic, and technological society, and a regret of this loss (Cobet, personal interview). In the Spanish American texts, Germans search for that element and find it. Latin America and its literature continued to fulfill a certain *Ersatzfunktion*, particularly for liberals:

> [...] dort schien die Umgestaltung der Gesellschaft, die sich [in Deutschland] nicht bewerkstelligen ließ, schon im Gange zu sein. Und da man sich mit dem schon verbürgerlichten deutschen Arbeiter nicht solidarisieren konnte, solidarisierte man sich mit der Masse der Ausgebeuteten Lateinamerikas, vor allem mit dem Indio (Botond, personal correspondence, 13 Sept. 1989).

Evidence of such solidarity may also be seen in German literature in the popularity of B. Traven's books, such as *Der Karren*, which depicts the life of Indians in America.

The importance the concept of humanity has for Germans is revealed in the fact that it can be found in titles of reviews like this of one of *Geisterhaus*:

> "Der menschliche Faktor"[34]

The human factor extends to the whole spectrum of figures in these novels, from main to minor characters:

> *Chronik eines angekündigten Todes*:
>
> Die Randfiguren werden zwar voll Ironie in ihren Schwächen geschildert, wie der Pfarrer, der Bürgermeister und der General. Am Schluß bleiben sie aber doch in ihrem jeweiligen Wahn verständlich und menschlich.[35]

This critic informs his audience that the human quality found in *Chronik* extends to the minor characters, that the author is capable of portraying even these figures with detailed idiosyncracies which convey their *Menschlichkeit*. Other reviews acclaim the knowledge that the Spanish American writers have of humanity and their representation of humanity in their works:

> *Geisterhaus*:
>
> Isabel Allendes abwägende, zugleich ungemein poetische Prosa, die Spannweite ihrer Welt- und Menschensicht läßt das Fadenspiel der Tragödie durchschaubar werden, sie schafft beklemmende Situationen, vermittelt Einblicke, ist frei von Klischees.[36]
>
> *Eva Luna*:
>
> [...] mit prallen Geschichten [...], die staunen lassen über diese Quelle der Erzählkunst voll Menschenkenntnis [...][37]
>
> *Liebe in den Zeiten der Cholera*:
>
> *Die Liebe in den Zeiten der Cholera*, der neue Roman des kolumbianischen Literaturnobelpreisträgers Gabriel García Márquez, ist ein ästhetisches Monument der Menschenkenntnis und der Menschenfreundlichkeit [...][38]
>
> [...] scheint er [García Márquez] uns in seiner Anmut, Weltklugheit, Menschenfreudlichkeit zuzurufen: Kein doppelter Boden. [...] Alles da, greifbar, sichtbar![39]

These reviews demonstrate the regard German critics have for Isabel Allende's and in Gabriel García Márquez's understanding of humanity and for the human factor that plays a large part in their novels. Neither author characterizes any of their antagonists as totally negative; some plausible explanation of their plight is given so that the audience attains some comprehension of the reasons behind their actions.

Another aspect of *Menschlichkeit* that Germans see in Allende's and García Márquez's novels is the frequent depiction of protagonists with human foibles. The best example is García Márquez's *General in seinem Labyrinth*, in which García Márquez shows the human side of a man who has been made almost superhuman with the passage of time:

> Die Figur des alten, allmählich resignierenden Bolívar jedoch wird sehr eindringlich dargestellt: eine lebendige Gestalt aus Fleisch und Blut jenseits des Heldenklischees.[40]

> [García Márquez] hat ihn [Bolívar] vom hohen Denkmalssockel herabgeholt und als Moribunden gezeigt, als einen Menschen mit seinen Stärken und Schwächen.[41]

> Trotz des ungewohnten Stils handelt der "neue" Márquez wieder von der menschlichen Seite der Krise Lateinamerikas--und ist insofern doch ein "alter" Márquez.[42]

The last critic sees not only the human side of García Márquez's main character in *General*, but also recognizes that one of the characteristics in García Márquez's writing is to make his characters human. We also detect the critic's perception that in *General* García Márquez had otherwise employed a style not anticipated by the German public.

Other critics recognize not just the Spanish American novelists' understanding of humanity, but also their call for humanity in their works:

Von Liebe und Schatten:

> Isabel Allendes Roman ist ein Appell zur Menschlichkeit, zur humanen Tat und Bedeutung der Liebe. Während hierzulande Liebe zur "Beziehung" und damit zum "Problem" degeneriert, ist Isabel Allendes Darstellung der Liebe eine Parabel des Widerstandes gegen die Willkür eines Despotenstaates.[43]

The critic here not only identifies Allende's appeal for humanity but also the distinction made in the meaning of "love" in *Von Liebe und Schatten* and in German society and literature. Allende was quoted in several reviews explaining her belief in love as a means of dealing with a problem:

> Die Liebe ist für mich wie ein Licht, das es erlaubt, mit der Gewalt zu leben, das Leben unter dem Zeichen der Gewalt erträglich macht.[44]

In the view of the critic mentioned above, love in Germany often develops into a problem. Love as a positive manifestation of humanity takes a prominent position in the Spanish American best sellers and contrasts with the above critic's opinion of love in German society.

A more explicit statement regarding the attitude perceived in West Germany toward humanity and its portrayal in literature compared with that perceived in Spanish America and its literature is found in this critique of *Geisterhaus*:

> Die Figuren leben. Welch ein Unterschied zur zeitgenössischen deutschen Literatur, bei der man immer wieder den Eindruck hat, daß die in ihr geschilderten Menschen gar nicht existieren.[45]

This idea of the "alive" characters contrasting to those barely existing figures in German literature brings us back to the German appreciation of *Lebendigkeit* and vitality in Spanish American literature.

While German critics consider the characters in Allende's three novels to be alive, little mention is made about them being so in her *Geschichten der Eva Luna*. Likewise, in at least one review of Vargas Llosa's *Geschichtenerzähler*, there is noted disappointment:

> Doch die Story ist allzu glatt, ihr fehlen lebendige Charaktere.[46]

References to polarity and extremes in Latin American life and nature are thus seen repeatedly in German critiques of Spanish American literature. Manifestations of polarity are the juxtaposition of opposites; vibrant colorfulness, vivacity, vitality, and feelings; spontaneity; humanity; and the more extreme forms of nature. These are not perceived to occur with such regularity in German life, nor in German literature or in literatures translated from most other languages. Their regular treatment in the Spanish American works discussed here thus accounts in part for the special attraction that Spanish American novels hold for the German reader. The Latin American best sellers display a wide range of polarity without such tremendous extremes that they become distasteful or "frightful" to Germans. By 1989, we find reactions of disappointment when the reader does not find the expected characteristics in subsequent Spanish American works.

Polarity, vitality, spontaneity, and humanity, which Germans perceive to be a function of Latin American life and literature, are, then, often concretized by readers in the form of sensual experiences, feelings, passions, and emotions, with which German readers can identify on a personal level. These characteristics are seen in Germany in connection with Spanish American literature and so collectively constitute the final feature of the Spanish American sub-genre as perceived in West Germany.

Notes

[1] Helmut Hein, "Eine andere Kultur," *Die Woche*, Regensburg, 15 Mar. 1990.

[2] Walter Haubrich, "Wo die Wirklichkeit phantastische Züge annimmt," *Frankfurt Allgemeine Zeitung* 26 Jan. 1985.

[3] Eva Karnofsky, "'Sie sind eine schlechte Journalistin' sagte Pablo Neruda . . . 'aber vielleicht geben Sie eine gute Romanautorin ab.'" *Börsenblatt* 13 Jan. 1989: 133.

[4] Lothar Schmidt-Mühlisch, "Ein Mord gegen den Willen der Täter," *Die Welt* 14 Oct. 1981.

[5] Heinz G. Konsalik, "Bücher für den Weihnachtstisch," Bayrische Rundfunk 23 Dec. 1984.

[6] Effi Horn, "Isabel Allende erzählt ihre prallen Geschichten," *Münchner Merkur* 2 Sept. 1988. Future references to this review will be noted as: Horn, "Allende erzählt."

[7] Wilfriede Eichler, "Haß, Gewalt und Leidenschaft," *Der Morgen*, Berlin, 31 Dec. 1990/1 Jan. 1991.

[8] Miriam Zink, "Generalsfrau im Dschungel der Politik," *Welt am Sonntag* 18 Sept. 1988: 57.

[9] Gisela Huwe, "Alltag in der Welt der Liebe und des Schattens," *Berliner Morgenpost* 7 Sept. 1986.

[10] Susanne Steufmehl, "*Eva Luna*," *Bücherei aktuell* (Munich) St. Michaelsbund 4 (1988).

[11] Reinhard Baumgart, "Eine schöne Bescherung," *Die Zeit* 1 May 1987. Future references to this article will appear as: Baumgart, "Bescherung."

[12] José Reina, "Triumph der Vergänglichkeit," *Buch Journal* I Frühjahr 1990.

[13] Claudia Theurer, "Ins Chaos der Lüste," *Abendzeitung* Munich 11 Aug. 1989: 14. Future references to this review will be noted as: Theurer, "Ins Chaos."

[14] Wolfram Schütte, "Ein bravouröses Kunststück über alles & nichts," *Frankfurter Rundschau* 5 Aug. 1989: ZB4.

[15] Karl Krolow, "Tropische Familien-Saga," *Süddeutsche Zeitung* 18 July 1970.

[16] Elisabeth Zeitler, "Exotisches Märchen," *Städtemagazin 'Plärrer'* 9 (1988).

[17] Rolf Brockschmidt, "Bolívars letzte Reise," *Tagespiegel* 31 Dec. 1989.

[18] "Portrait eines Menschen im Labyrinth seiner Leiden und verlorenen Träume," *Elmhorner Nachrichten* 26 May 1990.

[19] *Buch Journal* Heft 3/1990.

[20] Lorenz Tomerius, "Unerschöpfliche Phantasie," *Industriemagazin* Nov. 1984.

[21] Thomas Schreiner, "Sturz in die Barbarei," *Nürnberger Zeitung* 13 Apr. 1985.

[22] Bernhard Lassahn, "Tango in der mörderischen Macho-Welt--der preisgekrönte Roman von Angeles Mastretta," *Szene* Hamburg Aug. 1988.

[23] Günther Engels, "Die verlorene Ehre der Angela Vicario," *Kölnische Rundschau* 25 Nov. 1981.

[24] Jörg Drews, "Isabel Allende bei Suhrkamp," *Merkur* Dec. 1986: 1066. Future references to this review will be noted as: Drews, "Allende bei Suhkamp."

[25] Baumgart, "Bescherung."

[26] Theurer, "Ins Chaos," 14.

[27] Drews, "Allende bei Suhrkamp," 1068.

[28] Walter Haubrich, "*Hundert Jahre Einsamkeit*," *Frankfurter Allgemeine Zeitung* 8 May 1971.

[29] Baumgart, "Bescherung."

[30] See for example stories by the Uruguayan Horacio Quiroga and the Colombian José Rivera's *La Vorágine*.

[31] Christine Wischmann, "Was ein Schriftsteller im Urwald suchte," *Berliner Volksblatt* 29 July 1990. Even though this review appeared in a former East Berlin newspaper, it was written after the coming down of the Wall and by the West German critic who reviews Spanish American novels for the Deutsche Presse Agentur news wire service.

[32] "Züge einer Autobiographie," *Alfelder Zeitung* 11 Aug. 1990.

[33] Wolfgang Kunath, "Zwischen Natur und Kultur," *Stuttgarter Zeitung* 6 Nov. 1990.

[34] Helene Schreiber, "Der menschliche Faktor," *Rheinischer Merkur/Christ und Welt* 27 April 1984.

[35] Tom Königs, "Eine Novelle macht Furore," *Frankfurter Rundschau* 27 July 1981.

[36] Günther W. Lorenz, "Absage an die Verzweiflung," *Die Welt* 14 July 1984.

[37] Horn, "Allende erzählt."

[38] Jochen Hieber, "Der Hymnus der absoluten Liebe," *Frankfurter Allgemeine Zeitung* 31 Jan. 1987.

[39] Baumgart, "Bescherung."

[40] Walter Haubrich, "Der General in seinem Labyrinth," *Frankfurter Allgemeine Zeitung* 20 Apr. 1989.

[41] Hans F. Nöhbauer, "Der Held im Labyrinth der verlorenen Träume," *Welt am Sonntag* 8 Apr. 1990.

[42] Kalle Burmeister, "Das traurige Ende eines amerikanischen Traums," *Hamburger Morgenpost* 5 Dec. 1989.

[43] Sulamith Sparre, "Hoffnung auf Harmonie," *Nürnberger Zeitung* 2 Aug. 1986.

[44] Quoted here in Holger Schlodder, "Bekehrung wie in einer Legende," *Hannoversche Allgemeine Zeitung* 16/17 Aug. 1986.

[45] Bernhard Almes, "Der Tip des Buchhändlers," *Hamburger Abendblatt* 16 Aug. 1984: 20.

[46] Charlotte Bernau, "'Stürmische Wolke stößt an den Baum'--der magische Realismus," *Berliner Zeitung* 15/16 June 1991.

Chapter 9

Epilogue

Übrigens sind es ja gerade die Deutschen, seit neuestem meine zahlreichsten Leser, die dazu neigen, Geheimnisse in meinen Büchern unterzubringen. (Gabriel García Márquez, Die Welt 11 Jan. 1988)

It has been my purpose to study the cross-cultural reception of contemporary Spanish American best sellers in West Germany and by doing so to give support to the norm and deviation concept of genre by illustrating this specific case. The readership studied here is not exclusively that of the elite intellectual reader nor those who were already knowledgeable about Spanish American literature but rather that of the average West German reader. In order to answer the question of why these specific eleven works of fiction attained best seller status in West Germany during the 1980s and early '90s, factors both extrinsic and intrinsic to the novels were taken into account.

Readership of Spanish American literature in German translation among the general public was shown to have been minimal before the 1980s. Statistics attest to the fact that translations from Spanish into German remained behind translations from other European and Western Hemisphere languages during the '60s and '70s. This was found to be true in spite of the great number of offerings from Spain and Spanish America and in spite of the Latin American "boom," i.e., that time during the '60s of international recognition of Latin American literature. German Hispanists further attested to the West German lag behind other countries in the reception of this literature prior to the 1980s.

9.1 Extrinsic Factors

West German reception of Spanish American literature showed a dramatic increase during the '80s. This was found to be due in part to a variety of extrinsic circumstances, including the 1976 Frankfurt Book Fair, the Latin American Program at Suhrkamp, Berlin Horizonte 1982, the awarding of the 1982 Nobel Prize for Literature to García Márquez, the "Allende phenomenon" beginning in 1984, and political developments in Latin America. With the exception of the political events, which were also occasionally tied to literary production, all the other extrinsic factors dealt directly with literature. At the same time, the overall image of Latin America in West Germany--while perhaps more optimistic than it had been in earlier decades--remained for the most part negative during the 1980s, even though some countries, such as Argentina and Uruguay, were already taking steps toward democratic reforms. Thus, the increased interest in Latin America was primarily a literary phenomenon. West German publishers capitalized on this interest and effectively marketed the Spanish American novels for the targeted German audience.

The reception of Spanish American novels in West Germany was augmented in the '80s to the point that García Márquez and Isabel Allende singled out West Germans as being among their most numerous readers and avid fans. All four of Allende's works and every novel written by García Márquez since *Chronik eines angekündigten Todes* (1981) have become best sellers in West Germany.

9.2 Intrinsic Factors

The evidence indicates that the popularity of García Márquez and Allende was not an isolated phenomenon; it was no coincidence that Angeles Mastretta and Mario Vargas Llosa also became best-selling authors in West Germany during the latter half of the '80s and into the '90s. Intrinsic features associated with Spanish American writing also led to the success of Spanish American novels. West German reviews of Spanish American books mentioned "Latin American literature" as a definite type of literature that was in vogue as a consequence of intrinsic characteristics of the novels and that had attained popularity because of its distinctive literary features. Spanish American novels were viewed in West Germany as being a specific category of novel, and West German readers began to look for fiction with characteristics that those books written by Spanish American authors had to offer. Germans noted the trend toward Latin American literature as a type and recognized Latin America as a place producing quality writing:

> Immer mehr mittel- oder südamerikanische Autoren werden gelesen, da ist die Gefahr groß, minderwertige Mitläufer, vom Latinoboom profitierend, zu erwischen, die sich an den Erfolg der großen Vorbilder anhängen wollen.[1]

> Literarisch gilt Lateinamerika als Kontinent des Romans [...][2]

> LITERATURKONTINENT LATEINAMERIKA[3]

The Germans of the '80s were apparently ready for well written, quality literature that was at the same time accessible and made a point of simply telling a good story. German literature at that time was considered by many to be dry, inward-looking, and often overly didactic. In an article in *Spiegel*, German literature was described as attracting fewer readers as a result of its "langweilige Nabelschau, Innerlichkeit und Ichbesessenheit" as well as "[d]er reflektierende Stil, das Kreisen der Sprache um sich selbst."[4]

German literature of the '70s was often politically complex, and this gave way to the "Nabelschau" and often unreadable (Pracht-Fitzell, personal interview) qualities of works during the late '70s and '80s. Novelist Nicolas Born's *Die erdabgewandte Seite der Geschichte* (1976) and P. Handke's *Die Stunde der wahren Empfindung* (1975) mark the decade's *Tendenzwende* turn toward New Subjectivity and New Inwardness. Bernward Vesper's *Die Reise* (1977) takes the protagonist from political opposition to the isolated world of drugs. The new women's literature, together with works by older generation authors like Uwe Johnson (*Jahrestage* vol. 1-4) and Peter Weiss (*Ästhetik des Widerstands*), offers a certain counterbalance.

But in the '80s even this impulse of political-cultural commitment stagnates in favor of a concentration on private fear and New Motherhood, in short, New Obscurity ("Neue Unübersichtlichkeit," Jürgen Habermas). German literature was thus not meeting the needs of the general reading public. In the '90s in the area of belletristic literature, of approximately 9,000 titles produced in Germany, almost half were from abroad. In comparison, only 450 German works were "exported."[5]

In contrast, the ability of the Spanish American writers of the 1980s *zu erzählen*, not just to describe or teach, filled that gap for the average German reader, largely due to their ability to offer basic story-telling enhanced with other features sought by the German audience:

> Zutreffend scheint mir--was andere gesagt haben--daß die lateinamerikanische Literatur noch mehr erzählt als die deutsche Gegenwartsliteratur und daß sie welthaltiger ist [...][6]

Spanish American literature was able to offer the reading public political-, historical-, and social-oriented literature in a structure easily grasped by the general reading public. While none of the texts studied here is to be considered as explicitly political literature, there is a comprehensible political theme or background in the majority of them. The combination of the political message with the accessible story (in the form of structure, language, style, and characters) that is interesting for the general public allows a greater audience to be reached. In the case of West Germany, which had a deficit of both native popular political novels and of Spanish American literature reception prior to the '80s, the combination of politics and "massenwirksam" but sound story-telling within the Spanish American framework offered Germans what they were not finding elsewhere.

Before the 1980s, West Germans were not inclined to read about Spanish American politics; the image of Latin American politics at that time was a negative one of rightist dictatorships, torture, and exploitation. With dictators being turned out of office, democratic reform movements springing up, and elections taking place in the 1980s, however, hope for political change was added to the German image of Latin America. The fact that the novels discussed Spanish American politics, history, and culture in a realistic vein but often with an optimistic message supported the West German perception and desire for change.

The idea of a vicarious change, of "experiencing" another culture through its literature, was another appealing aspect for German readers. In contrast to the relative safety, harmony, and homogeneity of German life, Spanish American literature offered polarity, vitality, "risk," and very human and colorful characters. We observe in West German reviews of the Spanish American best sellers the frequency with which the critics exalt sharp contrasts by integrating the juxtaposition found in the works into their critiques. This celebration of vitality, spontaneity, and extremes in feelings and in nature takes place in a country in which one strives toward social conformity and in which one rarely experiences the types of natural phenomena that occur in Latin America. This is not to suggest that other countries do not experience the same sort of uniformity and homogeneity; however, this feature is seen readily in relation to the German situation.

Exoticism and magic realism are two more components that Germans considered to some extent to be inherent in Latin American literature. Many German Hispanists deem the perceived exotic and magical realism features of Spanish American literature as the principal enticements for the German general reading public to this literature, yet evidence indicates that the attraction of these qualities has been exaggerated. The general public was likely drawn to these features, but to a lesser extent and in less extreme forms than is generally assumed.

The German view of its own reality contrasted tremendously with its perception of that which is Latin America, as we have seen in the observed features and neatly summarized by Claudia Wiese:

> Die Lateinamerikaner setzen der deutschen Gleichformigkeit Exzessivität und Phantasie entgegen, der Farblosigkeit setzten sie Tupfer auf, der strengen Struktur und Ordnung setzen sie Maß-

> losigkeit und extreme verbale Flexibilität, der schwächer werdenden europäischen Erzählkraft etwas Eigenes und Einzigartiges entgegen. Anstatt der "tautologische[n] Klaustrophobie" einer Person aus der Feder Peter Handkes handeln ihre Geschichten (angeblich) von "Abenteuern dieser einfachen Menschen." "Fabulierfreudigkeit" und Geschichtenerzählen--lange vermißt in der deutschen Literatur--statt Kälte, Sterilität und Abstraktion. (*Die hispanoamerikanischen Boom-Romane* 109-10)

In reviewing the intrinsic characteristics of the novels as recounted by West German critics in conjunction with the scope of readership, we can see how often the German readers associated certain features with the Spanish American works.

9.3 The Reviews

A brief overview of the principal and most respected newspapers and magazines in West Germany reveals the general consistency with which the critics reviewed the eleven Spanish American best sellers. The critiques in these publications--*Frankfurter Allgemeine Zeitung*, *Frankfurter Rundschau*, *Der Spiegel*, *Süddeutsche Zeitung*, *Die Welt*, and *Die Zeit*--usually contained the most thorough analyses of the works. They also offered some continuity with regard to the reviewers, such as Walter Haubrich with the *Frankfurter Allgemeine Zeitung*, Dieter E. Zimmer with *Die Zeit*, Günter Lorenz with *Die Welt*, Wolfram Schütte with the *Frankfurter Rundschau*, and Albert von Schirnding with the *Süddeutsche Zeitung*. However, in no case did any one critic review all of the best sellers in the respective newspapers, so no definitive deductions regarding continuity can be made. Rather, generalizations can be observed.

The reviews of *Hundert Jahre Einsamkeit* and *Chronik eines angekündigten Todes* in the major publications were uniformly positive. It is interesting to note that Haubrich (*Frankfurter Allgemeine Zeitung*) and Tom Königs (*Frankfurter Rundschau*) discuss the universally accepted themes of *Chronik* as being fate and the machismo honor code; others--Walter Boehlich (*Der Spiegel*), Dieter E. Zimmer (*Die Zeit*), and Lothar Schmidt-Mühlisch (*Die Welt*)--recognize the theme of the honor code but place more emphasis on the theme of collective guilt.

In Haubrich's critique of *Geisterhaus*, he lists reasons for the popularity of the novel in Europe. These features are fairly complete and insightful; other reviewers offer comprehensive analyses of the book, but few come so close to discussing the actual reasons for the work's success in Europe. It was noted above that Haubrich was also one who identified the theme of fate in *Chronik*, one of the novel's more universally accepted themes, while some other German critics accentuated the theme of collective guilt. Haubrich's insight into Spanish American literature and its reception in Germany is one manifestation of the fact that during the 1980s a more knowledgeable German reading public had arisen, in contrast to the same public in prior decades.[7]

We notice the consistency with which the various publications rate *Liebe in den Zeiten der Cholera*, *Geisterhaus*, *Von Liebe und Schatten*, *Eva Luna*, *Geschichten der Eva Luna*, and *Lob der Stiefmutter*. For the most part, *Liebe* was either praised with some criticism or praised and criticized in equal portions, *Geisterhaus* and *Lob der Stiefmutter* were praised while *Liebe und Schatten*, *Eva Luna*, and *Geschichten der Eva Luna* were heavily criticized. *Mexikanischer Tango* received more mixed reviews, ranging from praise (Adriane Barth in *Spiegel*) to Verena Auffermann's very negative critique in the *Frankfurter Rundschau*.

The German response to *General in seinem Labyrinth* and *Geschichtenerzähler* are of note. While the reviews were positive, a number of critics record their belief that the public will be disappointed in the novels: The reader would encounter difficulties in the geographical and historical names and facts in *General in seinem Labyrinth* and in the Indian names and structure of *Geschichtenerzähler*,[8] and the texts did not offer the reader what he or she had come to expect in Latin American fiction. Both novels, together with *Geschichten der Eva Luna*, were on the best seller list for significantly shorter periods than previous novels by these three respective authors.

We can thus conclude that among the reviews of the Spanish American novels of the 1980s in the principal West German publications, little difference is found regarding whether the individual publications are considered conservative, moderate, or liberal.

9.4 Assessment of Theories and Methodologies

Having employed a neopositive approach to Jauß's reception aesthetics and genre theory, I can now evaluate their effectiveness in a cross-cultural reception study such as this one. These primary theories will be reviewed as follows: neopositivism, Jauß's reception aesthetics, his concept of concretization, and norm and deviation in genre theory.

Contemporary literary scholars in the West tend to prefer traditional philosophical, structuralist, and new critical in-depth analytical approaches. Hence, the neopositive investigation of best-selling novels tends to incur less favor with them. This approach, as I have applied it in Part I, nevertheless lends itself to the study of reception aesthetics, the study of the genre, and and the study of best sellers. Neopositivism examines the cultural-historical basis for judgment and interpretation of a literary work. It is used here to determine how the cultural-historical setting aided in the formation of the particular collective set of West German reader variables during the 1980s; the reader variables in turn influenced the German reception and interpretation of the Spanish American novels.

As discussed in the Introduction, the concept of the genre used here is based on historical and geographical factors and is used to classify this group of Spanish American novels. Jauß sees literary forms and genres as primarily social phenomena; they depend on functions in the lived world. Cultural-historical conditions thus provide the context for that lived world of the West Germans during the '80s and early '90s.

Finally, it was indicated that best sellers and society stand in direct relationship: Best sellers can reflect the hopes, dreams, and fantasies of a society as a whole during the time frame in which they become best sellers. Since they mirror cultural, social, historical, and political conditions (Arnold, *Bestseller* 5), they have been examined here through a neopositive approach.

Reception aesthetics offered a framework in which the collective set of reader variables could be observed in the West Germans' encounter with the Spanish American works of fiction and their respective text variables. West German reception of these Spanish American novels was shown to have been greater than in other European countries, and García Márquez and Allende have both noted the exceptional West German readership of their works. The aggregate set of variables then influenced the particular West German readings of the Spanish American books and led to interpretations and observations at times unique to West Germans.

Reception aesthetics demonstrates the interaction between the production of the work, the work itself, and the audience, i.e., the interaction between the audience's set of expectations and its reception of that work, which then influences future production of later works. Cross-cultural contemporary reception introduces new considerations into this triadic model. The Spanish American authors do receive feedback from their readers in West Germany, directly through readings there and letters from German readers and indirectly from agents' reports, sales statistics and so forth. But it is almost impossible to determine how and to what degree this cross-cultural feedback influences future production. Furthermore, since I was studying works written for the most part during the last ten years, I was not able to utilize the historical perspective that helps discern clearer patterns in reception and its influence on future production.

The distinction is thus made between the primary intracultural influence and secondary cross-cultural influence toward future production and continued reception. "Intracultural" feedback from within Spanish America is also problematic. The individual countries of Spanish-speaking America do not comprise a single cultural unit: Reader variables will vary from country to country within Latin America. The issue of feedback is additionally complicated by the Chilean author Allende living in Venezuela and the United States and the Colombian writer García Márquez living in Mexico. Even though Latin America is made up of many different cultures, the German reading public considers it to be a homogenous cultural unit. This impression often leads to German perception of Latin American stereotypical characteristics which are continuously reinforced by the Spanish American literature selectively read by the public.

Thus, in examining contemporary cross-cultural reception, Jauß's theory provides a practical procedure except for the final stage. This final step of reception conventions, which then influences future prose production, needs adjustment in an international context. German reader feedback to authors had minimal influence on future production of Spanish American works. Instead, German reaction to Latin American literature chose which future texts from Latin America would be translated, marketed, bought, read, and reviewed by the receiving culture. The process reinforced and crystallized the German set of impressions and expectations of Latin American literature; and these perceptions, when viewed through the eyes of a different social, political, cultural, and historical context, created a new concept of the literature from the producing culture.[9] The situation of Spanish American best sellers in Germany can be used as a case study to see how the final phase in Jauß's cycle can thus unfold along even more complex lines within the cross-cultural context and may thereby produce a newly conceived genre.

More helpful in this study was Jauß's notion of concretization, that public and accepted view of an author or work. Concretization can be established by evidence of the extent of an audience and critical reactions to a text. The best seller status of all the Spanish American works displayed some testimony of the extent of the West German audience, while the reviews offered consistencies in their descriptions and interpretations of the novels.

Although there are difficulties in determining how any group of readers in fact receives and perceives a novel, the corpus of reviews renders a viable and researchable set of data. I found perceptions emanating from the West German--and particularly post-World War II--situation; and these perceptions contributed to the set of variables exemplifying that link in cross-cultural reception. West Germans did indeed receive these works more than did readers in most other non-Latin American countries, and the union of text variables and German reader variables contributed to new interpretations of the novels. Furthermore, consistencies in the descriptions and interpretations of the novels demonstrated those expectations that West Germans had concerning these Spanish American best sellers collectively.

The application of the genre theory used here enabled me to consider how the West Germans perceive the Spanish American works as a group. The manner in which the reviews consistently described the works in certain terms demonstrates how the Germans considered the texts to have similar characteristics. A pattern of reception of the Spanish American books was established based on the German expectation of these similar features. In a few cases, critics interpreted a perceived characteristic as inherent in one work, while other evidence (interviews with authors, Spanish American critics' interpretation of the works, etc.) does not indicate such a feature of that book. Such is the case, for example, of the "political message" of Vargas Llosa's *Lob der Stiefmutter*.

The West German readers came to expect the shared qualities and continued to buy and read the Spanish American novels on this basis. Each new work reinforced for the Germans the set of similarities while at the same time offering variation. The West German publishers, media, and critics promoted the concept of these shared features for the reader; and the works assumed a perceived genre quality in West Germany. Genre theory, then, proved to be a valuable means of investigating the reception of this collective set of the Spanish American works in West Germany.

9.5 Final Comments

From the material that I have presented, several final observations can be made.

Of the eleven texts that I examined, Gabriel García Márquez's *Hundert Jahre Einsamkeit* has already established itself as a "classic" on the international literary scene as well as in Germany. Isabel Allende's *Geisterhaus* was frequently compared to *Hundert Jahre Einsamkeit* in many German reviews. Although *Geisterhaus* was never considered a better work than *Hundert Jahre Einsamkeit*, there are strong indications (sales figures and length of time on the best seller list) that *Geisterhaus* was much more widely read in West Germany than was *Hundert Jahre Einsamkeit* among the general reading public. Allende's first novel thus helped to popularize Spanish American novels.

Together, *Hundert Jahre Einsamkeit* and *Geisterhaus* aided in establishing the qualities that would come to be associated by West German readers with Spanish American novels. *Von Liebe und Schatten*, *Eva Luna*, and *Geschichten der Eva Luna* were considered to have many of the same characteristics encountered in *Geisterhaus*, and *Liebe in den Zeiten der Cholera* combined features that Germans found in *Hundert Jahre Einsamkeit* and *Geisterhaus*. Advertising for *Chronik eines angekündigten Todes* was built in part on reference to the already highly acclaimed *Hundert Jahre Einsamkeit*. Mastretta's *Mexikanischer Tango* was very often compared to Allende's works. García Márquez's *General in seinem Labyrinth* was very different from his previous novels. German critics nevertheless found association with his earlier works (e.g., in this review title: "Chronik eines Seite für Seite angekündigten Todes"[10]) and more so in name recognition and in the genre-type of literary qualities which terms like "unverkennbar 'garciamarquesisch'" elicit.[11] Vargas Llosa's *Lob der Stiefmutter* and *Geschichtenerzähler* are evidence of the continued popular trend of the Spanish American novel in the late 1980s and early '90s. Thus, the German public's ability to relate these novels to one another may be viewed as a function of the perceived sub-genre.

The West German general reading audience was searching for certain features that it found in the Spanish American best sellers, and the elements were collectively associated with the works, which therefore came to be perceived in West Germany as if they constituted a distinct genre. At least two noted critics, Jörg Drews and Joachim Kaiser, intimated that Allende's works would not have been published by Suhrkamp Verlag had they been written by an equivalent German writer.[12] This would suggest that Suhrkamp Verlag realized the potential market needs that were not being met in other literary works and that these needs were met in Allende's works.

The reviews of *Mexikanischer Tango* consistently compared Mastretta with Allende and noted the similar marketing of their works by Suhrkamp. This indicates the critics' views that Suhrkamp purposefully built the marketing strategy for Mastretta's work on that of Allende's works. This idea contributes to the notion of Spanish American literature being viewed and treated as a separate type, or sub-genre, of literature in West Germany.

Reviews of *General in seinem Labyrinth*, *Geschichtenerzähler*, and *Geschichten der Eva Luna* registered disappointment or anticipated disillusionment on the part of the general reading public. *General in seinem Labyrinth* and *Geschichtenerzähler* presented the German reader with a number of cultural impediments and deviations from the perceived norm, while *Geschichten der Eva Luna* offered little variation from her preceding work *Eva Luna*. Many reviews simply list the characteristics--the same features repeatedly--such as in the following review:

> [...] 23 Geschichten, in denen Erotik, Leidenschaft, Liebe, Gewalt, das zwischenmenschliche Miteinander, der südamerikanische Dschungel, das Geld und die Armut dominieren.[13]

German disappointment is marked by the shorter length of time that these texts were on the best seller list and likely indicated the end of the Latin American literary trend in Germany.

Several of the Spanish American novels elicited special readings particular to West Germany through the critics. Especially noteworthy are the German readings of *Geisterhaus* and *Chronik eines angekündigten Todes*. The reviews of *Geisterhaus* repeatedly refer to "overcoming the past," a phrase which appears to be a product specifically of the West German post-World War II situation. In fact, Allende wrote the novel in order not to forget the past.[14] *Chronik eines angekündigten Todes* was also shown to reflect the theme of collective guilt, a troubling philosophical issue much on the mind of post-World War II West Germans.

The West German interest in Spanish American novels during the 1980s and early '90s was thus the result of better preparation, a literary system that successfully marketed and promoted the Spanish American works for the West German public, and a set of perceived features that met certain literary needs of the West German readers. These literary characteristics as discerned by the West Germans show how the aggregate set of variables of the readers from a common cultural background can influence the interpretation of a literary work. This study has therefore examined cross-cultural reception aesthetics and demonstrated that the process can create new perceived interpretations, themes, and sub-genres.

Notes

[1] Ennelyn Schmidt, "Warten auf den Tod," *Stadtblatt Osnabrück* Oct. 1988.

[2] Jan-Barra Hentschel, "Eigenständige Tradition mit Weltgeltung," *Harburger Anzeiger und Nachrichten* 2 Feb. 1991.

[3] Found on a bookmark and a brochure marketed by Suhrkamp Verlag for bookstores to give to their customers.

[4] "Gedankenschwere Nabelschau," *Spiegel* 12 (1992): 263.

[5] "Gedankenschwere," 260.

[6] Botond 13 Sept. 1989. Professor Dieter Janik, translator Monika López, and Kiepenheuer & Witsch editor Bärbel Flad also echoed this sentiment to me.

[7] Rafael Gutiérrez Girardot would undoubtedly disagree with this statement. In his article "Borges in Germany" in *Borges and his Successors. The Borgesian Impact on Literature and the Arts*, edited by Edna Aizenberg (Columbia: University of Missouri Press, 1990), 59-79, he writes that Haubrich's 1976 article "Dichter sollte man erschiessen: Die seltsamen Ansichten des Jorge Luis Borges" revealed "a painful lack of critical penetration, an intellectual dishonesty, a total unawareness of Borges's characteristic irreverence, and a complete ignorance of the simplest facts of literary sociology" (69). In contemplating Gutiérrez Girardot's reasoning, we find that his assessment may indeed be correct, at least to the point that Haubrich lacked comprehension of Borge's irreverence. We must then question the difference between Haubrich's article on Borges in the mid-1970s and those written by Haubrich on Spanish American novels in the 1980s. It may be that time has aided Haubrich's judgment or that his deficient understanding of the complicated Borgesian way of thinking may have been an isolated situation.

[8] See, for example, Hanspeter Brode, "Sprung in den Dschungel," *Frankfurter Allgemeine Zeitung* 16 Mar. 1991.

[9] I would like to thank Dr. Vittoria Borsò for her thoughts on this subject.

[10] Andrea Köhler, *Badische Zeitung* 26 Feb. 1990.

[11] Dieter E. Zimmer, "Der Held in der Hängematte," *Die Zeit* 2 June 1989.

[12] Jörg Drews, "Isabel Allende bei Suhrkamp," *Merkur* Dec. 1986: 1069 and Joachim Kaiser, "Die neue Lust am kulinarischen Roman," *Stern* 16 Feb. 1989: 71.

[13] Susanne E. Giegerich, "Eva Luna zum Zweiten," *Aachener Nachrichten* 29 Dec. 1990.

[14] Uta M. Reindl, "Schwieriger Weg in die Literatur," *Kölner Stadt-Anzeiger* 16 Nov. 1984: 22.

Bibliography

Works Cited

Allende, Isabel. *Eva Luna.* Trans. Lieselotte Kolanoske. Frankfurt/M: Suhrkamp Verlag, 1988.

---. *Das Geisterhaus.* Trans. Anneliese Botond. Frankfurt/M: Suhrkamp Verlag, 1984, 1988. Trans. of *La casa de los espíritus.* 1982.

---. *Geschichten der Eva Luna.* Trans. Lieselotte Kolanoske. Frankfurt/M: Suhrkamp Verlag, 1990. Trans. of *Cuentos de Eva Luna.* 1990.

---. *Von Liebe und Schatten.* Trans. Dagmar Ploetz. Frankfurt/M: Suhrkamp Verlag, 1986, 1988. Trans. of *De amor y de sombra.* 1984.

Allport, Floyd Henry. *Social Psychology.* Boston: Houghton Mifflin Co. 1924.

Arnold, Heinz Ludwig, ed. *Deutsche Bestseller--Deutsche Ideologie.* Stuttgart: Ernst Klett, 1975.

Bangerter, Lowell A. *German Writing Since 1945. A Critical Survey.* New York: Continuum Publishing Company, 1988.

Böll, Heinrich. *Aufsätze, Kritiken, Reden.* Cologne: Kiepenheuer & Witsch Verlag, 1967.

Börsenverein der Deutschen Buchhandels, E.V., ed. *Buch und Buchhandel in Zahlen.* Ausgaben 1979-1988. Frankfurt/M: Buchhändler-Vereinigung GmbH, 1979-1991.

Boulding, Kenneth, E. "National Images and International Systems." *International Politics and Foreign Policy.* Ed. James N. Rosenau. New York: The Free Press, 1969. 422-431.

Broyles, Yolanda Julia. *The German Response to Latin American Literature and the Reception of Jorge Luis Borges and Pablo Neruda.* Heidelberg: Carl Winter Universitätsverlag, 1981.

Bullivant, Keith. *Realism Today. Aspects of the Contemporary West German Novel.* New York: St. Martin's Press, 1987.

von Bülow, Gabrielle, et al. "Roßtäuschung. Hildegard Knefs *Der geschenkte Gaul.* Analyse des Bestsellers und seiner Aufnahme." Arnold 7-40.

Castellanos, Helga. "Das Lateinamerikabild der Deutschen und das Deutschlandbild der Lateinamerikaner." *Zeitschrift für Kulturaustausch.* 24 (4) 1974: 54-56.

Cowley, Malcolm. "Classics and Best-Sellers." *The New Republic* 22 Dec. 1947: 25-27.

Daus, Ronald. "Der deutsche Leser und seine Schwierigkeiten mit einer fremden Realität." *Zeitschrift für Kulturaustausch--Lateinamerika-Colloquium 1976* 24 (1) 1977: 53-57.

---. Quoted in "Colloquiums-Protokoll." *Zeitschrift für Kulturaustausch--Lateinamerika-Colloquium 1976* 24 (1) 1977: 75.

Desleal, Alvaro Menén. "Zur Situation der lateinamerikanischen Literatur in den Ländern deutscher Sprache." *Zeitschrift für Kulturaustausch* 24 (1) 1974: N. pag.

Engelsing, Rolf. *Der Bürger als Leser. Lesergeschichte in Deutschland 1500-1800.* Stuttgart: J. B. Metzler, 1974.

Escarpit, Robert. *The Book Revolution.* London: Harrap, 1966.

Faulstich, Werner. *Bestandsaufnahme Bestseller- Forschung. Ansätze - Methoden - Erträge.* Wiesbaden: Otto Harrassowitz, 1983.

---. *Domänen der Rezeptionsanalyse. Probleme, Lösungsstrategien, Ergebnisse.* Kronberg/Ts.: Athenäum Verlag, 1977.

---. *Thesen zum Bestseller-Roman. Untersuchung britischer Romane des Jahres 1970.* Bern: Herbert Lang, 1974.

Faulstich, Werner and Ricarda Strobel. *Bestseller als Marktphänomen. Ein quantitiver Befund zur internationalen Literatur 1970 in allen Medien.* Wiesbaden: Otto Harrassowitz, 1986.

Fricke, Harald. *Norm und Abweichung. Eine Philosophie der Literatur.* Munich: Verlag C. H. Beck, 1981.

Friedl Zapata, José A. "Die Rolle der Literaturkritik bei der Rezeption lateinamerikanischer Literatur in den deutschsprachigen Ländern." *Zeitschrift für Kulturaustausch--Lateiname-rica-Colloquium 1976* 24 (1) 1977: 77-80.

García Márquez, Gabriel. *Chronik eines angekündigten Todes.* Trans. Curt Meyer-Clason. Cologne: Kiepenheuer & Witsch Verlag, 1981. Trans. of *Crónica de una muerte anunciada.* 1981.

---. *Der General in seinem Labyrinth.* Trans. Dagmar Ploetz. Cologne: Kiepenheuer & Witsch, 1989. Trans. of *El general en su laberinto.* 1989.

---. *Hundert Jahre Einsamkeit.* Trans. Curt Meyer-Clason. Cologne: Kiepenheuer & Witsch Verlag, 1970. Trans. of *Cien años de soledad.* 1967.

---. *Die Liebe in den Zeiten der Cholera.* Trans. Dagmar Ploetz. Cologne: Kiepenheuer & Witsch Verlag, 1987. Trans. of *El amor en los tiempos del cólera.* 1985.

"Gedankenschwere Nabelschau." *Spiegel* 12 (1992): 258-63.

Glotz, Peter. *Buchkritik in deutschen Zeitungen.* Hamburg: Verlag für Buchmarkt-Forschung, 1968.

Göpfer, Herbert G. *Vom Autor zum Leser. Beiträge zur Geschichte des Buchwesens.* Munich: Carl Hanser Verlag, 1977.

Grimm, Reinhold and Jost Hermand, eds. *Popularität und Trivialität.* Frankfurt/M: Athenäum Verlag, 1974.

Gutiérrez Girardot, Rafael. "Borges in Germany. A Difficult and Contradictory Fascination." *Borges and His Successors. The Borgesian Impact on Literature and the Arts.* Ed. Edna Aizenberg. Columbia: University of Missouri Press, 1990. 59-79.

---. "La recepción de la literatura latinoamericana en la República Federal Alemana." *Humboldt* 30 (97) 1989: 26-33.

Heller, Heinz B. "Literatur als Institution in der BRD." *Tendenzen der deutschen Gegenwartsli-teratur.* 2nd ed. Ed. Thomas Koebner. Stuttgart: Alfred Kröner Verlag, 1984. 446-99.

Hermand, Jost. *Kultur im Wiederaufbau. Die Bundesrepublik Deutschland 1945-1965.* Munich: Nymphenburger Verlagshandlung, GmbH, 1986.

Heydenreich, Titus, ed. *Der Umgang mit dem Fremden. Beiträge zur Literatur aus und über Lateinamerika.* Lateinamerika Studien 22. München: Wilhelm Fink Verlag, 1986.

Hintzenberg, Dagmar, Siegfried J. Schmidt, and Reinhard Zobel. *Zum Literaturbegriff in der Bundesrepublik Deutschland.* Wiesbaden: Friedr. Vieweg & Sohn, 1980.

Hohendahl, Peter Uwe. "Promoter, Konsumenten und Kritiker. Zur Rezeption des Bestsellers." *Popularität und Trivialität.* Eds. Reinhold Grimm and Jost Hermand. Frankfurt/M: Athenäum Verlag, 1974. 169-209.

Hübner, Hans. "Lateinamerika--Berichterstattung im Fernsehen." Wilke 73-90.

Hübner, Raoul. "Der diffamierte-integrierte 'Anarchismus.' Zu Heinrich Bölls Erfolgsroman *Gruppenbild mit Dame.*" Arnold 113-44.

Jauß, Hans Robert. *Aesthetic Experience and Literary Hermeneutics.* Trans. Michael Shaw. Minneapolis: University of Minnesota Press, 1982.

---. "Interaction Patterns of Identification Patterns with the Hero." *Aesthetic Experience and Literary Hermeneutics.* Trans. Michael Shaw. Minneapolis: University of Minnesota Press, 1982. 152-188.

---. *Literaturgeschichte als Provokation.* Frankfurt: Suhrkamp Verlag, 1970. Published in English as "Literary History as a Challenge to Literary Theory." In *Toward an Aesthetic of*

Reception. Trans. Timothy Bahti. Minneapolis: University of Minnesota Press, 1982, 3-45.

---. "Racines und Goethes Iphigenia. Mit einem Nachwort über die Partialität der rezeptionsästhetischen Methode." *Neue Hefte für Philosophie* 4 (1973): 1-46.

---. "Theory of Genres and Medieval Literature." Bahti 76-109.

King, Lynda J. *Best-Sellers by Design. Vicki Baum and the House of Ullstein.* Detroit: Wayne State University Press, 1988.

Koebner, Thomas, ed. *Tendenzen der deutschen Gegenwartsliteratur.* 2nd edition. Stuttgart: Alfred Kröner Verlag, 1984.

Lauterbach, Burkhart R. *Bestseller. Produktions- und Verkaufsstrategien.* Tübingen: Tübinger Vereinigung für Volkskunde E.V. Schloß, 1979.

Lorenz, Günter W. "Lateinamerika-Colloquium 1979 oder Bilder, Gleichnisse und Wirklichkeiten zweier Welten." *Zeitschrift für Kulturaustausch--Lateinamerika-Colloquium 1979* 30 (1) 1980: 4-8.

---. "Zur Krise der Rezeption lateinamerikanischer Literatur in den Ländern deutscher Spache." *Zeitschrift für Kulturaustausch* 24 (4) 1974. 98-100.

Machill, Horst. "Das Weihnachtsgeschäft des Sortimentsbuchhandels 1968." *Börsenblatt* 25 (1969): 593-619.

Marjasch, Sonja. *Der amerikanische Bestseller. Sein Wesen und seine Verbreitung unter besonderer Berücksichtigung der Schweiz.* Bern: Verlag A. Francke AG., 1946.

Mastretta, Angeles. *Mexikanischer Tango.* Trans. Monika López. Frankfurt/M: Suhrkamp Verlag, 1988. Trans. of *Arráncame la vida.* 1986.

Mertin, Ray-Güde. "Desbrozando el camino a la literatura latinoamericana en Alemania. La labor de una agente literaria." *Humboldt* 30 (97) 1989: 38-45.

Meyer-Clason, Curt, ed. *Lateinamerika über Europa.* Frankfurt: Suhrkamp, 1987.

---. "Möglichkeiten und Grenzen der Vermittlung lateinamerikanischer Kultur in Deutschland." *Zeitschrift für Kulturaustausch* 24 (4) 1974. 101-103.

Minta, Stephen. *Gabriel García Márquez: Writer of Colombia.* London: Jonathan Cape Ltd., 1987.

Mott, Frank Luther. *Golden Multitudes.* New York: Macmillan, 1947.

Müller, Hans Joachim. "Die Rolle der Literatur in Lateinamerika und ihre Möglichkeiten als Medium des Kulturaustausches mit Europa." *Zeitschrift für Kulturaustausch--Lateinamerika-Colloquium 1976* 24 (1) 1977: 49-52.

Ojeda, Jorge Arturo. "Amerika ist Europa." *Lateinamerika über Europa.* Ed. Curt Meyer-Clason. Frankfurt/M: Suhrkamp Verlag, 1987. 178-80.

Quandt, Siegfried. "Die Bundesrepublik Deutschland und Lateinamerika--Kommunikationsverhältnisse, Images." Wilke 136-42.

Rectanus, Mark W. *Literary Series in the Federal Republic of Germany from 1960 to 1980.* Wiesbaden: Otto Harrassowitz, 1984.

Reichardt, Dieter. "Bestandsaufnahme der Rezeption lateinamerikanischer Literatur in den Ländern deutscher Sprache." *Zeitschrift für Kulturaustausch--Lateinamerika-Colloquium 1976* 24 (1) 1977: 64-69. Published in Spanish as "Inventario de la recepción de la lectura latinoamericana en los paises de habla alemana." *En busca del texto. Teoría de la recepción literaria.* Ed. Dietrich Rall. Universidad Nacional autónoma de México: Mexico City, 1987. 423-434.

Rollka, Bodo. *Vom Elend der Literaturkritik. Buchwerbung und Buchbesprechung in der "Welt am Sonntag."* Berlin: Verlag Volker Spiess, 1975. Schnell, Ralf. *Die Literatur der Bundesrepublik. Autoren, Geschichte, Literaturbetrieb.* Stuttgart: J. B. Metzlersche Verlagsbuchhandlung, 1986.

Schonauer, Franz. "Die Prosaliteratur der Bundesrepublik." *Literatur Nach 1945 I. Politische und Regionale Aspekte.* Ed. Jost Hermand. Wiesbaden: Athenaion Akademische Verlagsgesellschaft, 1979. 250-72.

Seger, Imogen. "Bestseller-Soziologie--eine Forderung unserer Zeit." *Für Willi Droemer zum 18 July 1971.* Munich: N. p., 1971. 191-194.

Siebenmann, Gustav. "Das Lateinamerikabild in deutschsprachigen literarischen Texte'." G. Siebenmann and Hans-Joachim König, eds. *Das Bild Lateinameriamerikas im deutschen Sprachraum.* Tübingen: Max Niemeyer Verlag, 1992 (Beiheft zur *Iberoromania*, 3d. 8). 1881-207.

---. *Die neuere Literatur Lateinamerikas und ihre Rezeption im deutschen Spachraum.* Berlin: Colloquium Verlag, 1972.

Siebenmann, Gustav and Donatella Casetti. *Bibliographie der aus dem Spanischen, Portugiesischen und Katalanischen ins Deutsche übersetzten Literatur 1945-1983.* Tübingen: Max Niemeyer Verlag, 1985.

"*Spiegel*--Bestsellerliste: Orientierung für Millionen. Woche für Woche mit dem Computer ermittelt." *Buchreport* 5 Oct. 1988: 34-35.

Strausfeld, Mechtild. "Die großen Multiplikatoren: Autorentreffen, Festivals, Messen und andere Zusammenkünfte." Forthcoming in *Begegnungen in 500 Jahren. Lateinamerika und Deutschland.* Eds. D. Briesemeister, K. Kohut, G. Siebenmann. Frankfurt/M: Vervuert Verlag.

---. "Lateinamerikanische Literatur in Deutschland. Schwierigkeiten und Kriterien für ihre Vermittlung und Veröffentlichung." *Iberoamérica. Historia - sociedad - literatura. Homenaje a Gustav Siebenmann. Tomo II.* Eds. José Manuel López de Abiada and Tutus Heydenreich. Munich: Wilhelm Fink Verlag, 1983. 927-39.

Sutherland, John. *Bestsellers. Popular Fiction of the 1970s.* London: Routledge & Kegan Paul Ltd., 1981.

Tellechea, Juan Carlos. "Das Bild Lateinamerikas in der Bundesrepublik Deutschland." Wilke 116-20.

Timm, Uwe. "Zwischen Unterhaltung und Aufklärung." *Kürbiskern* 1 (1972): 79-90.

Unseld, Siegfried. *The Author and His Publisher.* Trans. Hunter Hannum and Hildegarde Hannum. Chicago: University of Chicago Press, 1980.

Vargas Llosa, Mario. *Der Geschichtenerzähler.* Trans. Elke Wehr. Frankfurt/M: Suhrkamp Verlag, 1990. Trans. of *El hablador.* 1987.

---. *Lob der Stiefmutter.* Trans. Elke Wehr. Frankfurt/M: Suhrkamp Verlag, 1989. Trans. of *Elogio de la madrastra.* 1988.

Wagner de Reyna, Alberto. "Hindernisse für das Verständnis zwischen Lateinamerika und den deutschsprachigen Ländern." *Zeitschrift für Kulturaustausch--Lateinamerika-Colloquium 1976* 24 (1) 1977: 75.

Wiese, Claudia. *Die hispanoamerikanischen Boom-Romane in Deutschland. Literaturvermittlung, Buchmarkt, und Rezeption.* Frankfurt/M: Vervuert Verlag, 1992.

---. "La recepción de la literatura hispanoamericana del 'boom' en Alemania." *Hispanorama* Mar. 1989: 50-53.

Wilke, Jürgen and Siegfried Quandt, eds. *Deutschland und Lateinamerika. Imagebildung und Informationslage.* Frankfurt: Vervuert, 1987.

Zeller, Nancy Anne McClure. "Ulrich Becher: A Computer-Assisted Case Study of the Reception of an Exile." Diss. U of Texas, 1981.

Zimmer, Dieter E. "Die Diktatur der Bestseller. Steht der Büchermarkt vor dem Ruin?" *Die Zeit* 15 Oct. 1971: N. pag.

---. "'Die Herzen großer Publikumszahlen . . .' Über die Karriere eines Bestsellers." *Literaturbetrieb in Deutschland.* Ed. Heinz Ludwig Arnold. Munich: Richard Boorberg Verlag, 1976. 98-134.

Zimmermann, Bernhardt. "Das Bestseller-Phänomen im Literaturbetrieb der Gegenwart." *Neues Handbuch der Literaturwissenschaft: Literatur nach 1945, II: Themen und Genres.* Ed. Jost Hermand. Wiesbaden: Akademische Verlagsgesellschaft Athenaion, 1979. 99-123.

Personal Contacts

The following are entries of personal interviews except where indicated as correspondence or as conducted by telephone.

Allende, Isabel, novelist. Frankfurt/M, 3 June 1989.
Arias, Arturo, writer and professor. University of Texas at Austin, 4 April 1990.
Bamberg, Maria, translator. Berlin, 3 April 1989. Letter, 24 June 1989.
Böhringer, Wilfried, translator. Saarbrücken, 27 Feb. 1989.
Borsò, Vittoria, professor. Mannheim, Erpolzheim, in June 1989 and 31 May 1992.
Botond, Anneliese, translator (*Geisterhaus*). Letter, 2 July 1989. Letter 13 Sept. 1989.
Buch, Hans Christoph, novelist. Telephone interview, 26 July 1989.
Cobet, Christoph, book dealer. Frankfurt/M, 9 Dec. 1988.
Dormagen, Jürgen, editor, head of the Latin American Program at Suhrkamp Verlag. Frankfurt/M, 18 May and 31 May 1989, 4 June 1992. Telephone interviews 12 Feb. 1990 and 1 July 1991.
Dorn, Knut, book dealer, Otto Harrassowitz. Wiesbaden, 21 Feb 1989.
Flad, Bärbel, foreign editor, Kiepenheuer & Witsch Verlag. Cologne, 13 and 15 Feb. 1989, 10 June 1992. Telephone interviews, 29 June 1989 and 12 Feb. 1990. Letter 21 Mar. 1990.
Floh, Goetz-Erich, book dealer for Latin American books. Munich, 2 May, 1989.
Groffy, Christoph, head of the Press Department, Suhrkamp Verlag. Frankfurt/M, 20 June 1989. Telephone interview 12 Feb. 1990.
Gustafsson, Lars, writer and professor. University of Texas at Austin, 26 Apr. 1990.
Heydenreich, Titus, professor. Universität Erlangen-Nürnberg. Erlangen, 22 Feb. 1989.
Hooge, Eckard, reader, editor, Bertelsmann Lesering. Rheda-Wiedenbrück, 17 July 1989.
Hörisch, Jochen, professor. Universität Mannheim, 22 May 1989.
Janik, Dieter, professor. Universität Mainz, 13 April 1989.
Kohut, Karl, professor. Katholische Universität Eichstätt, 19 Dec. 1988.
Kolanoske, Lieselotte, translator (*Eva Luna* and *Geschichten der Eva Luna*). Hamburg, 18 July 1989.
López, Monika, translator (*Mexikanischer Tango*). Letter 14 May 1990. 11 June 1992.
Meyer-Clason, Curt, translator (*Hundert Jahre Einsamkeit, Chronik eines angekündigten Todes* and other works by García Márquez). Munich, 27 June 1989.
Meyer-Minnemann, Klaus, professor. Ibero-Amerikanisches Forschungsinstitut. Universität Hamburg, 18 July 1989.
Neuschäfer, H. J., professor. Universität des Saarlandes. Saarbrücken, 27 Feb. 1989.
Ortega, Julio, writer and professor, Brown University. Austin, Texas, 3 Sept. 1989.
Ploetz, Dagmar, translator (*Von Liebe und Schatten, Liebe in den Zeiten der Cholera, Der General in seinem Labyrinth*). Herrsching, 27 June 1989.
Pracht-Fitzel, Ilse, writer, translator. Wichita, Kansas, 6 Apr. 1990.
Reichardt, Dieter, professor. Hamburg, 18 July 1989.
Ripken, Peter, head of Gesellschaft zur Förderung der Literatur aus Afrika, Asien und Lateinamerika, e.V. Frankfurt/M, 25 Jan. 1989 and 9 June 1992.
Siebenmann, Gustav, professor, Hochschule St. Gallen für Wirtschafts- und Sozialwissenschaften. Wolfenbüttel, 16 Mar. 1989. St. Gallen, Switzerland, 26 April 1989 and 15 June

1992.
Strausfeld, Mechtild, scout for Suhrkamp Verlag. Cassette recorded interview, Sept. 1989. 9 July 1991.
Timm, Uwe, novelist. Herrsching, 26 June 1989.
Vargas Llosa, Mario, novelist. Düsseldorf, 24 June 1992 at a reading and during a conversation with him afterward.
Wilke, Jürgen, professor. Katholische Universität Eichstätt, 19 Dec. 1988.
Wulschner, Hans Joachim, head of InterNationes. Bonn, 7 Mar. 1989.
Zurbrüggen, Willi, translator. Heidelberg, 9 Feb. 1989.

Works Consulted

Alcántara, Marco. "Claras Geist ist in mir gegenwärtig. Interview von Marco Alcántara mit Isabel Allende." *Nachrichten der Deutsch-Venezolanischen Gesellschaft.* Dec. 1984: 202-204.

Alfaro, Gustavo. *Constante de la historia de Latinoamérica en García Márquez.* Cali and Colombia: Biblioteca Banco Popular, 1979.

Anderson, Danny J. "Displacement: Strategies of Transformation in *Arráncame la vida,* by Angeles Mastretta." *Journal of the Midwest Modern Language Association* 21 (1) Spring 1988: 15-27.

Arciniegas, Germán. *America in Europe. A History of the New World in Reverse.* Trans. Gabriela Arciniegas and Vitoria Arana. Harcourt Brace Jovanovich, Inc., 1986.

Bell-Villada, Gene. "Banana Strike and Military Massacre: *One Hundred Years of Solitude* and What Happened in 1928." *From Dante to García Márquez.* Eds. Gene Bell-Villada, Antonio Giménez, and George Pistorius. Williamstown, MA: Williams College, 1987. 391-403.

Coddou, Marcelo, ed. *Los libros tienen sus propios espíritus. Esudios sobre Isabel Allende.* 1st ed. 1987 Veracruz: Universidad Veracruzana, 1986.

---. *Para leer a Isabel Allende. Introducción a la casa de los espíritus.* Concepción, Chile: Ediciones Literatura Americana Reunida, 1988.

Collazos, Oscar. *Gabriel García Márquez. Sein Leben und sein Werk.* Trans. Uli Langenbrinck. Köln: Kiepenheuer & Witsch, 1987. Trans. of *García Márquez: La soledad y la gloria. Su vida y su obra.* Barcelona: Plaza y Janés, S.A., 1983.

Drews, Jörg. "Die Entwicklung der westdeutschen Literaturkritik seit 1965." Lützeler 258-69.

Grimm, Gunter. "Einführung in die Rezeptionsforschung." *Literatur und Leser. Theorien und Modelle zur Rezeption literarischer Werke.* Ed. Gunter Grimm. Stuttgart: Philipp Reclam jun., 1975.

Heise, Hans-Jürgen. *Die zweite Entdeckung Amerikas.* Kiel: Neuer Malik Verlag, 1987.

Henry, H., ed. *Readership Research/Theory and Practice.* Amsterdam: North-Holland, 1987.

Lützeler, Paul Michael and Egon Schwarz, eds. *Deutsche Literatur in der Bundesrepublik seit 1965.* Königstein/Ts: Atheäum, 1980.

McLeod, James and Mark W. Rectanus. "Die westdeutsche Literatur seit 1965 auf dem bundesrepublikanischen Buchmarkt." Lützeler 246-57.

Mertin, Ray-Güde. "Zweiundzwanzig Namen für den Teufel--und wie übersetzt man sie?" *Literatur Nachrichten* (Informationsdienst Afrika--Asien--Lateinamerika). Sept. 1988: 1-4.

Meyer-Clason, Curt. "Die literarische Übersetzung." *Hispanorama* Nov. 1979: 33-41.

---. "Macondo auf Deutsch." *Hispanorama* Nov. 1981: 133-139.

Müller, Hans Joachim. "Isabel Allende zwischen Frauen- und Exilliteratur." Heydenreich 211-221.

Müller, Jürgen. *Literaturwissenschaftliche Rezeptionstheorien und empirische Rezeptionsforschung.* Frankfurt/M: Peter D. Lang, 1981.

Pietschmann, Horst. "Lateinamerikanische Geschichte als historische Teildisziplin: Versuch einer Standortbestimmung." *Historische Zeitschrift,* Band 248, Heft 2 April 1989: 305-42.

Rühle, Günther. *Die Büchermacher.* Frankfurt: Suhrkamp Verlag, 1985.

Rünger, B. *Das reduzierte literarische Lesen. Europäische Hochschulschriften: Reihe 1, Deutsche Sprache und Literatur, 1045.* Frankfurt/M: Lang, May 1988.

Schopf, Federico. "Über die Rezeption der hispanoamerikanischen Literatur in der BRD." *Nachrichten der Deutsch-Venezolanischen Gesellschaft.* 2 (4) Dec. 1984: 200-202.

Schulz, Winfried. "Das Bild des Auslandes in den Massenmedien der Bundesrepublik Deutschland." *Kommunikationspolitische und kommunikationswissenschaftliche Forschungsprojekte der Bundesregierung (1978-1985). Eine Übersicht über wichtige Ergebnisse. Teil I* Ed. Presse- und Informationsamt der Bundesregierung. Bonn, 1986. 265-73.

Siebenmann, Gustav. "Ein deutsches Requiem für Borges. Feststellungen und Materialien zu seiner Rezeption." *Iberoromania* 36, Neue Folge, Okt. 1992: 52-72.

---. "Erzähltechnik und Publikumerfolg: Ihre Korrelation am Beispiel des lateinamerikanischen Romans." *Referate der 1. wissenschaftlichen Tagung des Deutschen Hispanistenverbands.* Eds. Haensch, G. and R. Werner. Augsburg 25-26 Feb. 1977. 241-263. In Spanish published under the title "Técnica narrativa y éxito literario: Su correlación a la luz de algunas novelas latinoamericanas." *Iberoromania* 7, Neue Folge, Sept. 1978: 50-66.

---. "García Lorca en el recuerdo." *Colección El Arcaduz.* München: Spanisches Kulturinstitut, Dec. 1988: 24-47.

---. "La literatura latinoamericana en los países de habla alemana." *Revista Hispánica Moderna,* XLIV, 1 Jun. 1991: 124-137.

---. "Von den Schwierigkeiten der deutsch-hispanischen Kulturbegegnung." *Essays zur spanischen Literatur.* Frankfurt/M: Vervuert Verlag, 1989: 12-34.

"Sobre el Eurocentrismo." *Hispanorama* June 1988: 48.

Steenmeijer, Maarten. "El itinerario de la literatura hispanoamericana por el occidente." *Iberoromania* 32, Neue Folge, Okt. 1990: 110-118.

Stefanovics, Tomás. "Die literarische Übersetzung." *Hispanorama* Nov. 1979: 33-41.

Stegmann, Wilhelm, ed. *Deutsche Iberoamerika--Forschungen den Jahren 1930-1980.* Berlin: Colloquium Verlag, 1986.

Steinlechner, Birgit. "Nicht alles, was Schein ist, ist schon Verrat. Beitrag zur Rezeption der lateinamerikanischen Literatur." *Machete. Lateinamerikanische Identificationen.* Oct. 1988: 31-33.

Strausfeld, Mechtild. *Aspekte des neuen lateinamerikanischen Romans und ein Modell: "Hundert Jahre Einsamkeit."* Frankfurt/M: Peter Lang, 1976.

---. "Haus des Übersetzers." *Literatur Nachrichten* (Informationsdienst Afrika-Asien-Lateinamerika) Sept. 1988: 5.